AF512679

Emerging Conflicts and Regional Security in South Asia

Emerging Conflicts and Regional Security in South Asia

Editor

Pramod Jaiswal

ADROIT

Adroit Publishers

NEW DELHI • KATHMANDU

ISBN : 978-81-87393-68-9

2019

Copyright © : Author

No part of this publication may be reproduced or transmitted in any form or by any means, electronic or mechanical, including photocopying, recording or any information storage and retrieval system, without permission in writing from the publisher & author.

Published by
ADROIT PUBLISHERS 4675/21, Ganpati Bhawan, Ansari Road,
Daryaganj, New Delhi-110 002 Phone : 011-23266030
adroitpublishers@gmail.com

Typeset in Garamond Premier Pro by Arun, Akriti Graphic
Solution, Delhi-110081 E-mail: arun263923@gmail.com,
Ph: 9999414390

Dedicated

to

Ahana and Rayan

Contents

Preface

South Asia is one of the most ethnically, culturally and linguistically diverse, as well as most populous, in the world. However, the social, political and economic development of South Asia has been seriously hindered by conflicts. It is host to deeply entrenched ethnic hostility, communal violence and numerous wars, both inter- and intra-state. A vicious cycle of poverty, with deprivation and underdevelopment of South Asian countries has provided a fertile ground for intolerance and extremism. There is a need to overcome the bitter legacies of the past in order to create an enabling environment for peace and security in South Asia. Diverse political experiences, ideologies, ethnic identities and economic conditions across and within the states pose significant challenges for conflict management in the region. Similarly, the region has been characterised by the dynamic inter-play of security, economic and diplomatic factors reinforcing each other owing to the complex nature of territorial claims and religious extremist activities. This is evidenced by the competing political and strategic interests between the three nuclear weapon countries of the region viz: China, India and Pakistan. Unfortunately, the region has witnessed three major wars between India and Pakistan and one between India and China besides several other border skirmishes on and off at various times. Thus, there is a need of broader framework of Regional Security in South Asia for lasting peace and security in the region.

The discourse on regional security in South Asia tends to be focused on the inter-state rivalry between the two largest states in the region—India and Pakistan. The overt introduction of a nuclear dimension into the India-Pakistan relationship has generated international interest in a South Asia preoccupied to no small extent with the threat of a nuclear confrontation and its potential effects on regional and global security.

The book consists of 12 chapters by scholars from India, US and Bangladesh to point out some of these emerging conflicts of South Asia.

Dr. Binodkumar Singh looks at the insurgency of one of South Asia's hottest trouble spots- the North-East of India. He highlights that the insurgences of North-East India have trans-border linkages and most of the conflicts have acquired a criminalized character and display no resemblance to their original objectives and ideology.

Debalina Ghoshal analyses how Pakistan perceives its nuclear strategy and identifies some of the missing links in Pakistan's nuclear strategy.

Dr. Nishtha Kaushiki, Hilal Ramzan and Ghulam Mohiudin Naik trace the geopolitics of the power shifts– both the causes as well as the possible consequences of Afghanistan Peace Talks. They examine the failure of the quadrilateral talks and its outcomes and explore the power shifts and its implications to India. They also attempt to provide policy recommendations to India.

Nitu Kumari seeks to analyze the historical relations of India and factors of India's relations with the ASEAN. She carefully traces the gradual relations of India and ASEAN's non-traditional security relations as well as issues between them.

Similarly, Dr Shahnawaz Mantoo explains the meaning, the emergence, effects and consequences of extremism in Bangladesh.

Dr. Sanchita Bhattacharya minutely examines the internal conflicts in Pakistan which are mainly the results of the breakdown of state institutions. She believes that Pakistan is in the path of becoming a frail state, and government policies are making it weaker. She blames Pakistan's disastrous economy and their corrupt leaders as the major cause of its internal problems. She also points out Balochistan issue as one of the major irritants in the domestic sphere of Pakistan.

Monica Verma and Karnika Jain argue that Bangladesh's economic growth and the external Investment have led the country towards political stability. They also indicate that the threat of Islamic extremism is aggravating the security situation and explore whether the economic performance of Bangladesh can lead the country on a trajectory of peace and prosperity.

Dr. B.D. Mowell takes a critical look at the Sri Lankan insurgency and future prospects. He argues that the LTTE gained international attention for widespread suicide bombings, assassinations and other acts of violence that led the EU, the United States and many other foreign powers to ultimately label them as a terrorist organization. This was the factor that the international community turned a blind eye to the brutality of counterinsurgency efforts on the part of government forces, which militarily defeated the last remnants of the LTTE in 2009. He also remarks that transnational actors including the UN have been largely unsuccessful in pursuing accountability for claims of genocide and other human rights violations which both sides have levied against each other. He points out that many of the issues have been left unresolved and the Sri Lankan government has also become increasingly authoritarian since the war, which is one of many factors that indicates temporary dormancy rather than permanent resolution of the conflict.

Prasanta Kumar Sahu attempts to presume the relation of refugees in the realm of human trafficking, one of the transnational threats. The human security threats cum trafficking risks of refugees includes insecurity, sexual violence, lack of legal protection, socio-economic and political marginalization, social isolation and alienation, severe disruptions in family structure etc. Sahu tries to focus on the theoretical perspectives of transnational threats in the realm of refugees with reference to the Sri Lankan refugees and human trafficking issues. He points out that after civil war, the Sri Lankan Tamil refugees tried to flee to various countries and often got trapped in trafficking. He also tries to evaluate the human trafficking of refugees and human security threats confronting the Sri Lankan Tamil refugees mainly from Southern India whom tries to depart illegally to Australia. He analyzes the role of international organizations and the need for a global order to resolve the refugee crisis as well as the transnational threats as the subject matters subsist beyond the paradigm of 'boarders and borderlands'.

Taslima Islam argues that in spite of rapid economic and social progress, the country is hit by Islamic extremism. The progress of Bangladesh is being deterred by the violent activities of Islamic extremists. She believes that the present government of Bangladesh has made visible strides for stamping out extremism from the society, but the stand of all political parties including the political party who is in power against extremism is questioned. She aims to explore the changing features of militant groups and the roles of the political parties against extremism.

Monoj Das traces the historical origin of terrorism in Pakistan. He discusses the complex security situation of Pakistan with an emphasis on the existing terrorist groups and makes a conscious effort to identify and assess the significance of the funding sources adopted by the terrorist groups in Pakistan in the globalised world providing ample opportunities to them. He also assesses the role of the Pakistani state in addressing the problem of terrorism/ insurgency and countering terrorist financing. He argues that the globalization has provided opportunities for the terrorists in the form of easing of trans-border mobility, advances in communication technologies and a global financial system networked through information technology.

Subodh Bharti explains ethnic Identity of Madhesis, socio-political conditions of Madhesis and perceptions about the Madhesis among the hill people. He also discusses the factors responsible for the origin of the Madhesi movement and highlights all the four phases of Madhes movement.

At last, I would like to mention that the authors have sole responsibility for all errors/ omissions and take full responsibility for the work being original.

Dr. Pramod Jaiswal

Editor

Acknowledgements

The book consists of 12 chapters by scholars from India, US and Bangladesh to point out some of these emerging conflicts of South Asia.

It is the outcome of the combined effort of the authors of various paper incorporated in the book along with my personal contribution as an editor. Here, I would like to thank all the authors Dr. Binodkumar Singh, Debalina Ghoshal, Dr. Nishtha Kaushiki, Hilal Ramzan, Ghulam Mohiudin Naik, Nitu Kumari, Dr Shahnawaz Mantoo, Dr. Sanchita Bhattacharya, Monica Verma, Karnika Jain, Dr. B.D. Mowell, Prasanta Kumar Sahu, Taslima Islam, Monoj Das and Subodh Bharti for their timely submission. I would also like to thank many other senior scholars and friends who helped me and guided me in finalising the draft of the book.

Last but not the least; I would like to thank Adroit Publishers for providing all help and support for publishing the book.

Contributors

1. **Dr. BD Mowell**, School of Security and Global Studies, American Military University, USA.
2. **Dr. Binodkumar Singh**, Research Associate, Institute for Conflict Management, New Delhi, India.
3. **Debalina Ghoshal**, Independent Consultant and Strategic Analyst, India.
4. **Ghulam Mohiudin Naik**, PhD Research Scholar, School of Global Relations, Central University of Punjab, Bathinda, India.
5. **Hilal Ramzan**, PhD Research Scholar, School of Global Relations, Central University of Punjab, Bathinda, India.
6. **Karnika Jain**, M. Phil Research Scholar, School of International Studies, Jawaharlal Nehru University, New Delhi, India.
7. **Manoj Das**, Coordinator, Centre for South East Asian Studies, Gauhati University (Assam) & Ph.D. Research Scholar, Jawaharlal Nehru University, New Delhi, India.
8. **Monica Verma**, PhD Research Scholar, Department of International Relations, South Asian University, New Delhi, India.
9. **Dr. Nishtha Kaushiki**, Assistant Professor, School of Global Relations, Central University of Punjab, Bathinda, India.
10. **Nitu Kumari**, PhD Research Scholar, School of International Studies, Jawaharlal Nehru University, New Delhi, India.
11. **Prasanta Kumar Sahu**, PhD Research Scholar, School of International Studies, Jawaharlal Nehru University, New Delhi, India.
12. **Dr. Sanchita Bhattacharya**, Post-Doctoral Fellow, School of International Studies (SIS), Jawaharlal Nehru University, New Delhi, India.

13. **Dr. Shahnawaz Mantoo**, Assistant Professor, Centre for International Relations, Islamic University of Science and Technology, Jammu and Kashmir, India.

14. **Subodh Chandra Bharti**, M. Phil Research Scholar, School of International Studies, Jawaharlal Nehru University, New Delhi, India.

15. **Taslima Islam**, Centre for South Asian Studies, Pondicherry University, India.

Abbreviations

AAD	:	Advanced Air Defence System
AAMEF	:	Ansar al-Mujahideen English Forum
ABT	:	Ansarullah Bangla Team
ADB	:	Asian Development Bank
ADCs	:	Autonomous District Councils
AHAB	:	Ahle Hadith Andolon Bangladesh
AHWR	:	Advanced Heavy Water Reactor
AIM	:	Alliance for Independent Madhes
AMLA	:	Anti-Money Laundering Act
AMLO	:	Anti-Money Laundering Ordinance
AMSA	:	Australian Maritime Safety Authority
ANF	:	Anti-Narcotics Front
ANFS	:	Afgan National Security Force
ANP	:	Awami National Party
APG	:	Asia Pacific Group
APS	:	Army Public School
AQIS	:	Al Qaeda in the Indian Subcontinent
ASEAN	:	Association of South East Asian Nations
ATTF	:	All Tripura Tiger Force
BDR	:	Bangladesh Rifles
BJI	:	Bangladesh Jamaat-i-Islami
BLA	:	Baloch Liberation Army
BMD	:	Ballistic Missile Defense
BMTA	:	Bangladesh Madrassa Teachers Association
BNP	:	Bangladesh Nationalist Party
BRA	:	Baloch Republican Army
BSF	:	Border Security Force

CHT	:	Chittagong Hill Tract
CI	:	Counter Insurgency
CMH	:	Combined Military Hospital
DAE	:	Department of Atomic Energy
DGFI	:	Directorate General of Forces Intelligence
DRDO	:	Defence Research and Development Organisation
EC	:	Election Commission
EU	:	European Union
FATA	:	Federally Administered Tribal Areas
FATF	:	Financial Action Task Force
FBI	:	Federal Bureau of Investigation
FDI	:	Foreign Direct Investment
FIA	:	Federal Investigation Agency
FMCT	:	Fissile Material Cut off Treaty
FMU	:	Financial Monitoring Unit
GDP	:	Gross Domestic Product
GoI	:	Government of India
HAT	:	Harbour Acceptance Trial
HMG/N	:	His Majesty Government of Nepal
HNLC	:	Hynniewtrep National Liberation Council
HoA	:	Heart of Asia
HRCP	:	Human Rights Commission of Pakistan
HT	:	Hizbut-Tahrir
HTB	:	Hizb ut-Tahrir Bangladesh
HuAM	:	Harkat-ul-Mujahideen al-Alami
HUJ	:	Harkatul-Jehad
HuJIB	:	Harkat-ul Jihad-al-Islami Bangladesh
HUM	:	Harkat-ul-Mujahidin
IAEA	:	International Atomic Energy Agency
IBP	:	Islami Biplobi Parishad
ICANW	:	International Campaign to Abolish Nuclear Weapons
ICS	:	Islami Chhatra Shibir
IDPs	:	Internally Displaced Persons
IDSA	:	Institute for Defense Studies and Analyses
IEDs	:	Improvised Explosive Devices
IIF	:	International Islamic Front

IIGs	:	Indian Insurgent Groups
IKNM	:	International Khatme Nabuwat Movement
ILA	:	Islamic Liberation Army
ILAA	:	Islamic Liberation Army of Assam
INF	:	Islamic National Front
INS	:	Indian Navy Ship
IOJ	:	Islamic Oyikko Jot
IPCS	:	Institute of Peace and Conflict Studies
IPI	:	Iran-Pakistan-India
IPSC	:	Ispahani Public School & College
IRBM	:	Intermediate Range Ballistic Missile
IRF	:	Islamic Revolutionary Front
ISAF	:	International Security Assistance Force
ISI	:	Inter-Services Intelligence
ISIL	:	Islamic State in Iraq and the Levant
ISS	:	Islamic Sevak Sangh
ITER	:	International Thermonuclear Experimental Reactor
IURPI	:	Islamic United Reformation Protest of India
JEI	:	Jamaat-e-Islami
JeM	:	Jaish-e-Muhammad
JMB	:	Jamaatul Mujahideen Bangladesh
JMJB	:	Jagrata Muslim Janata Bangladesh
JuD	:	Jammat-ud-dawa
JUI	:	Jamiat-ul-Ulema-e-Islam
KLO	:	Kuki Liberation Organization
KPP	:	Khyber Pakhtunkhwa Province
LeJ	:	Lashkar-e-Jhangvi
LeT	:	Lashkar-eTaiba
LTTE	:	Liberation Tigers of Tamil Eelam
MAD	:	Mutual Assured Destruction
MDGs	:	Millennium Development Goals
MEA	:	Ministry of External Affairs
MIRVs	:	Multiple Independently Targetable Re-entry Vehicles
MJF	:	Madhesi Janadhikar Forum
MKVs	:	Multiple Kill Vehicles
MLA	:	Muslim Liberation Army

MLO	:	Money Laundering Organisation
MNA	:	Mizo National Army
MNF	:	Mizo National Front
MQM	:	Muttahida Qaumi Movement
MRMM	:	Madhesi Rashtriya Mukti Morcha
MSCA	:	Muslim Security Council of Assam
MSF	:	Muslim Security Force
MTF	:	Muslim Tiger Force
MULTA	:	Muslim United Liberation Tigers of Assam
MVF	:	Muslim Volunteer Force
NAM	:	Non-Alignment Movement
NAP	:	National Action Plan
NC	:	Nepali Congress
NCA	:	National Command Authority
NCP	:	Nepal Communist Party
NDFB	:	National Democratic Front of Bodoland
NER	:	North Eastern Region
NGO	:	Non-Government Organisations
NIA	:	National Investigation Agency
NLFT	:	National Liberation Front of Tripura
NLFT-BM	:	National Liberation Front of Tripura - Biswamohan Debbarma
NNC	:	Naga National Council
NORINCO	:	China North Industries Group Corporation
NPT	:	Non-Proliferation Treaty
NSCN (IM)	:	National Socialist Council of Nagaland
NSCN-IM	:	National Socialist Council of Nagaland - Isak-Muivah
NSCN-K	:	National Socialist Council of Nagaland-Khaplang
NSG	:	National Security Guard
NSI	:	National Security Intelligence
PAD	:	Prithvi Air Defence
PIPS	:	Pakistan Institute for Peace Studies
PLA	:	Peoples Liberation Army
PPP	:	Pakistan People's Party
PWR	:	Pressurized Water Reactor
QCG	:	Quadrilateral Coordination Group

RAM	:	Rockets, Artillery, Mortars
RBA	:	Royal Bhutan Army
RIHS	:	Revival of Islamic Heritage Society
RR	:	Rashtriya Rifles
RVDP	:	Rapti Valley Development Plan
SAAT	:	South Asian Anti-Terrorism Taskforce
SAT	:	Sea Acceptance Trial
SATP	:	South Asia Terrorism Portal
SBP	:	State Bank of Pakistan
SDGs	:	Sustainable Development Goals
SEANWFZ	:	Southeast Asia Nuclear Weapons Free Zone
SFC	:	Strategic Forces Command
SHB	:	Shaheed Hamza Brigade
SIG	:	Special Investigation Group
SIMI	:	Students Islamic Movement of India
SIO	:	Students Islamic Organization
SLBMs	:	Submarine-Launched Ballistic Missile
SMP	:	Sipah-eMuhammad Pakistan
SoO	:	Suspension of Operations
SPA	:	Seven Party Alliance
SPD	:	Strategic Plans Division
SSBN	:	Sub Surface Ballistic Nuclear
SSGI	:	Servants of Suffering Humanity International
SSP	:	Sipahe-Sahaba Pakistan
SVBIEDS	:	Suicide Vehicle Improvised Explosive Devices
TAC	:	Treaty of Amity and Cooperation
TC	:	Terai Congress
TILM	:	Tehrik-e-Islami Lashkar-e-Muhammadi
TIP	:	Trafficking In Persons
TMDP	:	Terai-Madhes Democratic Party
TNFJ	:	Tehrik-e-Nifaz-e-Fiqh Jafaria
TNSM	:	Tehreek-e-Nifaz-e-Shariat-e-Mohammad
TNW	:	Tactical Nuclear Weapon
TTP	:	Tehrik-e-Taliban Pakistan
TUM	:	Tehrik-ul-Mujahideen
UAE	:	Money Laundering Organisation

UDMF	:	United Democratic Madhesi Front
UILA	:	United Islamic Liberation Army
UIRA	:	United Islamic Revolutionary Army
ULFA	:	United Liberation Front of Assam
ULFA-I	:	United Liberation Front of Assam- Independent
UMLFA	:	United Muslim Liberation Front of Assam
UNDP	:	United National Development Programmed
UNESC	:	United Nations Economic and Social Council
UNHCR	:	United Nations High Commissioner for Refugees
UNODC	:	United Nations Office on Drugs and Crime
UNPO	:	Unrepresented Nations and Peoples Organization
UNSC	:	United Nations Security Council
USAID	:	United States Agency for International Development
USSR	:	Union of Soviet Socialist Republics
WHO	:	World Health Organization
WoT	:	War on Terror
ZOPFAN	:	Zone of Peace, Freedom and Neutrality
ZRV	:	Zomi Revolutionary Volunteer

CHAPTER 1

Insurgency in North-East India

Binodkumar Singh

Abstract

The North Eastern Region (NER) of India is one of South Asia's hottest trouble spots, not simply because the region has many armed insurgent groups operating and fighting the Indian state, but because trans-border linkages that the groups have and strategic alliances among them making the conflict dynamics all the more intricate. Troubled by history and geo-politics, the NER has remained one of the most backward regions of the country. The people are racially, ethnically and culturally different from the people in the rest of the country. They take great pride in their village, tribe and ethnic identity. Their ethnic aspirations cannot be dismissed as an outburst of emotive and irrational sentiments. The many conflicts afflicting the region are reflected in breakdown of public order and deterioration of inter-community relationships. In their anxiety to protect and promote their own language and culture, various insurgent groups are currently being fought in NER. Over the years, each of these conflicts has developed a nexus and linkages with forces inside and outside the region, and these linkages have contributed immensely to their life span. Most of these conflicts have acquired a criminalized character and display no resemblance to their original objectives and ideology. While states like Tripura and Meghalaya have lately shown signs of breaking the shackles of militancy, other states like Manipur, Assam and Nagaland continue to be affected by a high degree of militant violence.

The North Eastern Region (NER) comprises eight States viz. Arunachal Pradesh, Assam, Manipur, Meghalaya, Mizoram, Nagaland, Sikkim and Tripura. This region is culturally and ethnically diverse having more than 200 ethnic groups which have distinct languages, dialects and sociocultural identities. The Region covers 8 percent of the country's geographical area and about 4 percent of the national population. Almost all of its borders of about 5,484 Kilometers is international border along Bangladesh (1880 Kms), Myanmar (1,643 Kms), China (1,346 Kms), Bhutan (516 Kms) and Nepal (99 Kms). (Ministry of

Home Affairs, 2016-17). North-East India as a geographical region is a colonial construct, the concept of North East Frontier Region evolved during the British period for administrative reasons (Bhaumik 1998). The region is rich in natural resources, covered with dense forests, has the highest rainfall in the country, with large and small river systems nesting the land and is a treasure house of flora and fauna. Marked by diversity in customs, cultures, traditions and languages, it is home to multifarious social, ethnic and linguistic groups (Das 2008).

Troubled by history and geopolitics, the North-East has remained one of the most backward regions of the country. The trauma of partition in 1947 not only took the region backwards by at least a quarter of a century but also placed hurdles on future economic progress. It isolated the region, sealed both land and sea routes for commerce and trade, and severed access to traditional markets and the gateway to the East and South-East Asia – the Chittagong Port in East Bengal (now Bangladesh). It distanced the approach to the rest of India by confining connectivity to a narrow 27-km-wide Siliguri corridor, making it a "remote land" and constraining access for movement of goods and people. The phrase "North-East" got wide currency only after the recognition of the region and liberation of Bangladesh (Kumar 2006).

Political Map of North Eastern Region

Source: Maps of India www.mapsofindia.com

The uneasy relationship with most of the neighbouring countries has not helped the cause of development of the region and private investment has shied away from the region. Poor infrastructure and governance are combined with low productivity and market access (Chaturvedi 2008). The inability of governments to control floods and river bank erosion causes unmitigated damage to properties and lives of millions of people every year in the region. If the quest for ethnic and cultural identities has sowed the seeds, frustration and dissatisfaction from seclusion, backwardness, remoteness and problems of governance have provided fertile ground for breeding armed insurgencies. There is overwhelming dependence for resources on the Central Government, public investment in the region has sub-optimal productivity due to weak forward and backward linkages (Ministry of Development of North Eastern Region 2008).

The North-East was a gateway of commerce and culture that linked India overland to East and Southeast Asia. It is a meeting place. Political frontiers converge and overlap here. It represents an ethno-cultural frontier, encompassing much of India's rich but lesser known Mongoloid heritage, a complex transition zone of linguistic, racial and religious streams (YOJANA 2006). It is also a unique bio-geographic frontier where the mingling of Indic, Sinic and Malaysian-Burmese strains has produced a treasure-house of floral and faunal bio-diversity. If imperial politics distanced the Northeast from its trans-border neighbour further east, Partition in 1947 physically separated the Northeast from the Indian heartland. It is today virtually landlocked, like Nepal and Bhutan, with less than one per cent of its external boundaries contiguous with the rest of India. The remaining 99 per cent represents international borders shared with Nepal, Bhutan, China, Myanmar and Bangladesh (Verghese 1996).

The people of North-East are by and large the youngest members of the Indian family. According to the Anthropological Survey of India's monumental "People of India" study, most communities in India see themselves as migrants. The bulk of them would be internal migrants within the confines of Indian territoriality, whereas communities in the North-East either have their roots outside India or have migrated into the region from the Indian heartland (Singh 1992). Of the 5653 communities in India, 635 are tribal. Of the latter, a little over 200 categories are found in the North-East. Of the 325 languages listed in "People of India" Vol. IX, the largest number belongs to the Tibeto-Burman family and 175 communities (mostly northeastern) are shown speaking them

(Manoharan 1993). This is confirmed by the amazing linguistic diversity found in the North-East.

The region is unique from every point of view. The people are racially, ethnically and culturally different from the people in the rest of the country. They take great pride in their village, tribe and ethnic identity. Their ethnic aspirations cannot be dismissed as an outburst of emotive and irrational sentiments. The many conflicts afflicting the region are reflected in breakdown of public order and deterioration of inter-community relationships (Upadhyay 2008). Far from being a homogeneous society, as commonly believed, it is a very diverse society with many races, religions and languages. Whether it is linguistic practices, dress, rituals or food habits, there are vast differences among the various ethnic communities. They do not always share the same customs and traditions. Moreover, the cultural distance between the landowners in the plains and the hill people has produced wide cultural differences over the years, more so after independence (Marwah 2009).

The political fragmentation of the Northeast has resulted in the creation of a number of mini-states or autonomous units within them. This, in turn, has given rise to issues of financial and administrative viability with former districts or even smaller units assuming all the trappings of full-fledged states, each heavily dependent on Central subsidies. Such top-heavy administration has proved burdensome and swelled overheads. On the other hand, development has been hampered by poor infrastructure, a paucity of trained manpower, shortages of capital and entrepreneurial skills, high costs of small scale production, and marketing problems when economies of scale are sought. This applies to large-scale exploitation of the region's abundant natural resources of hydro-power, oil and gas, coal, and limestone (Verghese 1996).

In their anxiety to protect and promote their own language and culture, various insurgent groups are currently being fought in North-East. Many of these movements are manifestations of local aspirations or discontents. Some are secessionist. There are three kinds of insurgent outfits in the North-East region depending on their demands. They are – (i) Secessionist outfits (ii) Outfits demanding separate state within India and (iii) Outfits demanding Autonomous District Councils (ADCs) (Kumar 2006). Over the years, each of these conflicts has developed a nexus and linkages with forces inside and outside the region, and these linkages have contributed immensely to their lifespan. Most of these conflicts have acquired a criminalized character and display no resemblance to their original objectives and ideology. While states like Tripura and Meghalaya have lately shown signs of breaking the shackles of militancy, other states like Manipur, Assam and Nagaland continue to be affected by a high degree of militant violence (Routray 2008).

The External Linkages

Countries surrounding India have been active in exploiting the volatile situation presented by the turmoil in the North-East. Not only countries such as China, Pakistan, Bangladesh and Myanmar, but also smaller powers such as Nepal and Bhutan have been involved in the region. Through political backing, economic assistance, logistic support, military training or arms supplies these countries have varyingly contributed to the ongoing violence in this region (Strategic Analysis 2000).

China

The Chinese support to insurgents in the North-East came early in the 1960s and continued through the 1970s. In May 1966, the Nagas approached the Peoples' Republic of China for 'any possible assistance'. Subsequently, after the arduous journey of three months through Arunachal Pradesh and the difficult terrain of Burma, Issac Muivah, leader of Naga National Council (NNC), with a band of 300 men reached Yunan province in January 1967. It was in Yunan that the Naga fighters were imparted with the knowledge of arms and guerrilla tactics and they were also taught Maoism. With the Chinese support, the Naga insurgency became stronger and more intense with better tactics and modern weapons. Apart from the Nagas, the Chinese also extended moral and material support to the Mizo and Meiti insurgents by arranging for their training in guerrilla warfare and subversion in training centres in Yunan province of mainland China and Lhasa in Tibet. In the late 1970s, Peoples Liberation Army (PLA) leader Biseshswar and his group of 16 visited Lhasa in Tibet to secure Chinese support for their cause (Sarin 1980).

Over the years, the Chinese in their endeavour to normalize relations with India have been assuring New Delhi that they have stopped all aid to the insurgents in the northeast. It has been discouraging insurgent groups from trekking to China for receiving instruction in guerilla tactics. Nevertheless, India is yet to be convinced about Chinese intentions (Datta 2000). In the biggest intelligence coup by an Indian agency in recent years, on 18 December 2015, a National Investigation Agency (NIA) team brought Thai national and alleged gunrunner Wuthikorn Naruenartwanich *alias* Willy Naru to India. Naru, 58, was arrested on the request of the NIA in Bangkok on 30 August 2013, on the basis of an Interpol Red Corner Notice. His name had come up during the interrogation of National Socialist Council of Nagaland - Isak-Muivah (NSCN-IM)'s self-styled 'Foreign Secretary' Anthony Shimray *alias* Nikhang Shimray. Shimray revealed that he had allegedly paid an advance of around USD 800,000 for an arms consignment in April 2010. In its charge sheet, the NIA said that the NSCN-IM used to get most of its arms from the Chinese arms company China North Industries Corporation (NORINCO) and Naru had allegedly negotiated the deal. The delivery of consignment was to take place at Cox's Bazar, Bangladesh, but could not go through (*Hindustan Times* 2015). During the first round of interrogation conducted by the NIA, Willy had blown the lid off the USD 1.2 million deal that he had signed with Shimray. Shimray was planning to bring 1,000 AK-74 and AK-56 rifles, 50 universal machine guns and as many rocket launchers along with a huge assortment of ammunition. The probe agency further said that Shimray had been frequently travelling to Beijing to seal the arms deal (*The Quint* 2016).

Separately, in what has alarmed the Ministry of Home Affairs, on 28 March 2017, a day before China launched its aggressive campaign against the visit of the Dalai Lama to Tawang in Arunachal Pradesh, United Liberation Front of Assam-Independent (ULFA-I) 'chairman' Abhizeet Asom in a statement addressing the Dalai Lama said, "Despite the deceitful drawing of the McMohan line then, and your Holiness's acceptance that your homeland is an autonomous region of China, you are perpetrating the fallacy of 1914 by reiterating that Tawang belongs to India." Security sources said that a few Chinese agencies drafted the statement. The sources also said that this was not the first instance ULFA-I was playing into the hands of China. In 2015, ULFA-I was instrumental in floating a "Tibet Support Group" in Assam to launch a proxy war against India at the behest of China (*Deccan Chronicle* 2017). Further, pointing out that elusive ULFA-I 'chief' Paresh Baruah was taking shelter in China, on 2 May 2016, Joint Secretary, Home (In-charge North-East) Satyendra Garg said that Paresh Baruah is constantly moving to avoid arrest and possible extradition, after he fled Bangladesh some years ago. Reports say Baruah is hiding in the jungles of Ruili in south-western Yunnan province of China (*Assam Tribune*, 2016).

Pakistan

The North-East was always a part of the scheme in the overall Pakistani strategy. From the very outset Pakistan had shown its disagreement over the territorial division. Prime Minister of Pakistan Zulfikar Ali Bhutto in his book, 'The Myth of Independence', laid claims to Assam and suggested that he wanted some areas of India's North-East to be included in Pakistan. He wrote: "One of the problems at least is nearly as important as the Kashmir dispute: that of Assam and some districts of India adjacent to East Pakistan. To these, East Pakistan has very good claims, which should not have been allowed to remain quiescent." (Bhutto 1969). His statement was an open confession of Pakistani designs to convert Assam into a Muslim majority state by pushing in hordes of infiltrators and finally annexing it.

In fact, Pakistan was involved in the North-East ethnic movements from the nascent stage. Since the establishment of the NNC in 1956, Pakistan was the first to step in with moral and material support (Hazarika 1994). In 1956, NNC leader A.Z. Phizo spearheading the Naga insurgency fled to Dhaka. From there he was flown to London on a false passport provided by Pakistan (Nibedon 1985). Another important insurgent group active in the region was the Mizo National Front (MNF), which started claiming their independence in the early 1960s. With the failure of MNF to capture the District Council in 1963, its leader Laldenga with a group of volunteers reached out to Pakistan for the acquisition of arms and training. When the MNF was declared unlawful by the Indian government following its declaration of independence in February 1968, Mizo National Army (MNA) was forced to go underground and cross the borders into the Chittagong Hill Tracts and Pakistan began training Laldenga and his volunteers there. Pakistan not only gave material support with weapons and training in guerrilla warfare but also attempted to internationalize the issue (Verghese 1996).

With the emergence of Bangladesh in 1971, the Mizo and Naga groups were deprived of their bases. The Mizos travelled to West Pakistan and developed further ties with Pakistan via Rangoon (Verghese 1996). From the 1980s, there was a quantum jump in the covert operations by the Pakistani intelligence agency, Inter-Services Intelligence (ISI). Pakistan had created a special liaison cell for contact and coordination with Naga and Mizo rebels. (*Indian Defence Review*, 2012) In 1990, ULFA established first contact with ISI through the

Pakistan High Commission at Dhaka. Meeting with ISI was a turning point in the annals of the outfit. A phase of gradual transformation started from insurgent mode to terrorist mode, and ISI played a key role in the 1990s in providing logistic support, such as advanced training on urban guerrilla warfare, handling of sophisticated arms, and preparation of improvised explosive devices (IEDs) (*Journal of Defence Studies* 2014). To facilitate its work, the ISI tried to take the help of fundamentalist elements within the Bangladesh government, army, bureaucracy and intelligence. The ISI is alleged to have supported a network in Bangladesh, which included the hard-line Jamaat-e-Islami (JeI), the Bangladesh Nationalist Party (BNP) and the North-East rebel groups, during the BNP's rule (*Daily Mail*, 2012).

Bangladesh

After the emergence of Bangladesh in 1971, the North-East insurgents operating under Pakistani intelligence cover within East Pakistan suffered a setback. The status quo was maintained till Sheikh Mujib's regime was pulled down in 1975. Immediately after the assassination of Mujibur Rahman, the new regime allowed the Mizo insurgents to establish their bases in Chittagong Hill Tracts (CHT). Since then, various Bangladeshi governments including the one headed by Sheikh Hasina had allowed Pakistan Intelligence operatives to launch their anti-India activities from Bangladeshi soil. In most of the cases, the government turned a blind eye to the ISI operations inside Bangladesh. This has facilitated the ISI channelization of money and materials through Bangladesh to insurgent groups in the North-East (Strategic Analysis 2000). The anti-India operations have been largely possible because of the presence of an overwhelming illegal immigrant Bangladeshi population in the North-East and the porosity of the Indo-Bangladesh border has led to many unanticipated problems for India.

In fact, almost all the major armed groups, the Nagas (NNC and NSCN) and the Mizos (MNF) to begin with and followed by groups based in Assam (ULFA and National Democratic Front of Bodoland), Manipur (People's Liberation Army, United National Liberation Front, People's Revolutionary Party of Kangleipak etc.), Tripura (All Tripura Tiger Force and National Liberation Front of Tripura) and Meghalaya (Hynniewtrep National Liberation Council and Achik National Volunteer Council) have received active or indirect support from Pakistani Inter-Services Intelligence (ISI) network in Bangladesh (Gopal 2004). Besides, there are elements in the Bangladesh Army and the

Bangladesh Rifles (renamed as Border Guard Bangladesh) which have pan-Islamic leanings and provide support to secessionist groups of India's North-East (Dialogue 2006). Bangladeshi support to Indian insurgents in Bangladeshi soil was proven with the confessional statement of Mohamad Hafizur Rahman and Din Mohammad, the two accused in the Chittagong arms haul case. This was the largest arms haul in Bangladesh, which had taken place on 2 April 2004, in the Chittagong area. It was bulky enough to equip an army brigade. Estimated at USD 4.5-5.7 million, the seizure in the ten trucks included: rocket launchers (150), rockets (840), over a million rounds of ammunition, grenade launchers (2000), grenades (25,000), and over 1700 assorted assault weapons (IDSA Strategic Comment 2009).

Further, proof of the Bangladeshi connection and support that the North-East insurgent groups get in its territory was revealed by Julius Dorphang, the surrendered Chairman of the Hynniewtrep National Liberation Council (HNLC) on 18 December 2007. Dorphang is the first leader of any insurgent group of the Northeast to have openly confirmed his stay in Dhaka and has endorsed the dominant view in India, that almost all North-East militant groups have bases in Bangladesh. He revealed that the top leadership of every outfit used to stay in Dhaka to ensure better coordination among cadres and leaders of the similar insurgent outfits. This was also necessary for active coordination with their support bases inside Bangladesh, be it the Directorate General of Forces Intelligence (DGFI) or other political parties that helped them. He also disclosed that the HNLC and other militant organizations such as the NSCN-IM, and the National Liberation Front of Tripura (NLFT) have operational presence and camps in the CHT of Bangladesh and that almost all the insurgent outfits had close relations with each other within Bangladesh (IPSC2007).

Myanmar

Myanmar has been another favorite base for Indian insurgents for three important reasons. The insurgents used this country as a safe base after East Pakistan (Bangladesh) became unavailable to them immediately after the liberation of Bangladesh. Myanmar is also used as a crucial link zone through which rebels can go to China for training and weapons. It also provides a safe training and regrouping zone where new recruits can be taught guerrilla warfare and active guerrilla units can be shifted to when under pressure in India. The drug trade further strengthens their activities, with Myanmar's insurgent groups (like the

Kachins) cooperating with Indian Insurgent Groups (IIGs) like ULFA and NSCN (USI Journal, 2012). Almost all insurgent groups operating in Manipur, Nagaland and Assam have their camps in Myanmar.

Indeed, Myanmar's stand towards the insurgents in the North-East is ambiguous. Their army has been selective in targeting Indian rebels. As a result, despite occasional crackdowns on National Socialist Council of Nagaland-Khaplang (NSCN-K), ULFA and People's Liberation Army (PLA), rebels have been functioning from there without any difficulties. The reluctance of the Myanmar government to act against IIGs can be explained in the light of the country's own severe internal security problems and the tenuous control the government exercises over the remote regions that border India. The ethnic affinity of populations on either side of the border, archaic rules and regulations governing the trans-border movement of people and trade and poor border security aggravate the situation (*Faultlines* 2006). Moreover, despite the success of the high-level visits between India and Myanmar, Myanmar has not been able to act in the manner that New Delhi has expected it to because many parts of northern and north-western Myanmar are not quite in the control of Naypyidaw. Also, there is some reason to believe that the lower echelons of the Myanmar's army have a tacit understanding with the IIGs (Vivekananda International Foundation 2011).

Nepal

The territory of Nepal is used as a safe entry point for intelligence operations by the ISI. Nepal is also recognized as an important factor in the terrorists' plans due to the fact that Nepal basically serves as a good contact point for the purchase of sophisticated armory by various insurgents groups based in North-East India. The insurgents do not face much hurdles sneaking into Nepa1 (Aakrosh 2004). The fact that Nepal was being used as a corridor to smuggle in ISI agents has been established after the tracking down of Yakoob Memon, one of the accused in the Bombay Blast case in 1996 from Kathmandu. The 1999 hijacking of an Indian aircraft from Kathmandu revealed the dangerous face of cross-border intelligence activities targeted at Indian national security.

Further, the arrests of two high-profile terrorists, Adul Karim Tunda and Mohammed Ahmed Sidibappa *alias* Yasin Bhatkal, have brought the India–Nepal border into sharp focus. The seeds for an 'open' border between India and Nepal can be found in the Treaty of Peace and Friendship which the two countries signed in 1950. The extent of misuse of the open border by terrorists and criminals has led to a clamor in some quarters to rethink the rationale for keeping the border with Nepal open. While it is true that the open border has facilitated terrorist and criminal activities which are adversely impacting national security, it is equally important to recognize that an open border has also helped India and Nepal to develop and deepen socio-cultural and economic relations. The open border also has a favorable impact on the two economies (*IDSA Strategic Comment* 2013).

Bhutan

Bhutan's tryst with the ULFA and the Bodo terrorists, by the government providing a safe haven to the insurgents, beginning in 1991, in return for their promise to drive out the Nepalese Ngolop refugees from Bhutan, is a story of utility degenerating into a liability. The insurgents, on the run following the Indian army operations Operation Rhino and Operation Bajrang, could not have asked for a better sanctuary. But, they started using the Nepalese refugees as porters and guides for their operations in the relatively unknown terrain. The presence of the insurgent outfits affected the country's developmental activities in the southern districts. Apart from these plans getting affected, the intrusion of insurgents in the region led to destabilizing developments with government officials found colluding with the terrorists. In July 2000, the Bhutanese government admitted that the ULFA was transferring funds abroad thorough its diplomatic baggage (IPCS 2001).

The royal government of Bhutan by and large chose to ignore their presence in the initial years as they set up camps, mainly in the Samdrup Jongkhar District of southern Bhutan along the Indo-Bhutan border (*Asian Survey* 1998). However, on 15 December 2003, a 6,000-person-strong Royal Bhutan Army (RBA) launched simultaneous attacks on the ULFA, NDFB, and Kuki Liberation Organization (KLO) camps in the southern districts of Bhutan as part of 'Operation All Clear'. According to a statement released by the Foreign Ministry, there were about 30 camps in Bhutan: 13 belonging to the ULFA, 12 to the NDFB, and 5 to the KLO (*Asian Survey* 2005). Whatever may be the reason behind the Bhutanese military action; 'Operation All Clear' was a landmark event and set an example of cooperation in counter-terrorism in South Asia. There has been substantial increase in vigil and intelligence sharing along Indo-Bhutanese border after this operation. Bhutan has assured the Government of India (GoI) of all sorts of cooperation in countering the menace of terrorism. There are no permanent insurgent camps in Bhutan at present. However, inaccessible forested areas along the Assam–Bhutan border continue to serve as temporary bases and safe havens for the insurgent groups, mainly NDFB (Songbijit), who seek refuge there to avoid contact with the security forces (*Journal of Defence Studies* 2014).

Changing Nature and Situation

The nature of insurgency in the North-East has radically changed from an earlier jungle-based, army targeting, ideal seeking and disciplined rebellion to an increasingly city-based, civilian targeting, politically rudderless and undisciplined violence (Nag 2002). Indeed, the nature of conflict in the North-East has transformed. Firstly, while the narratives on insurgency woven around the activities of the bigger outfits have lost much their relevance, in the absence of a strategy to deal with the evolving scenario, the vacuum has been filled in by smaller outfits - breakaway factions of the old outfits as well as new entities. Secondly, the tactic of insurgency has changed from one that aims to destabilize the existence of the state to one that benefits from its continuation. As a result, while killings have diminished, incidents of extortion has picked up. Thirdly, while the threat to India's territorial integrity has been diluted to a large extent as a result of the decline in the larger outfits, the smaller and new outfits remain potential contact as well as collaboration points for the external forces (*Times of Assam*, 2012).

The security situation in the North-Eastern States, which has remained complex for quite some time because of diverse demands of ethnic groups and various militant outfits, improved substantially in 2016. The number of insurgency related incidents in the region decreased by more than 15 percent compared to 2015 (2015 - 574, 2016 – 484). The year 2016 witnessed the lowest number of insurgency incidents since 1997. Similarly, security forces casualties in the region declined from 46 (2015) to 17 (2016). Civilian casualties declined in all States except Assam where it increased from 9 in 2015 to 29 in 2016, thereby leading to an overall marginal increase (2015 - 46, 2016 - 48). The number of kidnapping / abduction incidents also declined in the region (2015 - 267, 2016-168). Counter Insurgency Operation led to the killing of 87 militants, arrest of 1202 and recovery of 605 weapons in 2016 in the region (Ministry of Home Affairs 2016-17). The profile of violence in North Eastern Region as a whole during the last five years is given below:

Security Situation in North East Region since 2012

Years	Incidents	Extremist arrested	Extremist killed	Arms recovered/ surrendered	SFs killed	Civilians killed	Extremists surrendered	Persons kidnapped
2012	1025	2145	222	1856	14	97	1161	329
2013	732	1712	138	1596	18	107	640	307
2014	824	1934	181	1255	20	212	965	369
2015	574	1900	149	897	46	46	143	267
2016	484	1202	87	698	17	48	267	168

Source: Annual Report 2016-17, Ministry of Home Affairs, Government of India.

While the States of Sikkim, Mizoram and Tripura had no insurgency-related violence in 2016, there was a considerable decline in incidents in Meghalaya (44 percent) and Nagaland (43 percent) compared to 2015. In 2016, the State of Manipur accounted for about 48 percent of total violent incidents in the region and the State of Arunachal Pradesh experienced an increase in violent activities by 38 percent, primarily on account of violence by NSCN-K. In Assam, insurgency-related violence continued to decline and the year 2016 witnessed the lowest number of insurgency incidents since 1997(Ministry of Home Affairs 2016-17).

Among various factors contributing to the present improvement in the situation, the most prominent is the ongoing peace talks with several insurgent formations. It is pertinent to recall, however, that these peace talks were preceded by sustained and successful counter insurgency (CI) operations against these groups. These operations were backed by generous surrender-cum-rehabilitation policies, losses of 'safe havens' in Bhutan and Bangladesh, the death, arrest or surrender of top insurgent leaders, fatigue and disillusionment with violence, and loss of the limited popular support and legitimacy that many insurgent groups had in the past. According to the South Asia Terrorism Portal (SATP) database, at least 158 insurgent groups operated in the region at one point or the other. Currently, however, the total number of proscribed militant formations in the region stands at a modest 13: Assam (3), Manipur (6), Meghalaya (1), Nagaland (1), and Tripura (2). Apart from these, there are 23 active militant groups operating in NER: Assam (4), Manipur (6), Meghalaya (7), Nagaland (4), and Arunachal Pradesh (2). Mizoram and Sikkim have no proscribed or active militant groups. Thus, a total of 36 out of 158 insurgent formations are still operational. The Government is, however, in talks with one of the proscribed groups, the Tripura based Biswamohan Debbarma faction of the National Liberation Front of Tripura (NLFT-BM). Of the remaining 122 outfits which are neither active nor proscribed, 82 have become defunct. The Union Government and State Government have, meanwhile, entered into ceasefire and Suspension of Operations (SoO) with 40 of the remaining groups, which are willing to abjure the path of violence and pursue their demands within the framework of the Indian Constitution (South Asia Intelligence Review 2017).

Conclusion

The North-Eastern Region of India is at present experiencing a period of relative calm. Over the years, with almost all major insurgent outfits of the region entering into ceasefire agreements with the government, the incidents of violence have come down quite significantly. However, there is no reason to be complacent about this fact. The situation may soon turn for the bad within a short period of time. Moreover, the system of prolonged talks along with poor mechanisms for rehabilitation and poor oversight over the implementation of ground rules have been responsible for many instances of deviance. Indeed, some of these groups under the various ceasefire and SoO agreements continued to engage in abduction, extortion and killing, and thus continued to constitute an ongoing security challenge.

The very significant improvements in the security situation in India's Northeast need a vigorous effort of political consolidation. Taking peace talks with various militant groups under the ceasefire and SoO agreements forward in a time bound manner is one critical avenue of progress, absent which frustration, ongoing or escalating criminality, splits and internecine clashes can only mount, making a mockery of various ground rules established under the various transient agreements. At the same time, sustained counterinsurgency operations against those groups that remain outside the talks are an imperative.

In conclusion, some points need to be reiterated. Insurgency flourishes when the people have a feeling of separate identity on the basis of ethnicity, culture or history. This is compounded by a sense of neglect, exploitation and discrimination, and immensely aggravated by bad governance, corruption and economic backwardness. All these factors exist in the North East. The key to the situation, clearly, is to provide good, corruption-free governance, and economic development. It has been rightly said that when people in Delhi think of the Northeast, they think of the distance, and that translates itself into a mental gap. When the people of the Northeast think of Delhi, they think in terms of different levels of development, and this translates into an emotional gap. Let us hope that these gaps can be bridged, and that, with changes in attitudes, the North-East will take the high road to peace and prosperity.

References

Ahuja, Rajesh, NIA team brings Thai gunrunner with NSCN(I-M) links to India, *Hindustan Times*, 9 December 2015.

Anand, Manoj, China plans proxy war against India with support of northeast militant groups, *Deccan Chronicle*, 5 April 2017.

Annual Report 2016-17, *Ministry of Home Affairs*, Government of India.

Arya, Shailendra, 'Myanmar—Winds of Change and Opportunity', *USI Journal*, No. 588, April–June 2012.

Bhattacharjee, Giriraj, Northeast: Talks and Some Troubles, *South Asia Intelligence Review*, Volume 16, No. 2, 10 July 2017.

Bhaumik, Subir, 'North-East India: The Evolution of Post Colonial Region', in Partha Chatterjee (ed.), *Wages of Freedom,* Oxford University Press, New Delhi, 1998.

Bhaumik, Subir, Thai Gunrunner, Held by NIA, Reveals Naga Rebels' China Arms Deal, *The Quint*, 15 January 2016.

Bhutto, Z.A., *The Myth of Independence*, Oxford University Press, London, 1969.

Chasie, Charles, "North East: Strategies for Growth", *YOJANA*, December 2006.

Chaturvedi, B.K., "Planning for the North East", *YOJANA*, December 2008.

Das, Pushpita, 'IDSA's Focus on North East', in Pushpita Das and Namrata Goswami (eds.), *India's North East: New Vistas for Peace*, Manas Publications, New Delhi, 2008.

Das, Pushpita, 'Need to Effectively Manage India–Nepal Border', *IDSA Strategic Comment*. 19 September 2013.

Das, Raju, 'ULFA(I) chief constantly on move', *Assam Tribune*, 3 May 2016. Datta, Sreeradha, "Complicity of State Actors in Chittagong Arms Haul Case Revealed", *IDSA Strategic Comment*, 9 March 2009.

Datta, Sreeradha, Security of India's northeast: External linkages, *Strategic Analysis*, Volume 24, No. 8, 2000.

Gopal, Krishan, 'Islamic Fundamentalism in Bangladesh and Its Role in North-East Insurgency', in Dipankar Sengupta and Sudhir Kumar (eds.), *Insurgency in North-East India: The Role of Bangladesh*, Authors Press, Delhi, 2004.

Hussain, Wasbir, Insurgency in India's Northeast Cross-border Links and Strategic Alliances, *Faultlines*, Volume 17 February, 2006.

Kumar, B.B.,"Ethnicity and Insurgency in India's North-East" *Dialogue*, Vol.8, No.2, October-December 2006.

Manoharan, S., *Languages and Scripts*, Anthropological Survey of India, Vol. IX of People of India Series, Oxford University Press, New Delhi, 1993.

Marwah, Ved, *Inida in Turmoil,* Rupa. Co., New Delhi, 2009.

Mazumdar, Arijit, Bhutan's Military Action against Indian Insurgents, *Asian Survey*, Vol. 45, No. 4, July/August 2005.

Nag, Sajal, *Contesting Marginality: Ethnicity, Insurgency and Subnationalism in North-East India*, Manohar Publishers & Distributors, New Delhi, 2002.

Nibedon, Nirmal, *Night of the Guerrillas*, Lancer Book, New Delhi, 1985.

North Eastern Region - Vision 2020, *Ministry of Development of North Eastern Region*, Government of India.

Preisner, Stefan, "Bhutan in 1997: Striving for Stability," *Asian Survey*, Vol. 37, No. 2, February 1998.

Rahman, Mirza Zulfiqur, Northeast Insurgent Groups and the Bangladesh Connection, *IPSC*, Article No. 2449, 26 December 2007.

Routray, Bibhu Prasad, 'Northeast: Island of Peace and Ocean of Conflict', in Suba Chandran and P.R. Chari (eds.), *Armed Conflicts in South Asia- Growing Violence*, Routledge, New Delhi, 2008.

Routray, Bibhu Prasad, Nature of North East India conflict changes – But New Delhi strategy doesn't, *Times of Assam*, 2 December 2012.

Routray, Bibhu Prasad, Northeastern Insurgents in Bhutan: Time for a Pro-active Action, Article No. 556, *IPCS*, 28 August 2001.

Roy, Dipanjan, 'Pakistan ISI Admits Supporting Insurgency in India's Northeast', *Daily Mail*, 15 March 2012.

Saikia, Jaideep, 'NE Insurgent Groups and the Strategic Encirclement', *Vivekananda International Foundation*, 11 January 2011.

Sanjoy Hazarika, *Strangers in the Mist: Tales of War and Peace from India's Northeast*, Penguin Books India, New Delhi, 1994.

Sarin, V.I.K., *India's North-East in Flames*, Vikas Publishing House, New Delhi, 1980.

Sharma, Sushil Kumar, Insurgency in North-East India External Dynamics, *Journal of Defence Studies*, Vol. 8, No. 4, October–December 2014.

Singh, Anil Kumar, 'Insurgency in India: Internal and External Dimensions', *Aakrosh*, Vol. 7, No. 25, October 2004.

Singh, K.S., *People of India: An Introduction,* Seagull Books, Calcutta, 1992. Singh, Prakash, "India's Border Management Challenges", *Dialogue*, Vol.8, No.2, October-December 2006.

Sinha, S.P., 'Northeast: The Threat Posed by External Actors', *Indian Defence Review*, 30 October, 2012.

Upadhyay, Archana, 'Civil Society and Democratic Space in the North East: A Perspective', in Pushpita Das and Namrata Goswami (eds.), *India's North East: New Vistas for Peace*, Manas Publications, New Delhi, 2008.

Verghese, B.G., *India's Northeast Resurgent,* Konark Publishers Pvt. Ltd., Delhi, 1996.

CHAPTER 2

Understanding Pakistan's Nuclear Thinking: How Should India be Prepared?

Debalina Ghoshal

Abstract

Fathoming the nuclear strategy of adversaries is not cumbersome. However, to comprehend the logic behind adopting a strategy is complex. Nuclear deterrence is a psychological game and states adopt different means to strengthen deterrence vis-à-vis the adversary. Deterrence must be logical and credible and states may choose a strategy that they feel would strengthen their deterrence. Some states may choose to lower nuclear threshold vis-à-vis their adversaries in order to strengthen deterrence, while some would choose to keep the nuclear threshold high. However, ultimate objective remains the same: to deter the adversary.

It is in this context, that the paper analyses how Pakistan perceives its nuclear strategy and rationale behind this perception. The paper also aims to identify some of the missing links in Pakistan's nuclear strategy.

Pakistan's Perception of its Nuclear Weapons

Pakistan perceives that its conventional inferiority vis-à-vis India's conventional forces can be negated with its nuclear force. On the other hand, India views its nuclear weapons as means to strengthen deterrence and not for war-fighting. India believes that limited conventional conflict is possible even under a nuclear umbrella, evident from its adoption of the 'Cold Start' doctrine. Pakistan, on the other hand, argued that a conventional conflict, even of a limited scale, under a nuclear umbrella, could become according to General Ashfaq Parvez Kayani, previously the Pakistan Army Chief, "unintended and uncontrollable" (Lodhi 2012).

New Delhi has adopted a 'no-first-use' doctrine and by keeping the nuclear threshold high, it seeks to strengthen her nuclear deterrence. Pakistan rejected the 'no-first-use' doctrine (though it is yet to come out with a written nuclear doctrine) that has lowered the nuclear threshold. By 2011, Pakistan further lowered the nuclear threshold by testing 60 kms range tactical nuclear weapon (TNW), the Nasr. That Pakistan perceives that the introduction of TNWs as a counter to India's Cold Start doctrine, and a weapon that can prevent a war is evident from Khalid Kidwai's statement, former advisor to the National Command Authority (NCA), that possession of TNWs "would make war less likely" by narrowing down any opportunity for India to look for space for a limited conflict (*The Express Tribune* 24 March 2015).

Kidwai believes that TNWs could prevent any destabilisation and is a "defensive deterrence response" to an "offensive (Cold Start) doctrine". According to him, TNWs "blocked the avenues for serious military operations" by India and hence, "reinforced deterrence" by preventing any conflict in South Asia. As Pakistan aspires to achieve 'full spectrum deterrence', Kidwai believes, deterrence should be credible not only at the strategic and operational level but also at tactical level. It is evident that Pakistan believes that its nuclear weapons are solely meant for Pakistan's survival. According to Kidwai, nuclear strategy integrates the planned operations of conventional forces and also operations of nuclear forces.

In an interview conducted by the *Dawn News* in February 2015, General Musharraf, former President of Pakistan discussed Pakistan's military preparedness that he believed was evident from the modernisation of its conventional forces as well as its conducting cold tests of its nuclear-capable missiles. According to Musharraf, Pakistan adopts a strategy of deterrence, and deterrence is "not just possession of force" but, "will to use the force." (*Dawn News* 20 February 2015). Musharraf adds that the enemy must feel that Pakistan is irrational and can use these deadly weapons.

Quite evidently, Pakistan tries to coy with this weapon system to influence the psyche of Indian political leaders and military officials that a nuclear conflict is not far-fetched if New Delhi crossed the conventional threshold and this is done through the portrayal of irrationality in its nuclear strategy and by lowering the threshold. A.Q. Khan, the 'father' of Pakistan's nuclear bombs also views nuclear weapons as means of "ensuring peace by using it as a tit-for-tat threat." (*Time*, 7 July 2011).

One of the major reasons why Pakistan can afford to flirt with its nuclear strategy is because the Pakistani Army enjoys an unprecedented power in Pakistan and also in its decision making policy. In fact, when in 2010 Pakistan's then President Asif Ali Zardari suggested Pakistan should adopt a 'no-first-use policy' probably owing to the fact that Islamabad was developing a 'second strike capability', this suggestion was brushed aside by the then Chief of the Pakistan Army, General Ashfaq Parvez Kayani. (*The Times of India* 6 May 2011).

According to Pakistan's Prime Minister, Nawaz Sharif, nuclear weapons are "invincible" and "impregnable" (*Deccan Chronicle* 29 May 2014). Sharif also believes that nuclear weapons would ensure that Pakistan's military would not be defeated.

Pakistan's views on the Fissile Material Cut off Treaty (FMCT), a treaty which restricts the production of fissile materials, plutonium and enriched uranium is noteworthy. Kidwai in 2010, when he headed the Strategic Plans Division (SPD) viewed FMCT as "Pakistan specific" treaty. (*The Express Tribune* 13 November 2010). Kidwai feared that signing the FMCT meant that Pakistan would have to open its nuclear facilities to international inspection. Ambiguity in nuclear strategy has been practiced by India, China and Pakistan in order to strengthen deterrence. Probably, Islamabad felt that signing the FMCT would restrain Pakistan from maintaining this ambiguity in its nuclear strategy.

Pakistan's National Statement at the National Security Summit-2014, identified multi layered defence mechanism guided by five Ds: deter, detect, delay, defend and destroy (Nuclear Security Summit 2014).

Pakistan's Nuclear Weapons and the Concerns: An Indian Perspective

Pakistan claims that Pakistan's nuclear weapons are solely meant to deter India. However, its delivery mechanisms of the nuclear warheads are capable of reaching targets up to Israel. Some of its ballistic missiles of the Shaheen category can reach targets in Iran and other Middle Eastern countries.

In a recent analysis by Yousef Khalifa al Yousef, he writes that Iran is also apprehensive of Pakistan's nuclear weapons and therefore, desired to have its own nuclear weapons. Iran views Pakistan's nuclear weapons as in the words of an Iranian researcher Vali Nasr, a "Sunni bomb" and therefore, represents "the Pakistani Afghani threat on Iran's eastern border" (Yousef Khalifa Al-Yousef 2017). The Shia Sunni rival exists between Pakistan and Iran and now that the nuclear deal is in doldrums, Pakistan's apprehension that Iran could get the bomb will remain.

Pakistan's threat perception is not just confined to Iran in the Middle East. In the past there were reports of Israeli Air Force trying to bomb Pakistan's nuclear facility at Kahutathat has made Islamabad cautious of Israel's military capability. (*Pakistan Today*, 26 October 2015). At this point of time, some of the Middle Eastern countries could break out into nuclear weapon states and being close to their proximity, it is hard to believe that Islamabad eschews this threat.

Therefore, one could conclude that Islamabad is using the nuclear weapons are India centric psychology as a disguise to develop its deterrent capability against its adversaries in the Persian Gulf. The Shaheen 3 missiles which have a range of 2750 kms which Kidwai claims has been developed to check India's ability to launch a second strike from the Andaman and Nicobar Islands can reach targets up to Israel (*The Indian Express* 24 March 2015). In fact, for Pakistan, it would be wise if there is no effort to destroy India's counter strike and second strike capability since tampering with such a capability would only lead to destabilisation as India's counter and second strike capability would strengthen India's 'no-first-use' policy. Moreover, there are no details available on the trajectory of the Shaheen 3 missile. If the missile is following a depressed trajectory, then the original range of the missile could be close to 3500 kms-4000 kms or may be even more. India's Agni V Intermediate Range Ballistic Missile (IRBM) also follows a depressed trajectory and hence, the actual range of the missile exceeds 5000 kms. Depressed trajectory missiles are often an easy answer to diplomatic pressures that a state would have otherwise had to face should the missile have flown the actual range.

Moreover, by confining the nuclear game to counter-force targeting strategies, Pakistan has jeopardised the Mutual Assured Destruction (MAD) doctrine, premised on targeting counter-value targets, based on which nuclear deterrence is strengthened. Kidwai states that TNWs are defensive in nature to an offensive Indian Cold Start doctrine; however, counter force targeting is an offensive doctrine while counter value targeting is an defensive nuclear doctrine. But Pakistan's counter-force targeting strategy can be well fathomed if one goes by the Quranic Concepts of Warfare. It states that enemy should be targeted in a way that when the target is struck, should deprive the enemy of his weapons or combat strength in case aiming at enemy's vulnerable points is difficult to achieve (Malik 1986).

Pakistan's logic of developing Nasr is, however, illogical and misnomer to deterrence and stability. Every strategic weapon system is capable of being allocated for tactical employment and Pakistan's Shaheen missiles are capable of being used for tactical employment. Using strategic weapon systems for tactical employment reduces the stress on command and control as it minimises the opportunity of a decentralised command and control, while also maintains a high nuclear threshold thereby, strengthening nuclear deterrence. The likelihood of a conflict breakout is less likely with strategic nuclear weapons as opposed TNWs.

Further, if Pakistan's Nasr missile batteries are destroyed by Indian Army's heavy artillery or even by the Indian Air Force, there could be a nuclear fall-out in Pakistan's own territory and lead to catastrophe for Pakistan's own troops. To prevent this from happening, Islamabad would then need sophisticated defence system to protect its Nasr batteries. Countering rockets, artillery, mortars (RAM) and missiles could become a cumbersome task for Pakistan on the battlefield.

Not only is Pakistan developing the Shaheen category of ballistic missiles, but also Islamabad is developing Multiple Independently Targetable Re-entry Vehicles (MIRVs) which could enable Pakistan to attack multiple targets using just one missile. What makes matters worse is that these MIRVs according to Cold War literature are first strike weapon systems and thereby, strengthens Pakistan's 'first use' capability. This would also put a pressure on the Indian ballistic missile defence (BMD) system which would have to work towards a mid-course missile defence system then. At this point of time, New Delhi is only working on terminal phase missile defence system, not sufficient for intercepting MIRV-ed missiles. However, on a positive note, Pakistan's MIRVs would strengthen the arms race stability-instability paradox in the region. India was already progressing towards developing MIRV capability. As already mentioned, Cold War literature suggests that MIRVs could be used as first-strike weapons.

There are also reports that India is also developing MIRV capability could further create a doubt in Pakistan's mind regarding India's 'no-first-use' doctrine, which any way Islamabad does not trust. If Pakistan was not working on MIRV capability, this could have resulted in Pakistan resorting to a pre-emptive strike in order to nullify any option for India to launch a first strike with the MIRVs. However, MIRV capability on both the sides would balance the stability-instability paradox and therefore, is conducive for strategic stability. Nuclear instability is not a result of both states possessing a particular weapon system, but is a result of one state possessing a sophisticated nuclear delivery system while the other state does not. Therefore, parity on both sides will bring nuclear stability in South Asia.

Pakistan's nuclear weapons are also a cause of concern for proliferation of nuclear weapons to probably those friendly countries of Pakistan who would desire to develop nuclear weapons. Pakistan is not a member of the Non-Proliferation Treaty (NPT) and hence, no legal constraints could bind it. Though Pakistan confirms that it has implemented domestic export control mechanisms, all these mechanisms remain at the domestic level and therefore, subject to scrutiny.

Clearly evident from Kidwai's concerns is India's NSG waiver not viewed in the positive light by Kidwai as he believes it would lead to destabilisation of the region. However, what Kidwai failed to see was India's NSG waiving was as a result of its terrific record of non-proliferation, despite not being a party to the NPT. India has also held a record of being a responsible nuclear weapon state and therefore in sync with Kidwai's logic of the NSG membership being 'criteria based'.

India has also signed and ratified Physical Protection of Nuclear Materials and its 2005 Amendment and also the International Convention for the Suppression of Acts of Nuclear Terrorism. In 2014, New Delhi also ratified the International Atomic Energy Agency (IAEA) Additional Protocol which would provide the IAEA with enhanced transparency on India's civil nuclear program. This safeguards agreement with the IAEA covered 20 facilities that include the Nuclear Fuel Complex in Hyderabad, Tarapur atomic power plant, Rajasthan Atomic Power Station, both units at Kudankulam, and the Kakrapar Atomic Power Station (*The Hindu* 23 June 2014).

India is also taking steps to enhance nuclear safety and security measures in its nuclear facilities while for non-proliferation measures, India is working on developing proliferation resistant reactors, for example, the Advanced Heavy Water Reactor (AHWR) which reduces the scope of proliferation (*Indian Embassy in Kuwait*). India has also joined the International Thermonuclear Experimental Reactor (ITER) along with South Korea, USA, Japan, Russia and the European Union using fusion reaction and thereby lesser susceptible to proliferation (*Saran* 2005).

Way Forward: Towards Strategic Stability

On a positive note, Pakistan's command and control structure are well within the domain of the civilian control as is evident from its command and control structure. The Prime Minister heads the NCA along with civilian authorities assisting side by side the military. According to Pakistan's Tehreek-e-Insaf leader, Imran Khan, in a democratic country, nuclear weapons should be under the jurisdiction of civilian control. (*AAJ TAK News* 2012).

Stability and peace can be strengthened in the region through orchestrated and institutionalised dialogues on nuclear issues. Nuclear Confidence Building Measures would be a way forward. Secondly, disarmament is least likely to be a solution to any nuclear instability in the region. Therefore, nuclear arms control measures could be an alternative.

On Nuclear Confidence Building Measures, India and Pakistan already have an agreement in place of not attacking each other's nuclear facilities which came into force in 1991 under a bilateral agreement, Agreement on the Prohibition of Attack against Nuclear Installations. Both the states refrained from attacking each other's nuclear power and research reactors, fuel fabrication, uranium enrichment, isotopes separation and reprocessing facilities and other installations with fresh or irradiated nuclear fuel and material in any form and establishments storing significant quantities of radioactive material" (Nuclear Threat Initiative). Every year, on January 1, as a mark of nuclear confidence-building measures both the states exchange lists of their nuclear installations (*The Hindu* 1 January 2014). Both the states also commonly practice to inform each other of their missile test firing *apriori*.

On India's part, New Delhi should not rethink on its nuclear doctrine of 'no-first-use'. In fact, New Delhi needs to be firm on its no first use doctrine. Secondly, the political signalling needs to be clear on the 'no-first-use' doctrine that this adoption is because of our conventional capability which could defeat Pakistan even without crossing the nuclear threshold. The best option for Islamabad would be to adopt a bilateral 'no-first-use' treaty with India that would reduce nuclear instability and increase the nuclear threshold. Further, both New Delhi and Islamabad could work towards a framework to ban very short-range and short-range nuclear capable ground launched ballistic and cruise missiles of ranges up to 500 kms from their arsenals similar to the Intermediate -Range Nuclear Forces Treaty (INF Treaty) between the United States and Russia.

India does not need TNWs as a deterrent against Islamabad's TNWs. India must continue to reiterate its 'punitive retaliation' strategy in order to send a strong political to Islamabad that irrespective of the yield and type of nuclear weapons used by Pakistan, the response from India's side would be punitive as stated in the nuclear doctrine. This also implies that Indian political leaders would have to send a clear cut message to Islamabad that New Delhi does not draw any distinction between tactical and strategic nuclear weapons strike on its territory. India, therefore, should continue to work towards nuclear force survivability and also military personnel survivability against a nuclear attack.

A well-dispersed and capable command and control system reduces the vulnerability of being wiped off in the first strike itself. At present, the Prime Minister heads the Nuclear Command Authority (NCA), which further directs the Strategic Forces Command (SFC), heads New Delhi's command and control. The SFC will then need to work in collaboration with the Defence Research and Development Organisation (DRDO) and the Department of Atomic Energy(DAE). However, this dispersal of command and control system would need to be well supported by improved communication systems.

Also, at present, New Delhi lacks a Chief of Defence Staff with a fixed tenure as opposed to the Chairman Chief of Staff Committee appointed at present without a fixed tenure. New Delhi's nuclear weapons are in a de-mated state. Under sea-based nuclear deterrence, there could be serious command and control issues since the warheads may need to be mated with the delivery system.

India ventured into developing a two-tier ballistic missile defence (BMD) system, the Prithvi Air Defence System (PAD) and the Advanced Air Defence System (AAD). However, the credibility of this missile defence system still remains doubtful despite the Defence Research and Development Organisation (DRDO) announcing the interceptor tests of the PAD to be successful on several occasions. In addition, India has also collaborated with Israel to jointly develop air and missile defence system (*Times Now* 22 May 2017).

The PAD at present has only been tested against liquid fuelled missiles and from a low range. There remains scepticism whether the missile defence could intercept solid fuelled missiles since it is technically difficult to intercept solid-fuelled missile systems than to intercept liquid-fuelled missile system. Moreover, there is little doubt that adversary will fit countermeasures of missiles which could include MIRVs, manoeuvrable re-entry vehicles (MARVs), decoys and chaffs on their missiles to evade missile defence system.

The Shaheen missiles have booster separation from the warhead at their boost phase which would make interception difficult. Moreover, at this phase, the missile defence can only intercept ballistic missiles at the terminal phase. The ideal phase of interception would be boost phase interception, this may be a difficult phase for India to intercept as this would require intercepting the missile just when it has been fired which would mean to intercept the missile in the Pakistani territory itself which could be politically as well as technically challenging for India. Interception of missiles at midcourse would need multiple kill vehicles (MKVs) to be able to intercept ballistic missiles with MIRVs. These factors would have to be taken into consideration by the DRDO.

From a realist perspective, missile defence systems can be offensive as well as defensive tools for states possessing nuclear weapons. States can choose to launch a nuclear first strike against adversaries and aim to wipe out their retaliatory capability. Missile defence could then be used as a shield against any remaining retaliatory capability of the adversary that the attacking state could not eliminate with its first strike.

However, when a state adopts a nuclear no-first use policy, BMD serves as a defensive system. That is to say, BMD would be used to protect the state from an adversary's first strike. India has to firmly voice its rationale for BMD: that while it maintains a no-first use doctrine, a missile defence system is crucial to India's survival. This open declaration is necessary since the combination of BMD and MIRVs can confuse states on India's no-first use doctrine. Cold War literature suggests that MIRVs were usually meant as first-strike weapons in order to alleviate the "use them or lose them" dilemma.

It is also necessary for India to differentiate clearly between the terms counter-strike and second-strike, which are often used interchangeably. Second-strike capability is a capability of a country to absorb and respond to a nuclear attack from an adversary, and is common both to states with first-use or no-first--use doctrines.

Unfortunately, little has been done to delve into the concept of counter-strike. A counter-strike capability can be defined as the attack launched after a state with a no-first use doctrine has been struck with a nuclear weapon by an adversary. Like second strike, counter-strike places an emphasis on survivability of nuclear forces, but it involves a posture/capability/doctrine unique to states with a no-first-use doctrine. A state with a no-first-use doctrine should not use the term second strike to refer to launching its first nuclear retaliation against an adversary's first-strike.

Also, Islamabad not only possesses nuclear-capable ballistic missiles but also nuclear-capable cruise missiles which include the Ra'ad and the Babur cruise missiles. This would mean that New Delhi would also have to work towards building a credible cruise missile defence system which would be technically a herculean task.

New Delhi's 'credible minimum deterrence' resulted in India working towards three- legged nuclear deterrent capability. The versatility and diversity in the delivery system could leave the adversary with the dilemma of which tried to destroy first; the dilemma of triad destruction. India is working towards the mobility of its nuclear forces for improved survivability.

For a sea-based deterrent capability, India has already developed the Arihant SSBN and is also developing submarine launched ballistic missiles. The sea trials of the INS Arihant have already started, and it has been reported that the SSBN would join the Navy fleet in some time (*NDTV* 16 December 2014). In 2013, the Arihant also completed its 'harbour acceptance trial (HAT) and is now undergoing its 'Sea Acceptance Trial' (SAT) (*India Today* 10 August 2013).

Reports suggest that this SSBN is fitted with the K-15 submarine-launched ballistic missile. As the K-15 remains restricted in range with 750kms of strike range, New Delhi is also concentrating on longer versions of SLBMs, which include the K-4 with 3,500kms and the Nirbhay cruise missiles with 1200 kms (*Defense Update* 27 January 2013). In May 2014, the K-4 underwent its debut flight-test again from a pontoon similar to the K-15 launches (*The Hindu* 8 May 2014).

SSBNs would have the ability to remain submerged in waters for a considerable long time without being detected and therefore, lesser chances of being destroyed in an enemy first-strike. India's Arihant operates on the 80Mega Watt Pressurized Water Reactor (PWR), which would give them the ability of remaining submerged inside water for longer time than conventional diesel-powered submarines. In order to make the submarine lighter in weight, the PWR uses light water as coolant and enriched uranium for fuel as opposed to natural uranium which could increase the weight of the PWR. Further, the ability to stay undetected for long due to its stealth capability also enhances the survivability options of the SSBN.

However, until now, India's Sagarika category SLBMs have only been fired from underwater pontoons simulating a submarine and not from a real SSBN and hence, how successfully could they be launched from SSBN remains to be seen (*Defense Update* 27 January 2013). While the K-4 missile has proved successful in its maiden flight test, the DRDO would need to conduct several such tests to confirm its credibility and reliability. Some of these tests would also need to be conducted from SSBNs also especially when they are submerged to further strengthen their reliability.

While New Delhi declares that a 'credible minimum nuclear deterrence' would be India's nuclear posture, the minimum number of weapons that would be required has not been stated. Moreover, de-mated nuclear weapons only leave more scope for ambiguity regarding the quantity of nuclear weapons that New Delhi nuclear arsenal possesses. This deception and ambiguity further strengthens deterrence and thereby ensure survivability of the arsenal since the enemy would be unsure of what according to New Delhi is 'credible minimum'.

India must strategise conventional military plans to be able to choke Pakistan without the use of nuclear weapons which may include a naval and economic blockade, projecting to Islamabad that Indian soldiers are prepared to bear the implications of tactical nuclear weapons. Needless to say that there has to be better military preparedness to be able to fight a conventional war which even under the nuclear umbrella, which requires modernisation of the Indian Army, Indian Air Force and the Indian Navy. However, the role of India's counter-terroristcounter-terrorist force, the Rashtriya Rifles (RR) in Kashmir also needs to be analysed (*Air Power Journal* 2012). The RR also has to be modernised adequately to be able to successfully conduct counter-terrorist operations as it has always been doing. Performing counter-terrorist operations in Kashmir could have become a challenge for the infantry of the Indian Army had the RR not been there as a vital support system. The RR to an extent takes away the burden from the Indian Army to allocate its forces to fighting counter terrorism within Jammu and Kashmir. There is a little doubt that Pakistan uses its nuclear weapons as a shield to promote proxy wars in India. In addition to this, the National Security Guards (NSG) must also be modernised in order to seal any opportunity by Pakistan to launch proxy wars in India under the nuclear shield.

Conclusion

Nuclear disarmament in South Asia is not a possibility unless the big powers disarm the same. However, given the present global nuclear arms race, the big powers are least likely to accept any scope of nuclear disarmament. In fact, given the present global nuclear arms race, nuclear arms control measures like the INF Treaty remains much under criticism and both the parties to the Treaty, the United States and Russia have time and again threatened to withdraw from the Treaty. Nuclear arms control measures are the initial steps towards nuclear disarmament. While many could conclude that nuclear arms control measures could bring in nuclear strategic stability in South Asia, the reality is that nuclear strategic stability through nuclear forces survivability, parity in nuclear forces between India and Pakistan and nuclear confidence-building measures could in future lead to nuclear arms control measures in South Asia.

Reference

"Nuclear Security Summit 2014", *National Statement Pakistan,*http://www.nss2014.com/sites/default/files/documents/pakistan.pdf accessed on 15 March 2017.

AAJ TAK News (2012), Imran Khan in a conversation "Can India, Pak Turn the Page,?" https://www.youtube.com/watch?v=uK_dNybuhhk ,Accessed on 16 April 2017.

Air Power Journal, (2012), Debalina Chatterjee, "Rashtriya Rifles in Kashmir: India's Counter Terrorist Force," *Air Power Journal,* Volume 7, No.1, Spring 2012.

Dawn News, General Musharraf's interview on "Pakistan can defeat India without using Nuclear weapons," on 20 February 2015, https://www.youtube.com/watch?v=SYe16v5m5f0 , Accessed on 17 April 2017.

Deccan Chronicle, Shafqat Ali, "Nuclear weapons make Pakistan invincible: Nawaz Sharif,"29 May 2014, http://www.deccanchronicle.com/140529/commentary-op-ed/article/nuclear-wepons-make-pakistan-invincible-nawaz-sharif accessed on 7 March 2017.

Defense Update, "India's K-15 Sagarika Submarine Launched Ballistic Missile Completes Developmental Tests," 27 January 2013, http://defense-update.com/20130127_k5_slbm_complete_tests.html#.VRJHJ1OUfpA accessed on 12 April 2017.

India Today, Sandeep Unnithan, "INS Arihant reactor goes critical, submarine to start sea trails," 10 August 2013, http://indiatoday.intoday.in/story/arihant-reactor-goes-critical-submarine-to-start-sea-trials/1/298902.html accessed on 12 March 2017.

Indian Embassy in Kuwait, "Nuclear Security in India," http://www.indembkwt.org/NUCLEAR%20SECURITY%20IN%20INDIA%20English.pdf accessed on 15 April 2017.

Lodhi, Maleeha (2012), "Pakistan's nuclear compulsions," *The News,* November 6, 2012, http://www.thenews.com.pk/Todays-News-9-141314-Pakistan%E2%80%99s-nuclear-compulsions accessed on 10 March 2017.

Malik, SK (1986), The Quranic Concept of War (New Delhi: Himalayan Books) and also cited in Debalina Chatterjee, "Taking a Stock of Pakistan's Artillery," *CLAWS Journal,* Summer 2012.

NDTV, Sudhi Ranjan Sen, "India to Lease a Second Nuclear Submarine From Russia," 16 December 2014, http://www.ndtv.com/india-news/india-to-lease-a-second-nuclear-submarine-from-russia-714039 accessed on 12 March 2017.

Nuclear Threat Initiative, "India-Pakistan Non Attack Agreement," http://www.nti.org/treaties-and-regimes/india-pakistan-non-attack-agreement/ accessed on 1 March 2017.

Pakistan Today, "India, Israel almost attacked Kahuta: report", 26 October 2015, https://www.pakistantoday.com.pk/2015/10/26/india-israel-almost-attacked-kahuta-report/ accessed on 12 March 2017

Saran, Shyam (2005), "Nuclear Non Proliferation and International Security, Volume 29, Issue 3, July 2005 http://www.idsa.in/strategicanalysis/NuclearNonProliferationandInternationalSecurity_ssaran_0705.html accessed on 10 March 2017.

The Express Tribune, Kamran Yousaf, "Pakistan under renewed pressure for nuke freeze," 13 November 2010, http://tribune.com.pk/story/76731/pakistan-under-renewed-pressure-for-nuke-freeze/ accessed on 12 March 2017.

The Express Tribune, 'Pakistan needs short-range "tactical" nuclear weapons to deter India', 24 March 2015, http://tribune.com.pk/story/858106/pakistan-needs-short-range-tactical-nuclear-weapons-to-deter-india/ accesed on 2 March 2017.

The Hindu, "India, Pakistan exchange nuclear facilities list," 1 January 2014,http://www.thehindu.com/news/national/india-pakistan-exchange-nuclear-facilities-list/article5526188.ece accessed on 1 March 2017.

The Hindu, Atul Aneja, "India more open to n-inspections," 23June 2014, http://www.thehindu.com/news/national/india-more-open-to-ninspections/article6139494.ece accessed on 5 March 2017.

The Hindu, T.S. Subramanian, "Success on debut for undersea launch of DRDO's K-4 missiles," 8 May 2014, http://www.thehindu.com/todays-paper/tp-national/success-on-debut-for-undersea-launch-of-drdos-k4-missile/article5987663.ece accessed on 9 May 2017.

The Indian Express, Shaheen-3 missile to cover Indian second strike from Andaman: Lt. General Khalid Kidwai, 24 March 2015, http://indianexpress.com/article/india/india-others/shaheen-3-missile-to-cover-indian-second-strike-from-andaman-former-head-of-pakistans-nuclear-weapons/ accessed on 12 March 2017

The Times of India, "Kayani doesn't back Zardari's 'no-first-use' nuclear-policy: WikiLeaks," 6 May 2011, http://timesofindia.indiatimes.com/world/pakistan/Kayani-doesnt-back-Zardaris-no-first-use-nuclear-policy-WikiLeaks/articleshow/8179491.cms accessed on 12 March 2017.

Time, Ishaan Tharoor, "A.Q.Khan's Revelations: Did Pakistan's Army Sell Nukes to North Korea," 7 July 2011, http://world.time.com/2011/07/07/a-q-khans-revelations-did-pakistans-army-sell-nukes-to-north-korea/ accessed on 8 March 2017.

Times Now, "Israel to supply Advanced long range air and missile defence systems to India", 22 May 2017, http://www.timesnownews.com/india/article/india-navy-bharat-electronics-limited-israel-aerospce-industries-defense-deals/61465 accessed on 12 March 2017.

Yousef Khalifa Al-Yousef (2017), *The Gulf Cooperation Council States: Hereditary, Succession Oil and Foreign Powers* (Lebanon: Saqi Books).

CHAPTER 3

Geopolitics of Afghanistan Peace Talks and Power Shifts: An Indian Perspective

Nishtha Kaushiki, Hilal Ramzan and Ghulam Mohiudin Naik

Abstract

Kabul is now increasingly being recognised as the centre stage of the "Arc of Turbulence" owing to Iran-Afghanistan-Pakistan axis. At a simultaneous level, the Afghanistan peace talks (quadrilateral talks) have created significant geopolitical shifts in South and Central Asia. On the one hand, there is Pakistan, China and Russia, and, on the other hand there are trilateral talks between US, Afghanistan and India. The stage is set for the region to embroil itself again in the great power geopolitics for the coming decade that will have considerable irrevocable consequences.

The proposed study aims to trace the geopolitics of the power shifts– both the causes as well as the possible consequences, and, to analyze how India is adversely affected due to the developments on the issue. The first section of the study will examine the failure of the quadrilateral talks and its outcomes. The later part will explore the power shifts and will specifically include the challenges it brings about for India. Finally, an attempt would be made to humbly put forward some recommendations which India could possibly adhere to for achieving a balance between the geopolitical shifts.

Background

Called as a "graveyard of the empires", Afghanistan has always been a contested land where the superpowers have traditionally clashed with each other for its control as well as for their respective geopolitical outreach. Post 9/11, it constitutes not only the core of the "arc of turbulence" but has rightly been described as the "vortex" in South Asia i.e. the source of conflict between

Islamabad and Kabul. In fact, under the prevailing circumstances, it has the capacity to serve as a "vortex" for both South and Central Asia.

The idea of the Afghan peace talks was originally put forward by Michael Semple, Acting Representative for the EU in Afghanistan, and Mervyn Patterson, political officer with United Nations assistance mission who were expelled in 2007 for doing so. As the momentum gained pace in 2008 and 2009, the "original and active members" for the same were to be the US, Afghan government and the Taliban. It is important to note at this point of time that China, Russia and Pakistan were nowhere in this afghan talks quagmire. It was at a later stage owing to the stakeholders of the Taliban faction that Islamabad gained access to the talks and later was joined by Beijing and Moscow. The Afghan peace talks designed originally for attempting to contain Taliban in order to achieve the US interest of "securitizing" the region, have now become the centre of the geopolitical shifts of the two regions mentioned aforesaid.

Causes of the Failure of the Afghan Talks

The failure of the Afghan peace talks can be attributed to the objectives and geopolitical methodology of the major actors in the peace process and second with the parallel developments that have taken place. These two broader reasons have included within them the entire gamete of the interwoven reasons. Afghanistan is faced with mired developments with regard to the peace process- the first dealing within the factions and factors within Afghanistan and second, handling the geopolitics between the groups that portray themselves as the genuine peacemakers. The situation gets complicated due to the porous and open borders, local support of the extremist measures and especially to the various factions of the Taliban.

As the objective of the paper is to explore the geopolitical dynamics of the Afghan peace talks, in which there are two central powers – the US and China, it therefore, becomes imperative to first understand the geopolitical methodology of the two nations. Divergences in the interests of the powers involved and other external players have led to the actors behaving in chess move style- each one power attempting to outdo the other. Brezhinski's "grand chessboard" theory is truly applicable here. The US has been the main protagonist in the talks, and had a convergence of interest (overthrow) of Taliban with external powers such as China, Russia and Iran, although, it has been poorly placed to broker a peace settlement due to the fact that Taliban section has been fighting a Jihad or a holy war. This convergence was short-lived as once the talks began, individual players started asserting their own respective strategic and economic interests. This soon gave way to the geopolitics being involved in the talks.

In 2002, the Bush administration released a statement on its national security and pledged that the US, "will not hesitate to strike pre-emptively against its enemies ... and will never again allow its military supremacy to be threatened by a rival superpower". This signalled the attempts towards maintaining its hegemony. Beijing, on the other hand, stresses on a multipolar world order. In this context, Odgaard (2007) commented that "the Chinese version of multipolarity implies power balancing through the looser concept of strategic partnerships. It involves partial cooperation with powers that are willing to counter US security policies in their respective sub-regions, hence forming the basis for China's poaching on US alliances and partnerships" (Odgaard 2007: 68). Beijing has thus emerged as a "shadow boxer".

From a Chinese angle, Foundation of SCO with four Central Asian states along with Russia under the aegis of Chinese leadership in 2007 marked the beginning of a Sino-phobia in the US and its allies. In 2007, the Afghan government struck Aynak copper lease deal worth US USD 3 billion. Further, as soon as US announced NATO withdrawal, Beijing announced in 2012 that post-2014, it would play a bigger role in the country's stabilisation. In addition to it, China had already made economic and infrastructure inroads in Central Asia beginning since 1991. In the first half of the 2000s, China moved to establish itself vigorously on the Central Asian market, mainly in hydrocarbons,3 extractive industries, infrastructures, and communications. Finally, since 2005, Beijing has been trying to establish ways to promote its language and culture and to train Central Asian elites according to the Chinese model (Peyrouse 2016: 14).

For example, trade between China and Central Asia for 2007 stood at approximately USD 18 billion (Laruelle & Peyrouse 2009: 39). At a simultaneous level, given the Sino-Pak synergy at work, Islamabad continued its support to the armed insurgents based on its soil (Haqqani and Hekmatyar networks) and at the same time, offered its good offices to help broker a deal between Kabul and Taliban in order to gain a strategic depth in the region and beyond, and, in order to outdo India's strategic outreach. It has to be remembered that India, Iran and the Former Soviet Union had once supported the Northern Alliance.

On a parallel front, the early 2000's was also important from various geopolitical perspectives. First, the rapid military transformation of China along with its hardened stance on the South China Sea dispute; next, the 2003 Iraq invasion by the US forces; third, India signing and later withdrawing from Iran-Pakistan-India (IPI) pipeline owing largely due to the US pressure and security issues; fourth, Russian resurgence as envisioned by Alexander Dugin and implemented at a practical level by Putin; fifth, 2008 Mumbai attacks that brought closer the US and Indian intelligence agencies and finally, the Arab spring and the theories of Iran-Iraq-Syria pipeline.

Istanbul peace process or Heart of Asia was initiated in 2011. The sixth HoA (December 2016) meeting that was held in Amritsar witnessed geopolitical shifts. As Afghanistan and India stressed on dismantling of all the terror groups operating from Pakistan, Russia, on the other hand, appreciated Pakistan and stressed that the bilateral differences between India and Pakistan should not affect the Conference. As Russia seeks to strengthen its relations with both Islamabad and Beijing, one cannot deny the emerging geopolitics in the Afghanistan peace talks due to the power shifts.

At the same time and in the above background Bonn II conference was held in 2011 which witnessed the participation of over eighty-five countries. Regional cooperation was stressed upon for securing peace in Afghanistan. Also, it stressed upon a peace process which would be "Afghan-led and Afghan-owned". The role of TAPI pipeline, CASA-1000, railways and other projects were also affirmed in order to encourage economic development and peace in the war-torn country. It was in the above background that the Taliban opened their first overseas office in Doha, the capital of Qatar in 2013, although discussions for the same were held for around two years. The said objectives included "peace and reconciliation". Interestingly, the Taliban unlike previously was now ready to talk to the Afghan government. Hence, primarily the parties that were involved were the Taliban, The Afghan government along with its High Peace Council, USA.

It definitely meant giving political and diplomatic space to the Taliban, a move that actually could have opened the doors for other extremist and terrorist organisations such as Pakistan based Lashkar-e-Taiba (LeT) and Hizb-ul-Mujahideen (HM); Lebanon based Hezbollah in the Middle East etc. However, the three parties had differences over a range of issues which included the role and the status of Afghan women in the political process, complete or partial withdrawal of forces from Afghanistan, the return of the previously captured

Taliban prisoners from Guantanamo Bay. Serious issues between Afghanistan and the US emerged due to the display of the Taliban flag at the office and also to the use of the nameplate "Islamic Emirate of Afghanistan". Karzai was under the impression that political legitimacy was already granted to the Taliban and the US had not considered the Afghan interests. Although the nameplate was changed to "Political Bureau for Afghan Taliban", yet, in July 2013, the office was shut down. The talks did not start again until the new President Ashraf Ghani took over in September 2014.

Another side of the developments when unfolded, unravelled a "mutual distrust" between the two countries. Although, both the sides agreed that US forces would remain in the operational area beyond 2014, issues such as Legal immunity from prosecution for the US soldiers and Afghan demand of the operations being conducted by the Afghans themselves after upon the guidelines of the US intelligence, and, most prominently, US guarantee of Afghan security on the same guidelines as a NATO ally developed into a serious mistrust. From a geopolitical perspective, US could not provide Afghanistan with such a security cover since Pakistan became a major non-NATO ally status. Bringing Pakistan and Afghanistan on the same level playing field would have actually invited more trouble for the US. For instance, Afghanistan could demand raids into Pakistani territory on account of the attacks emanating from Pakistan based terror groups. Implementing such decisions would have disturbed the geopolitical balance between the US, Afghanistan and Pakistan. Although the bilateral security arrangement between the two countries was signed in 2014, yet, mutual distrust persisted.

President Ashraf Ghani took personal initiatives to involve Pakistan despite the mutual distrust between USA and Pakistan. This resulted in direct talks between Afghan representatives and Pakistani government in 2015. An important consideration has to be given to the location of the talks i.e. Pakistan and China. This gave an impetus to the quadrilateral peace process and soon China was too involved, thereby increasing the number of stakeholders as well as gave considerable opportunity to Beijing to assert itself on geopolitical terms.

The Mullah Rasoul faction (called as the renouncers) of the Taliban had split in 2015 after the announcement of death of Mullah Omar. From Islamabad's perspective, as it has been involved in controlling certain factions of the Afghan Taliban, it simultaneously toed the diplomatic line too. In 2015, Sirajuddin

Haqqani was given an important position of Mullah Mansour's deputy thereby strongly indicating towards the control of Taliban being exercised by Pakistan's Inter Services Agencies (ISI). Although Mansour was killed in the US drone strikes in 2016 and Haibatullah was appointed as the new Emir of the Taliban. However, various studies and reports suggest there is an acute deficit of obedience amongst the Taliban factions, thereby making him ineffective of joining the peace process. Thus, the Haqqani network has a strong hold in the Afghan Taliban.

Owing to the differences on the issue of Afghan peace process and historical animosities, the Afghan government has given strategic help in terms of intelligence, training as well as ammunition to the Raoul faction, thereby, provoking a fight between the Taliban factions. In parallel terms, the first meeting of the Quadrilateral Coordination Group (QCG) on Afghan Peace and reconciliation process was held in Islamabad in January 2016. Through this platform, a major geopolitical achievement for Pakistan is to bring both US and China on the same table, thereby ensuring first, a Chinese involvement because of its Sino-Pak strategic ties which have always been in Islamabad's favour, and, second, attempting to ensure its cooperative side to both the hegemonic as well as a rising power, thereby, resulting in being in the good books of both at a simultaneous level.

As Beijing has influenced Moscow to be strategically engaged with Islamabad through its defence deals, adding another dimension to the peace process in Afghanistan is the new tripartite talks between China, Pakistan and Russia which were held for the first time in December 2016 wherein Moscow decided to work on "working group on Afghanistan". Neither Afghanistan nor India was included in the talks. This is undoubtedly an important sign of an emerging Pakistan-China-Russia alliance and setting up a new platform for the future faultlines of South Asia. The main argument put forward by them is that the US led war in Afghanistan has actually done more harm than good to the country. The war in Syria and Iraq has further pushed the extremists to move towards Afghanistan in search of a new place. And, this is where the strategic interests of both Moscow and Beijing have been involved as Afghanistan is their strategic backyard.

Owing to the reservations on the nature of talks by both India and Afghanistan, the tripartite were converted into a six party talks wherein Iran was additionally invited in April 2017. Kabul raised objections to the "duplicity" in defining the scope of terrorism and objected to Islamabad's policy of "nurturing terrorism" from its soil. Moscow used the platform to reiterate that "Taliban must give up violence, abide by Afghanistan's constitution and break links with other terrorist organisations" (*The Wire* 16 February 2017). The proposal of including the Central Asian Republics in the process was also mooted.

Lately, there have been various reports that both Moscow and Iran have started funding the Taliban faction led by the Haqqani network to fight in order to undermine the US led mission in Afghanistan. Both Iran and Russia who view the US presence in their strategic backyard as more harmful than Taliban's resurgence have also broadened their diplomatic engagement with the Taliban leadership. Iran has hosted several Taliban delegations for talks and conferences in recent years; and in 2014, the Iranian government "formalized" its relationship with the Taliban by allowing the terrorist group to open an office in Mashhad, the capital of Iran's Khorasan-e Razavi Province (Majidyar 2017). Iran had encouraged the relations between Russia and Taliban on account of consideration of fighting against the ISIL fighters who are seeking refuge in Afghanistan. Further, Russia's support to Syria's Assad regime can also be another factor as to why Moscow needs to be more aware of the ISIL. Ex-Taliban factions/dissidents who had left the organization have now joined hands with the ISIL and now they are perceived as a common threat to Moscow and Tehran. Another important consideration from a political perspective is the inclusion of the Russian and Iranian interests in the shaping up of a political scenario when the hegemonic power (US) decides to leave. Of course, such a situation would also be eyed upon by China and the US, but the immediate interests would that be of the neighbouring powers because instability in Afghanistan can have a snowball effect in the near-by regions. Thus, from these positions, Russia and Iran are now attempting to turn the tide in their favour. Indeed, the main beneficiary remains ISIL and Taliban in these geopolitical moves and cross-moves.

India amidst the Changing Security Dynamics of Afghanistan

As the United States has decided to lessen its involvement in Afghanistan, it has become an area of contestation among the other major players of the world. Apart from India and Pakistan– the two sub-regional countries, China, Russia and Iran has also entered the scene. Except India all other countries seems eagerly waiting to see the US out of Afghanistan. On one side China and Russia are eagerly waiting to see the United States out of Kabul but on the other side, both are concerned about the future of Afghanistan because of the presence of instable factors that could undermine their security. As far as India and Pakistan's engagement with Afghanistan is concerned they are involved in an intense competition to outclass the other in this turbulent country. In fact, their rivalry has also extended to Afghanistan. It is because of their respective interests in this turbulent country these countries are strongly engaging themselves in enhancing their strategic outreach in Afghanistan.

The question arises here is why these powers want to establish their strong presence in this unstable country? Why they are eager to ensure stability in this volatile country? The reason for the rising significance of Afghanistan has been its geostrategic location that makes it attractive for other powers. Afghanistan is located at the cross roads of South and Central Asia and acts as a gateway for both the regions to have access to each other. Another significance of Afghanistan is it's being the hotbed of terrorism or in other words, we can say the Taliban factor. The countries in its neighbourhood want a stable Afghanistan and no one wants it to become safe-havens for terrorist outfits which could have spillover effects to the neighbouring countries. As the United States is leaving Afghanistan without stabilising it a wide array of predictions have been made regarding the future course of Afghanistan. However, it has been widely held that the future of Kabul is going to be one of long drawn instability and civil strife. Keeping these factors in mind several rounds of talks like the Doha Peace Talks, Heart of Asia Conference, Russia-China-Pakistan trilateral peace talks, United States-India-Afghanistan talks and Moscow Six Party talks, have been held so far with respect to the security and stability of Afghanistan. It is in the backdrop of these factors that the geostrategic landscape of this vital country is changing. In the current scenario we are witnessing a new "great game" in Afghanistan as the regional powers are involved in efforts to establish links with Taliban with the aim to outfox each other (Azami 2017).

India's Engagement with Afghanistan

India and Afghanistan share a strong historical and cultural links. The relationship between the two is not only confined to their respective governments, but has its foundations in the long standing historical connections and exchanges among the people on both the sides. All these factors lead to the maintenance of stable relations between New Delhi and Kabul.

After the ousting of Taliban from power in Afghanistan, India's engagement in this strategically vital country became multidimensional. An immediate development towards this end was the 2002 up-gradation of India's Liaison Office to a full-fledged Embassy in Afghanistan. New Delhi vigorously participated in the Bonn Conference and was quite influential in the development of post-Taliban political and governing authority in Kabul. Since then, supporting the government of Afghanistan and the political process as authorised under the 2001, Bonn agreement, remained the main focus of India. New Delhi continued to follow the policy of an effective engagement with Kabul through comprehensive and widespread humanitarian and infrastructure initiatives as well as under the banner of international efforts for bringing political stability and economic reconstruction in the war-torn country (Pant 2012: 6).

In the current century, the relations between India and Afghanistan witnessed a significant upward trend. Like other neighbouring countries, security and stability of Afghanistan stands at the heart of India. The reason behind this is that the stability of the Afghanistan is crucial for ensuring India's own stability. It is in this backdrop, New Delhi has vigorously supported the democratic establishments and its development in this geostrategically vital country which is undergoing through the difficult phase of instability and surging for stability.

During the visit of Afghan President Hamid Karzai to India on 4 October 2011, the two sides signed a landmark agreement on establishing "strategic partnership". The agreement formalized the framework for bilateral cooperation between the two sides in the areas of political, economic, social, cultural, capacity building, and people to people contacts. Apart from this, New Delhi under this agreement is also obliged to help Kabul in providing special training, equipment, and more importantly capacity building programmes to make the ANSF more well-versed and strengthened. Subsequently, India responded enthusiastically and has extended its considerable support to meet the above mentioned desires of Afghanistan. A large number of Afghan officers are being trained in India. Not only this, New Delhi has also signed an agreement with Moscow in April 2014, under which it will supply arms to Kabul and will pay Russia for the military equipment sourced from Moscow (Samanta 2014). The former Indian Prime Minister Dr. Manmohan Singh, while commenting on India-Afghanistan 'strategic partnership' said–

> "Our cooperation with Afghanistan is an open book. We have civilizational links, and we are both here to stay ... India will stand by the people of Afghanistan as they prepare to assume responsibility for governance and security after the withdrawal of international forces in 2014" (Balachandar 2012).

Afghanistan acts as a vital land-bridge for India to access the energy-rich Central and West Asia and is also significant for India's strategic, economic and security needs. Knowing the geostrategic vitality of Afghanistan, India has not left any stone unturned in enhancing its outreach in the neighbouring country. Since the last decade, New Delhi has made significant strategic inroads in this troubled country and has been able to gain a specific position in the political, economic and strategic space in this resource-rich country. The Indian policy of providing unconditional support with the aim of installing a much stronger and stable government in Kabul for lasting peace and prosperity has won India the hearts of ordinary Afghan people and even the international community as well (Nair 2015: 2).

With the aim of enhancing its cooperation with Kabul, New Delhi has made colossal investments in Afghanistan on project basis. India has also made it to the list of being one of the leading contributors for security, prosperity and stability of the troubled Afghanistan. Indian aid to Afghanistan now stands over USD 2 billion, thereby making it the fifth largest donor to the Kabul and the largest donor at the regional level. India has provided much needed assistance to Afghanistan for the development of infrastructure. The most significant among which include– more than 200 schools with over a 1000 scholarships in Afghanistan are sponsored by India, construction of the Zaranj-Dilaram highway; construction of Salma dam (India-Afghanistan Friendship Dam); setting up of power sub-stations and the construction of the Parliament complex. The construction of Parliament building is described by officials as "a symbol of India's support to Afghanistan's democracy and civil reconstruction support" (Haidar 2015).

The India's engagement with Afghanistan got further boost under the dynamic leadership of the Prime Minister Narendra Modi. In response to Afghan President Ghani's visit to India in April 2015, as reported by the Embassy of India Kabul, Afghanistan–

> "India has gifted Afghanistan three Cheetal helicopters; assistance for the annual maintenance of M/s Habibiyar School, Kabul and Indira Gandhi

Institute of Child Health; USD 5 million fund to ARCS to treat Afghan child with Congenital Heart Disease (CHD) in India for 5 years; extension of ICCR scholarship till 2020 and indicated readiness to sign a bilateral motor vehicle pact to allow vehicles from both sides to traverse each other's countries" (Embassy of India).

The eagerness of Prime Minister Modi to enhance India's engagement in Afghanistan is quite evident from the fact that in the shortest period of almost six months, he paid two visits to Afghanistan. The first one was in December 2015 when he visited there to inaugurate the newly built Afghan Parliament and second was in June 2016 to inaugurate the Indo-Afghan Friendship Dam (Salma Dam) in Herat, Afghanistan. However, the 2015 visit was significant because at that occasion Prime Minister of India gifted four Mi-25 Attack helicopters to Afghanistan. This marked a shift in India's policy towards Afghanistan. India previously was engaging with Afghanistan on 'soft power' tactics and had never thought of supplying military offensive to the war-ravaged Afghanistan. Modi government has changed the dynamics of India's engagement with Afghanistan and is now ready to be a hard power. Washington has also given a green signal to New Delhi for military role in Afghanistan. India's military engagement in the strategically significant country is going to be a new twist in South Asia. Therefore, the image of India as being soft-peddling in Afghanistan is changing gradually (Kumar 2017).

Indian Concerns

Despite enjoying close relations with Afghanistan and being the largest donor at regional level and the fifth largest overall donors, India is deeply concerned with the developments in Afghanistan. These concerns also depict challenges for India.

1. *Pakistan's rising importance*: Among all the powers which are engaging themselves in the war-torn country, Pakistan occupies a key position as far as the Afghanistan problem is concerned. Apart, from the Taliban factor, Pakistan's geostrategic location is also making it crucial for the future course in Afghanistan. Islamabad shares an open border with Kabul which makes the former as the most significant determining factor for the latter's future. All this makes it a pre-condition for other powers to bring Pakistan into confidence if they have to secure their interests in the strategically important Afghanistan. Pakistan is eager to use its

unique position in Afghanistan– which is engulfed in the long-drawn instability, as a bargaining tool against major powers thereby to seek more and more strategic leverages from these countries. All these countries need cooperation from Pakistan's army in order to secure their interests in this volatile country (Mohan 2012). All these developments seem to be putting Pakistan on the driver's seat as far as the future of Afghanistan is concerned. Pakistan being the archrival of India, it is, therefore, quite natural for the latter to be concerned about the formers strategic advantage as far as their position in securitising the Afghanistan is concerned.

2. *Russian revisions in its South Asia policy*: Given the changing dynamics in the South Asian security and more importantly in Afghanistan, Russia has made revisions in its policy towards the South Asian region. Russia wants Afghanistan to be stabilised otherwise the instability in Afghanistan might take the Central Asian region into its ambit which Russia claims to be its sphere of influence. Towards this end, realising the geostrategic significance of Pakistan vis-à-vis Afghanistan, Russia seems to have made revisions in its policy towards South Asia thereby warming its ties with Islamabad. Another reason for Moscow's positive overturns toward Islamabad might be the mounting New Delhi-Washington Strategic proximity particularly in Afghanistan. Whatever the cause might be, Russia's revision in its South Asia policy has become a major cause of concern for India as it gives Pakistan a further edge over India as far as the balance of power in South Asia is concerned.
3. *Russia-China-Pakistan Axis*: India in the current security scenario is facing the emerging axis of power re-alignment between China, Russia, and Pakistan and even Iran. Even, this axis is also raising its head in Afghanistan and is actively taking initiatives to stabilise the instable Afghanistan. India seems to be only of a secondary importance for this grouping as far as their involvement in securitising Afghanistan is concerned. All these developments are only simmering in the Indian concerns.
4. *China's rising strategic profile in Afghanistan*: The rising Chinese strategic outreach in Afghanistan also in one or the other manner is undermining India's strategic influence in this volatile country. China because of its own concerns is actively engaging itself in Afghanistan and it also wants to protect its mounting economic profile in resource rich Afghanistan.

Beijing also looks toward Islamabad– the 'all-weather' friend to meet its strategic interests in Afghanistan. China and Pakistan are also joining hands to meet their interests in strategically vital Afghanistan. China along with Pakistan has even brought Russia and Iran into their confidence over the issues of addressing the Afghan problem. Apart from this, the volume of Chinese investment in Afghanistan is almost four times larger than that of India's (Kumar 2017). All these developments are undermining India interests in Afghanistan.

5. *Taliban Factor*: The main problem for India in Afghanistan is the resurgence of Taliban. Which India feels is going to undermine its interests in Afghanistan and also may even undermine its security. The other concerning factor for India seems to be that of Taliban being the pro-Pakistan in its outlook. It is in this backdrop that New Delhi is engaging itself wholeheartedly with the Kabul dispensation to keep Taliban at bay.

However, as the developments in Afghanistan are unfolding, it seems that bringing Taliban into confidence is becoming more and more important in order to ensure stability in this country. This is also a cause of concern for New Delhi as it stands against Taliban. In the current scenario of developments which are taking place in relation to Kabul especially under the aegis of several peace talks for ensuring stability in Afghanistan, almost all other participants except India have recognised the Taliban as a significant Afghan entity. India seems to be an odd man out. India is way behind where the other countries concerned about Afghanistan has reached regarding the perceptions about Taliban (Bhadrakumar 2017).

The regional consensus, indeed the international consensus is that for the enduring Afghan settlement, reconciliation of Taliban– an Afghan entity is crucial towards this end. Apart from this, there is also a consensus that the continuation of war in no way makes any sense and except the application of political means the impasse cannot be broken. With the exception of India, all other countries who participated in the Moscow led Six-party talks on Afghanistan in one or the other way are maintaining contacts with Taliban and are even willing to recognise it (Bhadrakumar 2017). Therefore, the policy establishments in New Delhi needs to rethink over its Afghan policy and how far India can go for insisting on an all-out war against Taliban when others are seeing the conflict more as an internecine strife.

Conclusion

The Afghan peace process has been influenced by the power shifts towards China and Russia. As China has displayed its eagerness and capabilities to reframe the existing structure of South Asian security architecture, the Afghan peace process too has been affected by it. Multiple groups claiming to be the true guardian and protector of the Afghan people have emerged. Thus, one can witness in the emerging Afghan cauldron a US led Afghan mission that is supported by the Afghan government despite differences; Moscow-Beijing-Islamabad which is backed by the Tehran government; a large consortium of the countries supporting the Istanbul peace process and the various Taliban factions who seek refuge and aid through these stakeholders. As each group seek power and economic gains apart from strategically undermining the other group, the biggest loser is definitely Afghanistan. From an Indian perspective, as the peace process game is definitely slipping out of New Delhi's hands, it should attempt to convince the powers of different ideologies that one should not differentiate one form of terrorism over the other. India being party wherein deliberate choices are made between ISIL and Taliban, would be a wrong one because it would open up new issues and agendas such as a decision to send the armed forces to fight the ISIL in Afghanistan. Certainly the issue of fighting along with Taliban, Russian and Iran would crop up; then another issue of legitimizing the terrorists' organisations would also emerge, which will have serious repercussions in the Kashmir issue. Hence, although a party to the talks, India should abstain itself from going too far because as each power aspires to have a piece of cake in the on-going process, history might repeat itself and Afghanistan will yet again become a new battleground for the competing powers, this time with new additions.

References

Azami, D. (2017). *World powers jostle in Afghanistan's new 'Great Game'. BBC News.* Retrieved 25 June 2017, from http://www.bbc.com/news/world-asia-38582323 Balachandar, S. (2012). *India's Role in Afghanistan: Past Relations and Future*

Prospects. Foreign Policy Journal. Retrieved 20 June 2017, from https://www.foreignpolicyjournal.com/2012/11/30/indias-role-in-afghanistan-past-relations-and-future-prospects/

Bhadrakumar, M. (2017). *Afghanistan: An area of rivalry. Trinuneindia News Service.* Retrieved 25 June 2017, from http://www.tribuneindia.com/news/comment/afghanistan-an-area-of-rivalry/363176.html

Embassy of India, Kabul Afghanistan (2017). Indo-Afghan Relations. Retrieved 23 July 2017, from http://eoi.gov.in/kabul/?0354?000

Haidar, S. (2015). Modi Reaches Kabul. *The Hindu*. Retrieved from http://www.thehindu.com/news/national/modi-reaches-kabul/article8028394.ece.

Kumar, S. (2017). *Modi plays hardball in shifting Af dynamics. The Pioneer*. Retrieved 21 July 2017, from http://www.dailypioneer.com/columnists/oped/modi-plays-hardball-in-shifting-af-dynamics.html

Laruelle, M., & Peyrouse, S. (2009). *China as a Neighbor: Central Asian Perspectives and Strategies*. Washington, D.C.: Central Asia-Caucasus Institute & Silk Road Studies Program.

Majidyar, A. (2017). *Iran and Russia Team up with Taliban to Undermine U.S.-led Mission in Afghanistan. Middle East Institute*. Retrieved 20 July 2017, from http://www.mei.edu/content/io/iran-and-russia-team-taliban-undermine-us-led-mission-afghanistan

Mohan, C. (2012). *As Russia Warms to Pakistan: Analysis. Observer Research Foundation*. Retrieved 25 December 2014, from http://orfonline.org/cms/sites/orfonline/modules/analysis/AnalysisDetail.html?cmaid=42843&mmacmaid=42844

Nair, K. (2015). *India's Role in Afghanistan Post 2014: Strategy, Policy and Implementation. MANEKSHAW PAPER*. Retrieved 15 July 2017, from http://www.claws.in/images/publication_pdf/1330417563_MP55PreintversioninsideKirit.pdf

Odgaard, L. (2007). *The Balance of Power in Asia-Pacific Security: US-China Policies on Regional Order*. New York, NY: Routledge.

Pant, H. (2012). *India's changing Afghanistan policy: Regional and Global Implications*. Carlisle, PA: Strategic Studies Institute, U.S. Army War College.

Peyrouse, S. (2016). Discussing China: Sinophilia and sinophobia in Central Asia. *Journal Of Eurasian Studies*, *7*(1), 14-23.

Samanta, P. (2014). *India to pay Russia for arms, ammo it sells to Afghanistan. The Indian Express*. Retrieved 5 July 2017, from http://indianexpress.com/article/ india/india-others/india-to-pay-russia-for-arms-ammo-it-sells-to-afghanistan/

The Wire (2017). Moscow Six-Party Talks on Afghanistan Commit to 'Red lines' on Taliban Engagement, 16 February 20017. Retrieved 21 July 2017, from https://thewire.in/109617/moscow-six-party-talks-afghanistan-commit-red-lines-taliban-engagement/

CHAPTER 4

Historical perspective of India and ASEAN Non-Traditional Security Issues and Relation

Nitu Kumari

Abstract

This article seeks to analyze the factors of India's relations with the ASEAN. It explores the historical relations of India and ASEAN and traces the gradual relations of India and ASEAN's non-traditional security relations as well as issues between them. The historical approach to understand the India-ASEAN is played an important role because without an adequate grasp understanding of reason and continuing of India-ASEAN relation, it is very difficult to comprehend the current scenario as well as improve the future aspects. Economic relation is the key feature of India-ASEAN relation. But now it's extending in cooperation for peace, prosperity and security and other areas also. Why this relation emerged and how it's going on. With the specific attention on non-traditional security issues, it tries to find the causes that, where both India and ASEAN agree with each other (policy, plan issues, challenges). Where they differs and how these differences on security policies and strategies not much affect the relations of India and AEASN. With historical analysis it highlights why India's view is differ from ASEAN on traditional and non-traditional security issues. And how with this different thoughts India and ASEAN's relation become stronger day by day. Resolving security political conflicted issues through non-traditional ways for mutuality of their interest.

Introduction

The disintegration of USSR in 1991 has resulted in many changes in the world political scenario. The world paradigm has largely shifted from bi-polar to multipolar and from conflict to cooperation. The concept of regional cooperation in third world countries emerged (developed) with great importance. Dissolution of Soviet Union vitally affects India's foreign policy and India started to look to South East Asian region. The end of cold war and domestic politics and regionalism concept nudged India towards a readjustment of its foreign policy goals and strategies (Sridharan1997). The "Look East Policy" of India has started a new era with the South East Asian countries.

Historicity:

The historical approach is important because without a grasp of reason and continuing of India-ASEAN relation we cannot be adequate understand about the present and we cannot assessed about future, so past is important. India and ASEAN were connected with each other politically, socially, and economically from the historic period. They learn various things from each other and discover their self. They connected through the Soft and Hard power aspects and India's wider strategic towards of South East Asia is very strong in ancient period as well (Das 2013).

The end of cold war, promotion of globalization of national economies, world wider shift from bipolar to multi-polar were some of the key factors that have created an atmosphere for India to enhances its linkage with south Asian Region. Before 1990s Southeast Asian region was ignored by India. As USSR was a very big alliance country of India. And India-USSR has wider relations in the field of commercial, economic, cultural and many bilateral and multilateral relations. Therefore, disintegration of USSR affected the Indian foreign policy and India gave attention to regionalism and regional organization. And with this perspective, India's look for East Policy came into the floor. With Look for East policy (LEP), India's relation with ASEAN and South –East Asian countries have expanded and diversified. Since the end of cold war and initiation of India's Look East India policy, India-ASEAN relations have progressed from sectorial dialogue partnership to annual summit-level meeting. East and South East Asian countries have become more important region for India ((Limaye 2003).

South East Asian countries have hub of natural resource but they failed to attract India for trade or other national relations before LEP, because India always sow these countries as Trojan Horse of America. And South East Asian countries also sow India as a hub of paradox, they also ignored to stable direct relation with India (Majumdar 2013).

The other factor that played a vital role in India ASEAN relations during cold war era is India's traditional close relations with Vietnam. This relation complicated India's relations with ASEAN although both sides maintained a balanced level (Sridharan 1997). The relations between India and South East Asian countries are not new phenomenon which emerge in 1990s they were connected with each other politically, socially, and economically from the historic period. Ancient period to contemporary era there were have very strong connections to trace between these countries and India. Trade, culture, tourisms, pilgrims and many ways connect to both actors. These connections affect to each other such as South East Asian countries learn writing art from south India. In other words it said that India-ASEAN relations emerge on the twentieth century however they are related from the previous era.

India and ASEAN: Concept of Security

Security concern is an important aspect for every state and international relations. And relation with neighboring country also played a vital role in security concern. On the concept of security, India and ASEAN have their own different approach and process, and according to that, both formulate their policy and strategies.

The concept of security, according to ASEAN is, "Security is comprehensive terms; it consisted of political, military economics and social factors. It promotes the internal security and less vulnerability of its members (Narine 1998). Although ASEAN member states have many differences in security concept and practical forum but ASEAN promotes the regional security approach in ideal strategies for security and peace in region. At the same time Indian point of view on security concept is reflecting on Non-Alignment Movement (NAM). As India denied to be an alliance of any great power for its security,and it promotes the respect for all nations' sovereignty and non-interference in internal matter. Its deprive the idea of bipolar system. While in times of changing world scenario, there was various political and economic consequence affects the India. which forced India to rethink about its security concept, policy and strategies..

India and ASEAN Traditional Security Résumé and Gradual Changes

India and ASEAN have various similar opinion on national security and international relation but at the same time, both India and ASEAN have different experience, they have differences on traditional security approach, specifically on nuclear policies and strategies. On the matter of nuclear policy, India's view is very different from ASEAN. As ASEAN strongly oppose the nuclear weapons presents, promotion such nuclear tests in their region and excepting to follow these approaches by its neighboring and ally's states also. ASEAN's this approach is not exactly adopted for India also. For instance, , India's nuclear tests in 1998, were criticized by many states. While India faced criticism especially from individual countries of ASEAN. As well as Media also criticized India's nuclear tests, but these reactions did not find any negative reflects the ASEAN policy. Even, ASEAN-India relation progressed on various non-traditional security aspects. And these relation reflects on India consider and support in Treaty of Amity and Cooperation (TAC), Southeast Asia Nuclear.

ASEAN's opinion and policies regarding traditional and non-traditional security take major shift and changed after 11 September 2001 attacks on the US. South East Asian countries and WE (US) singed anti-terrorism agreement and they start many activities against terrorism. As India also faced vulnerabilities with regard to terrorism from very earlier of its independent so this is the opportunity for India to come together and counter against terrorism (Amador et al 2011).Especially in case of Indonesia, US identify Indonesia as a vital link in its Asia-Pacific region and India's nearest maritime neighbors of it, so makes it vital for India to develop lasting relation with Indonesia (Sundararaman, 2004). After 11 September attack, there were a larger change on ASEAN and US aspect and strategy on non-traditional security. ASEAN-US antiterrorism agreement come into the force. And also the US maintains its strategic dominance through its large military support in the East Asian region (David 2010).

Security issue and nuclear test where co-related on the point of India. Although India's nuclear test in 1998 was criticized by many countries and by forum of ASEAN, which promotes and follow the Southeast Asia Nuclear Weapons Free Zone (SEANWFZ). But they did not change relations with India after this nuclear test. While there was an initial reaction especially from individual countries and Media also criticized India's nuclear tests but these reactions did not reflect the in the India-ASEAN policy. India and ASEAN came together in many ways, such as their role and support in Treaty of Amity and Cooperation (TAC), Southeast Asia Nuclear Weapons Free Zone (SEANWFZ) (Amador et al 2011).

India's non-traditional security regime took vital changes after 1960s. As after China's nuclear weapons test, there was a wide range of debates and discussions emerged, and it include the Indian political elite, intellectuals, political parties, journalists. As India had very bitter experience with China as the time of Nehruvian Period. And India change its policy towards security after the war of India-China. As also it very well known that successive Indian governments have continued to adhere to the Nehruvian doctrine, as according to this, India not going for a complete nuclear weapons program. The 1974 nuclear test established a fact that India could make nuclear weapons without seeking any help from other country. Although since then India follow its policy of "nuclear option approach". It was an ambivalent policy of India, according to this India reserved the right to go for nuclear weapons, when the situation demanded. For instance, at the time of national security, war and so on. However, with the passage of time, things were changed and world political scenario were also changed. It change regional security environment aspects also. The disintegration of the Soviet Union, the end of Cold War and the emergence of the US as the sole and only superpower at the world map, changed the geopolitical situation of the world. Added to it, the Chinese agreement to join the NPT and its normalization of relations with Russia along with the starting of close contacts with the US provided certain new and significant dimensions to India's security concerns. It became widely evident to the Indian political establishment that India can no longer rely on a general deterrent and has to stand on its own and evolve its own strategy to ensure its security and status. Against the backdrop of any possible nuclear attack or blackmail from China or Pakistan, it became imperative for India to discard its previous dubious nuclear ambiguity policy and go for a full-scale nuclear weapon program. Thus, India's nuclear strategy can be seen evolving from a situation of complete rejection to an increasing but invisible factor in the Indian military agenda. With these factors, one other key factor is that, although ASEAN is also the various security related issue like, India such as challenges of terrorism and some extremist radical groups but at the same time the situation of ASEAN as its consider as big alley of the US. Security guarantees from the US are enough for Southeast Asian countries to neglect nuclear weapons program (Nair 2011). And after the disintegration of USSR, India is trying to raise its voice alone at the international floor.

The 'Indira Doctrine' enunciated by Mrs Gandhi in July 1987 which asserted Indian commitment not to intervene in the domestic affairs of any states in the region nor would tolerate any such interventions by any outside power enhanced the regional military role of India. And during the 1980's all the three services of Indian armed forces envisaged the nuclearisation of their forces. The army and the air force viewed 'nuclearization' in terms of acquiring nuclear weapons and the navy saw it in terms of a nuclear-powered platform; initially for defensive purposes and ultimately as a deterrence for purposive nuclear threats. Thus, India ultimately tested its nuclear bomb in 1998 under the Vajpayee government.

India's non-traditional security strategies were evaluated after the security threat from neighboring country. Such as India-China war in 1962, as well as India-Pakistan War 1971-72. These past experiences and China-Pakistan alliance against India there was various factor gave wider emphasis on India's strategies on non-traditional security. No hegemony propaganda in ASEAN group also played a vital role it means In ASEAN statesno member state were create hegemonic role in the region and all member states tried to follow the rule of equality and Participation for peace. And peaceful zone is the main aspect of ZOPFAN (Katanyuu, 2006).

India's Policy on Nuclear Prestige

After the end of the Second World War, and the use of nuclear bomb in Hiroshima and Nagasaki in1945, the nuclear question remains prominent in world politics. Nuclear weapons, thus, acquired the status of the highest form of scientific expertise of the 20th century and the obvious symbol of human kind's mastery over nature. In the post Second World War period, the acquisition of nuclear arms increasingly began to be associated with national prestige. Besides this justification, nuclear weapons also came to be seen as a great leveller against conventional weaponry and thereby reemphasizing its vitality as an important means of national security. The Indian establishment always justified peaceful nuclear explosion for its potential ability to bring forth economic benefits for the country and hence advocated for the availability of peaceful nuclear explosion technology to developing countries. In short, the Indian political elites sought to bring mastery over nuclear technology for India's national development program.

Analysis

In today's global world, the economic relation is very important but you cannot ignore the security matter, as all states prior aspect is related to the security. That is the reason today all states thought comprehensive international relation with state, comprehensive relation between states and region, as well as comprehensive relation between region-and region. There is no hegemonic dominance issue present in ASEAN group, that's why ASEAN always give priority to non-tradition security collaboration and aspects.

ASEAN involved in various activities with members states which promotes the securitization or the idea of security with non-tradition security aspect. They promote practical and policy for future confidence. At the same time India has its own security challenges and previous experiences therefore India not play a very vital role with ASEAN to promotion in total nuclear free zone (means India do not agree with ASEAN's all non-tradition security policy but the interaction between India and ASEAN in progressed).Although India and ASEAN came together on various factor. For example, terrorism is a major reason for instability and disturbance within the region and within the states for both India and ASEAN. Today entire world is facing difficulties due to the direct and indirect terrorism. . Terrorism is not new in Asia, infect Asia is considered as the hub of terrorism. As India is also facing many disaster of terrorism. As well as India always emphasis that terrorism is the main enemy and barrier for the world peace and development. However t before 11 September 2001 (Nine Eleven) attack on US,maximum states does not considered India's voice against terrorism and AEASN was also in one of them. After the attack of Nine/ Eleven terrorism became consider as global threat for peace. As ASEAN is consider as the Trojan horse of US therefore ASEAN has also been sincere after 11 September attack. And ASEAN-US antiterrorism agreement come into the force.

ASEAN targeted by Islamic radical extremist groups, as India also facing many termism difficulties and community violence as well as long time conflict of Pakistan. As both India and ASEAN is facing the similar terrorism problem. So they collectively being more cooperative relation between against this terrorism issue. For instancr, India-ASEAN came together for joint declaration for cooperation to combat international terrorism.

On the matter of Nuclear-non-proliferation policy both India and ASEAN have different approach. As discussed earlier that how ASEAN's policy is different from India's policy. For example ASEAN's nuclear free zone concept, India's no first use concept and so on. . However it is significant to discuss the India's big different from ASEAN. ASEAN's all 10 full member sign treaty ZOPFAN in

1997 which related to the Southeast Asian Nuclear Weapon Free Zone Treaty (known as a treaty of Bangkok). ZOPFAN is the declaration for the peace, freedom, nuclear neutrality in zone. According to this treaty, all the member states have to give emphasis on peace in zone with the action of not to develop, manufacture or control nuclear weapons. ASEAN members cannot organize any activities which related to nuclear weapons program directly or indirectly. As noticed that see the situation of ASEAN is different, although this region also faced challenges of terrorism and some extremist radical groups but this is the fact that ASEAN is a big alley of the US. Which gives them Security guarantees from the US,and its enough for Southeast Asian countries to neglect nuclear weapons program. However some ASEAN countries have Conflict with China which is true for fear, but all ASEAN's member states does not have conflict with China (example -Myanmar). No hegemony propaganda in ASEAN group, it means in ASEAN there are the issue of hegemonic dominance is a big matter or hot issue, all members participating and making policies and strategies for regional peace. And the peaceful zone is the main subject of ZOPFAN.

About India, it also does work on creating peace, prosperity and stability in his own state and neighbor states or region but ways are different from ASEAN. While India also appreciates ZOPEAN concept. But, due to the past experiences the India could not ignore Pakistan's nuclear program China's defence policy (such as Chania's GDP and its defence expenditure), North Korea's missile test mission and so on. In history (1962, 1972) India has very harsh experience with neighboring countries (China, Pakistan) so these historic evidence defiantly influence the Indian defence and nuclear policy and its reflects on India's nuclear policy. As ASEAN has also aware with these historic tragedy therefore nuclear weapons program of India has not affected India-ASEAN relation. India and ASEAN collectively working in several areas. For countries development food, health, eradication of numarious pandemics or disease , welfare of citizen subjects are always consider as the main and most important factor for state. Both actor (India and ASEAN) also participating together for these things. Both ASEAN and India share the same priorities principal and values when it comes to health. ASEAN and India always promoting the protection of human rights in their region. As ASEAN's human right commission and India's maximum human right policies are similar. Sorexample both promoting the rights of minority, rights of women, rights of children, protection of religious freedom and so on.

Conclusion

In conclusion as India and ASEAN has many similarities and differences but it is said that both (India and ASEAN) also have very strong historical relation which reflects in their present relation as well as it opens the gate for future cooperation also. As in India, honour killing and violence against women, child labor, tribes exploration (Jarwa tribes news Andaman Nicobar) are some matter where India facing many challenges and criticism by World Health Organization, United Nations and other international organization. And these matters very positively handled by the ASEAN therefore India also take advantage and evaluate that these matter were handled by ASEAN.

As in Indian context this is very famous that there are far deference between the policy on paper and practice, India could get inspiration from with ASEAN and not make policy only on paper it should come into the floor also. Other approach of collaboration is migration issue. As India has two types of migration challenges such as internal migration (caused by marriage) and external migration (caused by employment) which affects Indian economy and scarcity of human resources and human assets. While ASEAN is very well known for migration policy. And ASEAN countries have many opportunity and concession for member states India could avail benefits from this approach. Because India has very large human resources force, so if India-ASEAN makes some liberal policy for labor, employee migrant and other types of employee than both take benefits from each other. ASEAN has many natural recourses and many unexplored area, so if both of them create some policy for employment and skilled labor supplement then both India and ASEAN could get many opportunities and positive aspects for future cooperation. It is in favour both actors. After these issues, some challenges are also similar between India and ASEAN. First confidence building for future cooperation rather than fulfill national interest, countering the challenges with cooperation and collective approach. Both ASEAN and India must engage in more confidence building on the matter of migration, non-proliferation and other traditional and non-traditional security aspects.. India and ASEAN have many issues and challenges, if they adopt collective action and cooperative approach on these subjects and r address the problem collectively. It will get very effective outcome comparison to work alone on these hot issue such as terrorism, health, migration and so on. Tourism visa, trade and commerce and many other \, areas are significant where they both could work together and get benifited. India-ASEAN relation was established in a very difficult situation as discussed earlier it was the result of the decline of USSR. With the constant effort of both side this relation being more strongly and stable day by day. This is the reason India and ASEAN expand their policy and relation not only in trade or economic level even social and cultural level also. Although India and ASEAN do not agree in all concept and perspective of each other but they respects each other's concept and approach on various platform. India's previous view about Southeast Asian countries (India thought ASEAN is the Trojan horse of America) is changing now., And nowadays India does not very much worried about American interference and influence in ASEAN group. Although India always very much concern and alert about China's extreme interference (in Myanmar) in ASEAN.

... while ASEAN also interested in stable a broad and good relationship with India because they worry about the China's hegemony in this region, especially some ASEAN states individually also interested in India's relation.. In this entire discussion, it emphasis on to underline that how and why India changed its policy and strategy toward the ASEAN and comeup with wider bilateral and multilateral relation with ASEAN. It discussed the ASEAN's perspective, role and policy for region peace and prosperity. What are the significance of India and ASEAN's policy towards cooperation. As Globalization is very important aspect for economic growth and prosperity of any country. The world is always as like dependence theory where one alone state cannot survive, or difficult to survive therefore cooperation is compulsory aspect and fact for today's world. Also traditional security concept of nations security is also changing in these days, so all states came to gather to address the tradition security threat and non- traditional security threat. With globalization, state boundary growing its interaction between internal social grouping and external forces this is the impact of globalization. As America playing a very important role in ASEAN region therefore other state could not ignore the importance of ASEAN. Because of the big ally of America (security support any time, weapons and equipment support) ASEAN declare it policy about this region, as nuclear-free zone region. But India cannot do this with same approach because of its relations and experience with China, (1962), Pakistan (1971) as well as the defence policy of North Korea. Due to these types of peculiar challenges India could not completely agree with ASEAN's norms such nuclear free zone declaration but India always in favour of stabling peace in the region and world. For example India promote nuclear free world with the maximum use of nuclear energy for development. No first use of nuclear weapons, no use of nuclear weapons against nuclear weapon less (those countries who does not developed nuclear weapons)countries and so on. Therefore many ASEAN's group's countries established individual relation with India. for example India has very good relation with Vietnam, Indonesia, and Myanmar, so, this is the very positive point for India, became generate a good relationship with ASEAN. Acoording to ASEAN's article 2(2), ASEAN respects independence, promote sovereignty and equability for all ASEAN's member states. But as very well known that the situation of this region is not very peaceful and it suffering many difficulties such as internal conflict, community clashes and so on. And ASEAN's charter and norms and strategies are not successful to resolve these problems (International organization: politics, law, practice 2011). In this scenario ASEAN could get positive benefit from India. India's role is very important for stability because of its individual relationships with these Southeast Asian countries. As well as India has a very good experience of democracy and well known for democracy supporting aspects..About nuclear question ASEAN's non-proliferation policy is good but the region should think beyond great powers. Means in these global world, states should not libel or dependant on some other states for national security and national interest. And also that, the world politics and scenario is always changeable according to the situation, so may be our today's alley countries become tomorrow's enemy, so ASEAN should think beyond the ally of America. Although ASEAN very careful and concern about conflict with China and changing role of china in AEASN countries. While ASEAN security should be a prior comparison to other things in ASEAN. ASEAN's member states who criticized India's army in past (1980) however nowadays those countries taking some benefits with this army (eg; Myanmar, Vietnam). Indian technology also helpful for them to excursion natural resource. And they try to balance China's hegemony in the South China Sea with help the of Indian equipment (Vietnam –India oil excursion program). India-ASEAN relationship is now more progressive. It starts with trade and spells over in a larger area. ASEAN's groups are more interested in relations with China and they get preference to India. India also interested in ASEAN for trade, tourism, energy and many other sections. India-ASEAN relation should carry this progress and explore challenges or issues which come between them. Cooperate in future and try to create deepen relation between them its beneficial for ASEAN-India and its helpful to stable peace East Asia and the Asia Pacific. So this relation should be eye to eye contact and be stronger. In ancient to modern India-ASEAN relation was in progress.

References

Amador, Julio S. III, , Bobillo, Ariane and Peñalber, Amirah(2011), "Issues and Challenges in ASEAN-India Relations: Political-Security Aspects", *India Quarterly: A Journal of International Affairs,* 67(2):111-127.

Das, Kumar Ajaya (2013), "Soft and Hard power in India's strategy Towards Southeast Asia",*India Review*, 12(3):165-185.

David, Arase, (2010), "Non-Traditional Security in China-ASEAN Cooperation: The Institutionalization of Regional Security Cooperation and the Evolution of East Asian Regionalism", *Asian Survey*, 50(4):808-833.

Katanyuu, Ruukun (2006), "Beyond Non-Interference in ASEAN: The Association's Role in Myanmar's National Reconciliation and Democratization", *Asian Survey*, 46(6):825-845.

Limaye, P Satu (2003), "INDIA'S RELATIONS WITH SOUTHEAST ASIA TAKE A WING", *Southeast Asian Affairs*, 39-51.

Majumdar, Sayantisen *(2013)*, "Persistent Influx: Impact on the North East Region" India & neeghbours : Harmonious Co-operation and Economic Engagement, *world Focus Special Issue, July 2013.*

Nair, Deepak (2011), "ASEAN's Core Norms in the Context of the Global Financial Crisis" *Asian Survey*, 51 (2):245-267.

Narine, Shaun(1998), "ASEAN and the Management of Regional Security" Pacific Affairs, University of British Columbia, 71(2): 195-214.

Peng Kuan, Eric Koo. 2005. India's Look East Policy: Analytical perspectives from the political, economic and military lenses. What is India—Policy analysis. http:// www.whatisindia.com/editorials/wis200501019_indias_look_east_policy.html (accessed on 25/11/2015).

Sundararaman, Shankari (2004), "Politics and Security in South-East Asia: Prospects for India ASEAN Cooperation" *INTERNATIONAL STUDIES* 41(4) 371-385.

Sen, Rahul, Asher G.Mukul and Rajan S. Ramkishen (2004),"ASEAN-India Economic Relations: Current Status and Future Prospects", *Economic and Political Weekly, 39(29):3297-3308*

Sridhran, Kripa (1997), "INDIA AND SOUTHEAST ASIA IN THE 1990s", *Southeast Asian Affairs, utheast Asian Affairs. 46-63.*

CHAPTER 5

Extremism in Bangladesh

Shahnawaz Mantoo

Abstract

The world is heading certainly towards fragile and largely unknown future owing to the increasing extremism. All countries are facing uphill and astounding challenges to their sovereign status within as well as from the external suspicious security sensitive environment. The extremist groups in all its forms are alarmingly increasing and dangerously engulfing the whole south Asian region and it certainly has serious consequences and will lead to the downfall of south Asian synthetic and secular culture. Bangladesh, of course, was solidly founded on Bengali culture, and secularism and progressive liberalism were its basic principles and became the founding stones of the constitution. But due to the emergence of several politically insensitive and inimical factors which made the country's internal political stability fragile and flimsy and also gave rise to ideologically diverse groups who in the course of time used the state machinery for their own political benefits. The extremism is the product of several factors and among them is the institutional failure, miss-governance, deep political confrontation, corruption and the culture of intolerance. This extremism has largely engulfed and surrounded the whole social fabric of the country and if not given due considerations will surely become a menace and which may prove catastrophic to the whole country. The paper will try to explain the meaning of extremism, the emergence, effects and consequences of extremism in Bangladesh.

The word, 'extremism' is not properly defined but is politically and psychologically charged. It is used as an instrument by political organizations and other groups to further their objectives. The basis of the creation of East Bengal, later East Pakistan, was on the principle of religion, the "Two-Nation Theory." However, the freedom struggle of East Pakistan in 1970's was driven by, secularism, geographical factors, Bengali language, culture, economic exploitation and alienation and other external factors also contributed to the creation of Bangladesh in 1971. Presently, Bangladesh's long tradition of moderate Islam, secular culture and social inclusiveness are increasingly under threat from religious and political extremism. In fact, Bangladesh has presently been termed as the 'base of Taliban' and 'cocoon of terror.'

Political Radicalization

The political radicalization and extremism in Bangladesh date back to Mujib's period but there were only signs of it. During Ziaur Rehman's period, the radicalization started with immense government backing and which later on was substantiated by General Ershad. The role of religion in the politics and society of Bangladesh gained a thrust when Bangladesh adopted Islam as a "state religion" during Hussain Mohammad Ershad's regime (1982-1990). Earlier, President Zia-ur Rahman (1977-1981) initiated the process of cultivating religious parties for political support who in turn are presently alleged for patronizing extremist groups in Bangladesh (Hashmi: 2009). The trend to seek the political support of the extremists was sprightly encouraged by the successive governments. The fundamentalists and jihadi elements were the notable allies of Begum Khaleda Zia's, Bangladesh National Party (BNP). During her regime, she reportedly manipulated the Islamists in order to weaken the then opposition Awami League and its allies. The Jamaat-e-Islami of Bangladesh (also called Jamaat), which is the leading Islamist political party of Bangladesh and the largest Islamic party in South Asia, formed part of the government during Khaleda Zia's second tenure as Prime Minister (2001-2006). Jamaat had as many as 16 members elected to parliament (Abu Kala: 15). Leaders like Motiur Nizami Rahman and Ali Ahsan Mujahid, who fought against Bangladesh's liberation and took over Jamaat-e-Islami in late 2000, were made ministers during her regime. Azizul Huq, the Chairman of the Islamic Oyikko Jot (OIJ), a radical Islamist party and a member of the advisory council of Harkat-ul-Jihad-al-Islami Bangladesh (HUJI-B), Bangladesh's main fundamentalist group (banned in February 2005), was part of the coalition government of Begum Khaleda Zia (Karlekar 2005: 8).

It should be noted that Jamaat-e-Islami was banned until 1979 due to its support for the Pakistani army during the liberation war. The party has never apologized for its role and has been a target of the wrath of secular nationalism (Riaz 2008: 3). According to Lt. General Yogendra Bammi, the Jamaat has now claimed that they are nationalist to the core. They maintain that during the Indo-

Pak war of 1971, Bangladesh was a part of Pakistan so they opposed the anti-Pakistan Bangladesh liberation movement that was backed by India. The Jamaat-e-Islami former chief Ghulam Azam has confessed before the International Tribunal that they were involved in the general massacre in the Bangladeshi during the liberation war which clearly shows that they were opposing the dismemberment of Pakistan (Interview with General Bammi 2000).

The main motto of the Jamaat is, "Allah is our Lord; The Quran and the Sunnah is our ideal; Jihad is our means; and Salvation is our end" (Karlekar 2005: 136). The objectives of Jamaat-e-Islami, as per its constitution, is to establish peace in Bangladesh and in the world, to achieve the grace of the Almighty Allah through efforts to establish the Islamic way of life for the greater well being of mankind. It has four-point programme: Purification of thoughts through Dawah and Tabligh, Organization and training, Social reform and service, and reform in governance. It has been alleged that Jamaat-e-Islami has facilitated the terrorist groups with financial assistance and providing manpower. For example, November 2001 witnessed one of the most recent high-profile murders of Gopal Krishna Muhuri, principal of Nazirhat College in Chittagong and a leading secular humanist. He was killed by four hired assassins, who reportedly belonged to a gang patronized by Jamaat-e-Islami (Amnesty International). HUJI has also been responsible for the attack on poet Shamsur Rehman. Hard cores like Bangla Bhai and Jangi Bhai send death threats in the name of Islam together with kafan (the white clothing of Muslim corpuses) to those they declare as murtad (apostate). Professor Humayun Azad, who wrote a book on the pro-Pakistan elements titled *Pak Sarzamin Shad-Bad*, was also sent death threats, but the government plays down the strength of these fundamentalist organizations (Ahmad 2005).

The other party that formed part of Khaleda Zia's government was IOJ (Islami Oikya Jote). It has openly supported the Islamist forces, the Taliban and the Al-Qaeda.[1] IOJ is not a single political party but a conglomeration of six smaller radical organisations namely, Khelafat Majlis, Nezam-e-Islam, Faraizi Jamaat, Islami Morcha, Ulama Committee Bangladesh, Bangladesh Farayazi Jamaat, Bangladesh Nizam-e-Islam Party, and Jamiyate Ulama-e-Islam. Some of these parties have previously expressed solidarity with the Taliban regime (Riaz 2008: 31). Both IOJ and Jamaat promote anti-Indian and pro-Islamic policies which provide ideal breeding ground for the growth of militancy (RNP Singh 2002:

24). Their presence in the political power structure encouraged the extremist elements to act without any fear as they enjoyed the patronage of the authorities. Some other well-known Islam based political parties that are also based on anti-Indian posture are Jamaat-e-ulema-e-Islami; Muslim League; Nizam-i-Islami; Islamic Democratic League; Islamic Republic Party; and Bangladesh Republic Party. They have well-disciplined cadres among youth and students. In fact, the political environment of Bangladesh has changed. Even Sheikh Hasina Wajed promoter of secular ideology, during the latter half of her tenure as the Prime Minister of Bangladesh (1996-2001), changed her attire by dressing herself of a Hajj pilgrim and Black Muslim headgear. She was even accused of not taking any actions against the Islamic forces involved in the killing of the ethnic minorities like Chakmas of Chittagong. It was speculated that the reason for the change was to obtain their support for the 2001 elections. The pro-Islamic political environment offered by the Pakistani Inter-Services Intelligence (ISI) a ready ground to start its operations in Bangladesh.

According to Bertil Linter, a Swedish journalist, the importance of Islam grew as the Awami League fell out with the country's powerful military, which began to use religion as a counterweight to the League's secular, vaguely socialist polity (many hard-line socialists who termed Bangladesh as unfinished revolution, however, were opposed to the idea of a separate Bengali state in Bangladesh, which they branded as 'bourgeois nationalism') (Lintner 2003: 3). Ali Riaz, in his book *Islamist Militancy in Bangladesh: A Complex Web* identifies the main cause for the rise of Islamism as a political ideology as: the crisis of hegemony of the Bangladeshi ruling classes—both civilian and military; the crisis of legitimacy of the military regime post-1975; the politics of expediency of the secularist parties; and the ineffective resistance of civil society (Riaz 2008: 30). Political radicalization of Islam in Bangladesh provided an ideal platform for the escalation of activities of Islamic groups pursuing a pro-active Taliban agenda.[2]

However, according to Partho Ghosh, the Islamic politics is confined to the cities and it has not yet reached the small towns or villages. People in the towns and villages are more concerned about their basic needs than religious fanaticism. They are themselves concerned about the rise of Islamism that is affecting their security. The very victory of Awami League is a good reflection of the support of the local masses to the secular forces in Bangladesh (Interview with Partho Ghosh 2009).

Bangladesh in Turmoil

In 2001, two simultaneous events in the South Asian region took place—the formation of Begum Khaleda Zia's government (2001-2006) in Bangladesh and the United States (US) led "War on Terror" that led to the invasion of Afghanistan. The 9/11 and subsequent "War on Terror" brought many extremist outfits in Afghanistan under the US scanner. These outfits required an alternate place for abode. The Canadian Security Intelligence Service in its July 2003 report noted that the (Islamist) extremists in Bangladesh established links with al-Qaeda and Osama bin Laden's International Islamic Front (IIF). Also, the October 2002 Bali blast resulted in the shifting of some of the Indonesian and Malaysian terrorist groups bases to Bangladesh (RNP Singh 2002: 26).

The unstable social, political and economic setup with the absence of democracy for a long time made Bangladesh a weak country which created a vacuum for such Militant forces to establish their bases. Easy money laundering provided ideal conditions for making it a breeding ground for recruitment, motivation, support, infiltration and also provided a safe haven for international fundamentalist groups, gunrunners, smugglers, pirates and ethnic insurgents. Ali Riaz, recognizes certain internal factors that contributed to the rise of Islamic militancy in Bangladesh which include: favorable socio-political environment for rise of militancy, coercion as an acceptable mode of governance, criminalization of politics, absence of state institutions in certain geographical areas of Bangladesh, a civil administration which supported the rise of such forces particularly at the local level and popularization of the culture for Islamist objectives. He also points out four regional factors that contributed to the rise and proliferation of Islamist extremism in Bangladesh as: unfavorable Indo-Bangladesh relationship, cross-border cooperation between Bangladesh militant groups and the militant groups of Myanmar, antagonism between north-east India and Bangladesh, easy availability of weapons and the "proxy-war" between India and Pakistan (RNP Singh 2002: 44-48). According to Hiranmay Karlekar, a renowned journalist, "One of the reason that makes Bangladesh an ideal base for militant operations is that it is a weak state with ineffective governance and police force, which fundamentalist Islamist organisations like the Jamaat, IOJ, and HUJI-B, with their highly organized, trained and armed cadres, can dominate without much trouble, since they already have a foot in the government" (Karlekar: 7). According to Professor Sayeed, these Islamists control vast stretches of the country with help from the political parties like Jamaat and a section of the BNP who are ideologically akin to each other. With such support from mainstream political organizations Islamist militants have succeeded to place their people in all government departments and the other sections of society, including mosques, madrassas, educational institutions, the Secretariat, the judiciary, civil society, mass media and even the armed forces. These Islamists have also developed a strong countrywide network to capture power through Islamist revolution (Karlekar: 15).

In this respect, it may be noted that the 2005 serial bombing where more than 400 small bomb blasts within a span of half an hour rattled the capital and towns across Bangladesh, demonstrated a steady increase of the activities in the political and social setup of Bangladesh.[3] Although there are no reports of suicide bombing but there are worries about the rise of suicide bombing carried out by Bangladeshis in the region including India and diffusing their area of influence across borders.

These forces in Bangladesh have been able to establish themselves firmly also because they are receiving support of the security agencies within Bangladesh. Furthermore, they have infiltrated these agencies and institutions of governance. It is reported by the intelligence sources (Bangladesh Intelligence Service) within Bangladesh that February 2009 Mutiny by Bangladesh Rifles (BDR) had revealed some possible links with the Jamat-ul-Mujahedeen Bangladesh (JMB), a fundamentalist group banned in 2005 (Riaz: 49).

Major Islamist Groups in Bangladesh

There are reportedly more than 20 Muslim extremist (militant) organizations operating in Bangladesh. However, only a few of them have been reported by the news media. Security agencies in Bangladesh have reportedly identified 48 training centers across the country of some of the Islamic organizations. Some of the Islamist organizations in Bangladesh include: Jamiat-ul-Mujahedeen (Bangladesh), Islamic Brothers Cell, Muslim Ummah Sanghati Parishad, Islamic Markaz Party, Jagrata Muslim Janata-Bangladesh (JMJ-B), Zaker Party, Shahadat-e-al-Hikma, Khadimul Islam, Bangladesh Khelafat Majlis, Jaish-e-Mustafa, Lashkar-e-Jihad, Jamaat-e-Yahia Trust and Islami Shasantantra Aandolan. Amongst them JMJ-B is considered as one of the most dangerous Islamic outfits. Its operational commanders are commonly known as 'Bangla

Bhai' (Bengal Brothers) (RNP Singh 2002). Another group Shahadat-i-Al-Hiqma a strong group was banned in February 2003.

It is also stated that Sheikh Abdul Salam Mohammad alias Fazlul Rehman, leader of the 'Jihad Movement in Bangladesh', signed the official declaration of al-Qaeda's 'holy war' against US on 23 February 1998. It is believed that Harkat-ul-Jihad-al-Islami of Bangladesh (HUJI-B) was formed in 1992 with the aid of Osama bin Laden. Incidentally, HuJI-B also included Bangladeshis who had fought as volunteers in the war against the Soviets in Afghanistan.[4] HuJI-B is headed by Shawkat Osman alias Sheikh Farid in Chittagong and, according to the US State Department, has "at least six camps" in Bangladesh. According to Bangladesh Assessment 2003, HuJI-B has 15,000 members of whom 2,000 are 'hardcore'. The survey further stated that "Bangladeshi Hindus and moderate Muslims hold them responsible for many attacks against religious minorities, secular intellectuals and journalists." Amnesty International has also reported in December 2001 that Hindus-who now make up less than 10 percent of Bangladesh's population of 163 million- in particular have come under attack. The Hindu places of worship have been ransacked, villages destroyed and scores of Hindu women are reported to have been raped.[5] HuJI-B is also involved in attacking US establishments in the region, supporting terror attacks and aiding terrorist organisations outside Bangladesh. In 2000, it was also suspected of having carriedout the assassination attempt on the then Bangladeshi Prime Minister Sheikh Hasina, a secular leader considered friendly towards India (Raman 2005).

In its 2005 report, submitted to US Congress it was mentioned that the mission of HuJI-B is to establish Islamic rule in Bangladesh. It has connections with the Pakistani militant groups like Harkat-ul-Jihadi-al-Islami (HuJI) and Harkat-ul-Mujahidin (HUM), who advocate anti-Indian propaganda in Pakistan.

Jamaat-e-Islami and its students wing Islamic Chhatra Shibir (ICS) have maintained an anti-India stance and are reportedly supporting the insurgent groups in north-east India. Like the Jamaat, the Islamic Chhatra Shibir blames 'a secular society' for Bangladesh's wild decadence. The ICS, as per the reports of the South Asia Terrorism Portal shares close links with other fundamentalist outfits operating in South Asia[6] and Afghanistan. They maintained that the said organization is acting on their behalf in Bangladesh, helping them to recruit youth and indoctrinate the people with fanatical ideas. These also provide support and shelter for stockpiling weaponry in Bangladesh. ICS has sent a significant number of its members to Pakistan and Afghanistan during the reign of the Taliban regime where a large number of fanatic youth came under the direct command of Osama bin Laden. The members of the ICS are involved in murders and terrorist attacks inside Bangladesh.

ICS is also reportedly involved in the bombing within Bangladesh. In fact, Maulana Mirza Nurul Huq, former Convener of the Bangladesh Madrassa Teachers Association (BMTA) in a press conference had said that "the Jamaat-e-Islami and its student front Islami Chhatra Shibir are involved in radical activities in educational institutions using the name of Islam."However, no serious steps have been taken to curb its activities. Other groups which are also quite active in Bangladesh include Jagrata Muslim Janata Bangladesh and Purba Bangla Communist Party (here it is included because of its dreadful activities). Amongst them Hizb ut-Tahrir Bangladesh (HTB) is emerging as a distinct Islamist organization. It is active particularly in the universities of and is having international connections (Riaz 2008: 3).

The recruits of these militant organizations, referred to as "Bangladeshi Taliban," are students of Deobandi madrassas[7] that have mushroomed throughout the country including the border areas of Bangladesh and Assam and West Bengal in India. "Meetings have been reported in the bordering madrassas, such as Jagadal Dakhila Madarsa, Distt. Panchgarh of JEI-Bangladesh where local leaders discussed motivating of Muslims in the areas on both the sides of the border to arouse the feeling of Jihad. A number of such bordering madrassas are reported to have been visited by JEI-Pak leaders who have utilized the opportunity to criticize India on the Kashmir issue and to give calls for sending Mujahedis to India and other non-Islamic countries. JEI-Bangladesh and ICS-Bangladesh have also been noticed delivering lecture on the need to liberate the bordering villages in West Bengal from India and merging them with Islamic Bangladesh. Indian Muslims are urged to take up arms to defend their faith and are assured of training and supply of weapons" (RNP Singh 2002).

It is also reported that the members of HuJI-B easily cross over to India and hide in madrassas and mosques in West Bengal and Assam. Thus, it is important for India to become conscious about security of the north-eastern region and prevent it from becoming like Federally Administered Tribal Areas of Pakistan which is nominally controlled by Islamabad and a safe haven for Taliban particularly when connectivity with the north-east India remains a challenge and border between India and Bangladesh remains porous.

In May 2002, nine Islamist extremist groups, including HuJI-B, formed the Bangladesh Islamic Manch (Association) at a camp near the small town of Ukiah south of Cox's Bazaar. The Munch included Rohingiyas, a Muslim minority in Burma, and the Muslim United Liberation Tigers of Assam (MULTA), a small militant group operating in India's north-east. Members of MULTA were reported to be trained by the Bangladeshi veterans of the anti-Soviet war in Afghanistan of 1980s, in at least two camps of southern Bangladesh (RNP Singh 2002: 265). The surrendered MULTA cadres revealed in interrogation that most of them crossed over to Bangladesh and took military training there, mostly in private madrassas located in three adjoining districts of Bangladesh, i.e., Kutigram, Jamalpur and Sherpur, very close to Meghalaya and Cox Bazaar. The trainers were tall sturdy and Urdu speaking men who appeared to be Pakistanis.

Jagrata Muslim Janata Bangladesh (JMJB), classified as a fundamentalist organization by Dhaka, is an Islamist group based around north-western region of Bangladesh. It is believed to have links with Taliban and Al-Qaeda and espouse the ideals of the Taliban. There are significant reports that suggested that JMJB was supported by the members of BNP as the former Deputy Minister for Land, Ruhil Kuddud Talukder Dulu, was reportedly having close links with outfit. Besharat Ullah, the BNP Joint Secretary, purportedly addressed the first rally of JMJB.

Jamaat-ul-Mujahedeen Bangladesh (JMB), founded in 1998 is a banned Islamic organization that gained prominence in 2001 when bombs and documents detailing the activities of the organization were discovered in Parbatipur in Dinajpur district. JMB's youth front Al-Mujahedeen that began working in mid 1990s remains obscure even today. It is also said that JMB is another name for the vigilante Islamist group, the Jagrata Muslim Janata Bangladesh.[8]

Sanctuary for Indian Insurgent Groups

The radicalization in Bangladesh determines the intensity of its indulgence in extending support to the northeast insurgents in India. However, the links of the insurgent groups fall into two categories, namely: links with Indian insurgent groups including Islamic groups operating in the north-east and links with umbrella organizations to synergies the activities of the fundamentalist and terrorist groups in Bangladesh and India (RNP Singh 2002: 224-225). There are substantial reports of use of India's north-eastern territory as a transit route to infiltrate into Jammu and Kashmir by the Islamist groups of the region. There have also been apprehensions about occasional and potential strikes by the groups and separatist groups targeting West Bengal, Assam and other cosmopolitan cities of India.

In fact, Nagas and Mizo insurgent groups of India's north-east were able to establish their base in Bangladesh (then East Pakistan) immediately after the partition of India. Presently there are two armed militant groups in Nagaland, 39 groups in Manipur, 37 groups in Assam, 30 groups in Tripura and four groups in Meghalaya. Most of these groups are aided and provided safe havens in Bangladesh (Jafa: 2006: 2). It was under the regime of Begum Khaleda Zia (2001-2006) that the number of the extremist groups of the north-east increased.

In 1956 after the Indian Army called out to fight Naga insurgency, A.Z. Phizo, the leader of the Naga movement crossed over to Bangladesh (then East Pakistan). He established his base in East Pakistan from where he armed his group and mobilized international support (Prakash Singh 1972: 11).

In fact, with the birth of Bangladesh, the sanctuaries of the north-east groups in Bangladesh were eliminated for a short period. However, after the assassination of Sheikh Mujibur Rehman, Mizo rebels regained some of the lost grounds in Chittagong Hill Tract (CHT) as collaborators of the local authorities and helped them in settling Bengali Muslims in CHT and ensuring their own safe refuge in return.[9]

In 2005, the Ministry of External Affairs (MEA) Government of India had prepared a list of 172 Indian insurgent group camps located particularly in Dhaka, Chittagong Hill Tract, Sylhet, Mymensingh, Sherpar, Moulawi Bazaar, Sunamganj, Rangamali, Khagrachari, and Bandarban. Cox's Bazar in Chittagong District is particularly used for the transshipment of weapons and explosives. The route adopted is Cox's Bazar, Alikadam, Kasalang Reserve Forest, Mizoram, Silchar, Jiriban, Tamenglong and Paren. BSF had submitted a list of 79 militant camps in Bangladesh to the BDR officers during a meeting at Shillong on 22 October 2003 (Prakash: 173).

A more detailed involvement of Bangladesh hard cores support to north-east insurgents was disclosed in a 10-page press note released on the occasion of BSF Raising Day in November 1995. The note disclosed that most insurgent outfits in the north-east were acquiring sophisticated weapons from Thailand with the active connivance of Bangladesh intelligence (Krishna 2005: 70-77). The facilities enjoyed by them broadly are same as those available to the Islamic fundamentalist groups (RNP Singh 2002: 22). In fact, links between Bangladeshi militants with India's radical militant groups is one of the major security challenges to reckon with.

The Bangladeshi hard core groups have extensive contacts with the Muslim groups of the northeast India like Muslim Liberation Tiger of Assam (MLTA), Students Islamic Movement of India (SIMI), Students Islamic Organization (SIO), Islamic Liberation Army (ILA), Liberation of Islamic Tiger Force (LITF), Muslim Liberation Army (MLA), Muslim United Liberation Tiger (MULTA), People's United Liberation Front, Harkat-ul-Mujahideen, United Muslim Liberation Front of Assam (UMLFA), Muslim Liberation Army (MLA), Muslim Security Council of Assam (MSCA), Muslim Security Force (MSF), Muslim Tiger Force (MTF), Muslim Volunteer Force (MVF), Harkat-ul-Jehad (HUJ), Harkat-ul-Mujahideen (HUM), Islamic Liberation Army of Assam (ILAA), Islamic Sevak Sangh (ISS), Islamic United Reformation Protest of India (IURPI), Islamic Revolutionary Front (IRF), Islamic National Front (INF), United Islamic Liberation Army (UILA), United Islamic Revolutionary Army (UIRA) and Zomi Revolutionary Volunteer (ZRV).

The Jamiat-ul-Mujahedeen, a banned organization in India, has also reportedly been using Bangladesh as an important transit point for its cadres. The Tehrik-ul-Mujahideen (TUM), which has close links with Ahle Hadis, has been using Bangladesh for the outlet of its cadres by exploiting the sectarian feudalism prevailing along the route. Top TUM outfits, Ahmedullaj Nahami alias Ahmed Jan (arrested in 1997 in Delhi) and Mohammad Yousuf Rather (arrested in 1998) made disclosures about the Tehrik-ul-Mujahideen (TUM) network in Bangladesh. Reports have been received from time to time from the top Lashkar-e-Toiba (LET) leaders visiting Bangladesh to have a conversation with the leaders of the JEI (BD) and its student's wing the ICS. In June 1999, Abdullahil Arman and Mohammad Yaqub Ali of LET (Pakistan) visited Bangladesh to meet Motinur Akand, President of the ICS and requested him to send volunteers to join the Kashmiri militants. Again in July 2000, Maulana Abu Faiyaz of the LET (Pakistan) met Maulana Abdul Rauf and Mufti Nizamul

Qadir (both leaders of HuJI-B) and formulated plans for launching suicide attacks on Indian security forces (RNP Singh 2002: 232).

On 12 October 2005, the Hyderabad Police Special Task Force revealed a massive network of subversions, recruitments and radicalization in Andhra Pradesh as investigators discovered that as many as 500 Hyderabad youth had undergone arms training in Bangladesh and Baluchistan through HuJI-Bangladesh network. Other prominent joint operations involving Bangladeshi cadres have included the 7 March 2006 serial bombings at Varanasi executed by HuJI-B and Students Islamic Movement of India (SIMI) conspirators; the Delhi blasts of 29 October 2005, involving HuJI-B and LeT cadres; and the 28 December 2005 attack at the Indian Institute of Science, Bangalore, attributed to HuJI-B and JEM cadres. While investigations are still to establish the linkages in the Mumbai blasts of 11 July 2006, preliminary investigations do suggest that Bangladesh was used for transit and facilitation operations (Sahni 2006).

According to the Indian intelligence reports, leaders of various militant outfits of the north-east are based in Chittagong and Sylhet, both these regions having international airports which can be used to flee within a short notice. Some of the insurgent group leaders are living with their families in Bangladesh. These include Paresh Barua (C-in-C of ULFA), Ranjan Daimary (President NDFB), Julius Dorphang (Chairman, HNLC), Dilesh Mark (Chairman, ANVC), Bishwamohan Debbarma (President, NLFT), and Ranjit Debbarma (President, ATTF) (RNP Singh 2002: 22). It is reported that Paresh Barua and Arabinda Rajkhowa are having fake Bangladeshi passports and travel documents and are working under Bangladesh's direct 'diktat.' Until recently Bangladesh has maintained a policy of complete denial without verifying the details given to them. In fact, Dhaka counter alleges that anti-Bangladesh elements are operating out of India. Now the government in New Delhi and Dhaka seems committed to take on actions against the terrorists and insurgent groups in the north east India and Bangladesh.

NSCN (IM) had its camps in Jorhart near Cox's Bazar with the strength of 250 cadres, Vaital camp near Rangamati with a strength of 300 cadres, Galilee camp near Alikadam with strength of 50 cadres and H.Q. of NSCN (IM) at Dhaka in a four storied building near New Market. The Indian Border Security Force (BSF), as well as an intelligence agency in the Cachar district, has stated that there are approximately 25 training camps in the area with full knowledge of

Bangladeshi authorities. Outfits operating in these camps are United Liberation Front of Assam (ULFA), National Democratic Front of Bodoland (NDFB), National Liberation Front of Tripura (NLFT), All Tripura Tiger Force (ATTF), Peoples Liberation Army (PLA) etc.[10] It is widely reported that the ULFA is a constituent of the Bangladesh Islamic Manch, a united council under HuJI's leadership. In 1995 a consignment of arms A.K.47, A.K 56 and R.P.D 7.62 L.M.G and ammunition arranged from China was delivered from a Chinese naval ship of the coast of Cox's Bazar and transshipped in the hired vessel. The goods were meant for the insurgent groups of the north-east India.

In 1998, it was reported that "The ISI has set up a training camp about 30 km from the Indo-Bangladesh border between the hamlets of Chattak and Jaintipura in Bangladesh. About 315 ultras from different outfits of the NE states divided into 14 batches are undergoing three months of intensive training under the Camp Commander Major Meer Muammar Mushtaqeen."

There was a massive arms seizure at Chittagong port on 2 April 2004. It included rocket launchers-150, rockets-840, ammunition rounds-over a million, grenades-2500 and assorted assault rifles over 1700. According to Subhash Kapila, "The unloading of this over-sized arms consignment at a Bangladesh government owned jetty indicates that the Bangladesh Government, its intelligence agencies and administrative machinery would be in the know of it..." The arms consignment loaded on dozen trucks or so was headed for Maulvi Bazar in proximity to the Indian border and where Bangladesh permissively tolerates the anti-Indian insurgents' safe havens and training camps... The type of weapons like rocket launchers and grenade launchers and hundreds of rockets and thousands of grenades indicate that they were intended for anti-Indian insurgents being hosted in Bangladesh and equip them to launch devastating fire-power attacks on Indian Army regular forces posts, camps etc (Kapila 2004)." Kapila further notes that there were significant proof to suggest that the then Bangladesh's ruling party BNP was involved in this arms haul as "Salauddin Qader Chowdhury figures as the biggest name not only in the seizure but also in his involvement in the past in such activities, Chowdhury is a Special Adviser to the Bangladesh Prime Minister and a leading BNP MP from Chittagong. He owns a shipping line and the shipping vessel that brought the arms consignment to the Chittagong outer anchorage is either owned by him or facilitated by him, the two trawlers which off-loaded the arms consignment from the outer anchorage and brought to the Fertilizer factory Jetty are reported to be owned by Hajji Abdul Sobhan, a local BNP leader with proximate links to Chowdhury. Local BNP leaders and party functionaries along with the local police were present at the Chittagong Port to oversee and facilitate the transfer of this large consignment of illicit arms consignment and its onward movement. In a country where police and intelligence surveillance are as intense as that of the ISI in Pakistan, it is inconceivable that the then Bangladesh Prime Minister Begum Khaleda Zia would be unaware of the involvement of ruling party MPs in such anti-Indian activities. Earlier, on 10 April , the Mayor of Chittagong Mohiuddin Ahmad Chowdhury (AL) made the following observations: Arms shipment was sent by USA and Pakistan. It was intended for anti-Indian insurgent groups operating from Bangladesh."

There was also arrest of NSI (National Security Intelligence) DG Maj Gen (retd.) Rezzaqul Haider Chowdhury and Brig Gen (retd) M Abdur Rahim in connection with the sensational Chittagong arms haul case. Referring to the confessional statement of arrested former NSI director (security) Sahab Uddin, the public prosecutor said that both the former NSI chiefs helped transport the deadly consignment through Bangladesh from China before it was hauled at the Chittagong Urea Fertilizer Company Ltd. Jetty in the early hours of April 02, 2004. Sahab Uddin in his confessional statement said that former NSI DG Brigadier General (retd) Abdur Rahim held several meetings with the UAE-based ARY group that is involved in firearms business in Dhaka and Dubai. According to former NSI director (security) Sahab Uddin's confessional statement, Rahim received a Mobile Monitoring System and also a commitment from ARY group that could help him in setting up a private TV channel. The then DGFI director (Counter-Intelligence Bureau) Rezzaqul Haider, who later succeeded Abdur Rahim as the NSI chief, also had close links with United Liberation Front of Assam (ULFA) operational wing Chief Paresh Barua who used the name 'Ahmed' to hide his identity. Rezzaqul took Paresh (Ahmed) to Combined Military Hospital (CMH) in Dhaka to meet Sahab Uddin, P. P Kamal Uddin told the court quoting Sahab Uddin's confessional statement.

Lintner cites an internal document from HUJI which mentions "lists no less than 19 'training establishments' all over Bangladesh, but it is uncertain how many of them actually offer military training. What is certain, however, is that since a new coalition government led by the Bangladesh National Party (BNP) took over in October 2001, Bangladesh Islamist militants have become more vocal and active (Lintner 2002)." The training includes both indoctrination and handling of weapons and explosives (RNP Singh 2002: 14).

Earlier in November 1999, former Director of the CBI, S.K.Datta, wrote: "Abu Nasir, a Bangladeshi Laskar who was arrested in West Bengal revealed names of many Laskar who were operating in the country. The Siliguri corridor has been targeted by the ISI through Laskar for establishing bases... [Chief of LET] Hafiz Saeed visited Bangladesh in 1998 and managed to recruit Bengali Laskars. Incidentally, in 1998, Bangladesh has been the favorite shelter for ISI operatives, ULFA activists and other militants of the northeast. It was reported in April 2000 that Mohammad Nasim former Home Minister in Sheikh Hasina's government, admitted that with the help of an unnamed foreign intelligence agency, Indian separatists had long been provided training on Bangladeshi soil. He also accused India of encouraging and training the Chakmas (Datta 2004:14). Islamist militants in Bangladesh have established bases in India and are provided sanctuary by their counterparts as well as the Indian rebels whom they help (Karlekar 2005: 19). However, Nasim declared that after Sheikh Hasina came to power in 1996, both the countries agreed not to shelter each other's separatist groups. Sheikh Hasina government also signed a peace accord with the CHT insurgents to contain the insurgency in CHT.

Details of the data obtained by Assam Police on the activities of the ISI and the different Muslim groups were laid on the table of the Assam assembly by the Chief Minister of Assam on April 6, 2000.[11] This document clearly details the ULFA leader's regular movement to Pakistan from Bangladesh and of the training imparted to them in Mujahideen camps in Peshawar. Prior to this, the Assam Police had arrested four persons on suspicion on 10 August 1999 in Gauhati. The role of Directorate General of Forces Intelligence (DGFI), the military intelligence agency of Bangladesh in all these transactions remains shadowy. Throughout they have been the go-betweens or intermediaries in the operations of the ISI with the northeastern militant groups.

Madrassas as the Breeding ground for Extremism

The madrassas perform an important function in an impoverished country such as Bangladesh, where basic education is available only to a few. Today there are an estimated 64,000 madrassas in Bangladesh divided into two kinds (Aliya and Quami). The Aliya madrassas are run with government support and control, while the Dars-e-Nizami is totally independent. Aliya students study for 15-16 years and are taught Arabic, religious theory and other Islamic subjects as well as English, mathematics, science and history. They prepare themselves for employment in government service, or for jobs in the private sector like any other college or university student. In 1999, there were 7,122 such registered madrassas in Bangladesh. These are also the main recruiting place for the fundamentalist outfits. According to the Bangladeshi intelligence agencies in their initial assessment identifies 323 madrassas where training of these groups take place. The investigation by the Bangladeshi intelligence agencies zeroed down on 323 Quomi madrassas where militant training was taking place.

There are 5,230 Quomi madrassas with about 14 lakh students and the related clerics mainly belonging to IOJ. It was given official recognition in 2006 by the Khaleda Zia government (Majid 2009). Official recognition of these educational establishments was resisted because of fears that this would lead to a spurt in religious extremism in the Muslim-dominated country rocking its fragile democracy. The education of these madrassas is restricted to the teaching of Holy Quran, Arabic and little else. Samina Ahmed, South Asia project director for the International Crisis Group says that the education of Quomi madrassas is not well equipped to fit in the modern learning but can be clerics. According to Communist Party leader Mujahidul Islam Selim, "they create an unemployed youth who have no capacity to be employed in the productive sector of the economy. They are being lured into becoming carriers of bombs."

Links

The end of Soviet occupation in Afghanistan led to the unemployment of many Jihadis or mujahedeen (Islamic religious warriors). Their Pakistani leaders motivated them to move to Bangladesh to operate against India (RNP Singh 2002: 222-223). The former BSF Director General Ajai Raj Sharma in 2002 stated that there were "firm reports" that Pakistan's ISI had set up new training centers for these groups in Bangladesh. "The groups operating in Jammu and Kashmir are also being trained there... It [ISI] is now fully concentrating in Bangladesh," Pakistani former President General Musharraf's visit to Dhaka in 2002 led to the strengthening of links with Bangladesh army, the BDR, the DGFI, the NSI, important bureaucrats and political leaders including anti-Indian leaders and extremist parties. It also led to an increase in the strength of Pak High Commission staff in Dhaka including some additional ISI personnel.

By 2006 at the end of the BNP's regime madrassas supplied nearly 35 percent of the Army recruits.

It is reported that India even views the Pakistani High Commission in Dhaka as the 'nerve centre' of ISI activities in promoting these groups and insurgency in India. Institutionalization of fundamentalism in India's eastern neighborhood has facilitated India's north-eastern insurgent groups to incessantly misuse Bangladeshi territory as headquarters, sanctuaries, training camps, arms procurement and storage facilities and transit route. In fact, "Since 1950s erstwhile East Pakistan has been facilitating, encouraging and supporting various northeast insurgent groups. In *The Myth of Independence*, former Pakistani Prime Minister Zulfiqar Ali Bhutto laid claims to Assam and suggested that he wanted some areas of India's northeast to be included in Pakistan" (Datta 2004: 14). In 2005, the MEA prepared a list of 307 north-east insurgents supported by Bangladeshi extremist outfits sponsored by ISI, with money coming from the Gulf. The list was handed over by the BSF to the erstwhile BDR. In fact, these insurgent groups who are using Bangladeshi territory are said to be cooperating closely with the erstwhile BDR, DGFI and ISI for their anti-Indian activity.

It is important to note that it was after 31 years, that any military chief of Pakistan visited Bangladesh in 2001 after a few months of 9/11 and almost immediately after the US invasion of Afghanistan. Subsequently, links between Pakistani ISI and DGFI became evident in late 2001 after the fall of the Taliban in Afghanistan when a ship carrying several hundred Taliban and Al-Qaeda cadres along with arms and ammunition arrived in Chittagong port. This was made possible by the Islamist extremist friendly government at Dhaka. They were moved to the southeastern border area of Bangladesh. This could not have been possible without the knowledge and support of the security agencies within Bangladesh. According to Colonel Anil Bhatt, almost all groups of India's northeast were reported to have met the Al-Qaeda seniors and pledged their support to them.[12]

Sayed Abu Nasir, a Bangladeshi national who had worked for the international Islamist charity outfit established by Osama bin Laden, was picked by the ISI and posted to Dhaka and worked with DGFI. According to the Indian intelligence sources, he was also involved in coordination and providing assistance to India's north-eastern secessionist and sending them to training camps in Pakistan (Karlekar 2005: 70-71). It is also believed that there are as many, if not more, terrorist training camps in Bangladesh territory as there are in Pakistan and that more Indian fugitives wanted for their involvement in acts of terrorism in Indian Territory have been given shelter in Bangladesh than in Pakistan.

Three ATTF undergrounds, who surrendered before the Security Forces on October 2, 2002, revealed that the ISI had arranged six-month training for eight ATTF undergrounds at Kandahar (Afghanistan) and that they were flown to Kandahar from Dhaka. Two senior leaders of the NDFB, Dhiren Boro (Vice-President, arrested on 1 December 2003) and Gobinda Basumatary, General Secretary (arrested on 5 December 2002) disclosed the instrumentality of the ISI in training of NDFB cadres in Pakistan. A number of ULFA leaders including Pradip Gogoi (Vice-Chairman) and Lohit Deori revealed that several batches of ULFA cadres were flown to Pakistan from Dhaka for training which was arranged by the ISI" (RNP Singh 2002: 23). Nazir Ahmed Sodozey, a Pakistani fundamentalist, disclosed the hidden facts of Bangladeshis undergoing training in the HuA camps in Afghanistan, provision of shelter to HuA cadres in Bangladesh, involvement of Bangladeshis in terrorist activities/ kidnappings of foreign tourists etc. Abu Baker Siddiquei, another hard core revealed that he had motivated and assisted recruitment of Bihari Muslims to undergo arms training at the RIF training centre in Arakan hills near Chittagong. Thus the rogue elements of Afghanistan and Pakistan possibly want Bangladesh to be an important base, if not headquarters and a staging center of their activities.

The recruits of these outfits are taken to Pakistan mostly via Nepal. In Pakistan, these recruits are trained and subsequently sent to military camps in Afghanistan. It is not known how many people from Bangladesh, including Rohingyas, have fought in Afghanistan. The Prothom Alo, a Bangla daily newspaper, reported in 2004 that 3000 Bangladeshis fought along with the Taliban fighters in Afghanistan. They have even served in Kashmir and Chechnya.

In this respect, it may be noted that in certain quarters it is believed that entire ULFA leadership has shifted its base to China. In 1960s, China was providing training facilities to the insurgent groups mostly in the Sajek range of Hills of CHT in late 1960s (RNP Singh 2002: 184). According to the recent investigation in Bangladesh, Hafiz Rehman, one of the accused of March 2004 weapons offloading consignment from China for ULFA, confessed before Metropolitan Magistrate that Paresh Barua was helped by Chittagong Urea

Fertilizers Limited, Coast Guard, the then chiefs of the Directorate General Forces Intelligence and National Security Intelligence to offload weapons and ammunition which were enough to arm a whole military division.

Financial Sources

With huge funds coming from Pakistan,[13] Afghanistan, Saudi Arabia, Jeddah, Qatar, Kuwait,[14] and United Arab Emirates the Jamaat-e-Islami and the group of related fundamentalist organisations turned into a formidable political force and became strong in the countryside as a result of being instrumental in setting up Deobandi madrassas. Deobandi madrassas are the main recruiting institution for the fundamentalist outfits. Other sources of funds include huge revenues and profits from investments and enterprises; institutionalized extortion; regular contributions of the members and associate members; Zakat (religious tax); profit from the sales proceeds of its literature. Jamaat has also set up a dozen of trusts, welfare and financial organizations like Islamic banks throughout the country. According to Abul Barakat, "the net profit from fundamentalist economy in Bangladesh is approximately Taka 12,000 crore." These organizations are almost entirely manned by Jamaat and Shibir members.

These groups of Bangladesh have reportedly been receiving financial assistance from madrassas and several Muslim Non-Governmental Organizations in West Asia and Bangladesh (RNP Singh 2002: 15). In Bangladesh, Adarsha Kutir, Servants of Suffering Humanity International (SSGI), Al Faruk Islamic Foundation, Hatadin, Rabita Al-Alam Al-Islam, the World Assembly of Muslim Youth, Al Haramain Islamic Foundation, the International Islamic Relief Organization, the Revival of Islamic Heritage Society (RIHS), the Ishra Islamic Foundation, International Islamic Relief Organization and Revival of Islamic Heritage Society are the main financing NGO's. Saudi Arabia, Gulf countries, Afghanistan and Pakistan also provide the Jihadis with logistic support (Riaz 2008: 83). The DGFI revealed that the militants are involved in the arms-trafficking and arms training at madrassas in Dhaka sponsored by a Saudi organization called al-Haramain, which is known to have links with Osama's money distributing infrastructure, operating in 37 branches in different parts of Bangladesh.

Conclusion

The society in Bangladesh is divided into two groups, one dominated by secularists and the other by Islamic forces, but the fact of the matter is that secularism is still a fundamental base of Bangladesh society. Both the groups are at loggerheads with each other which is very much dangerous for the stability of the country. Bangladesh as a nation cannot survive until and unless there is unity among all the stakeholders of the society. The interest and survival of the country is fundamental and the country in this globalized world has to show maturity in handling domestic conflict and also has to be careful regarding the external forces which may sacrifice Bangladesh interests for the sake of their own. The unity among the two big political parties is also very important for the overall positive progress of the society.

Ali Riaz suggest that to curb any kind of fundamentalism it is important to improve law and order situation, rounding up the known militants, dismantling the support infrastructure, investigating any links with the local administration, bringing the patron of justice, identifying the sources of weapons of the fundamentalist forces, commitment to education, balanced social and economic development, and human right protection. International pressure, particularly from the investors or developmental partners, can also check the militancy in Bangladesh. According to E N Rammohan, former Director General of the BSF for counter-insurgency, certain lessons that need to be taken into account include: first is to find the cause, analyze it and take drastic steps to effect remedial measures. Secondly, it is important to ensure that in operations the people should not be alienated. In a situation where there has been economic discrimination and corrupt governance it is important to ensure that there is good clean governance, can wean the people away from the insurgent. The present government of Bangladesh, however, seems committed to driving out the militant groups from its soil. In this regard, Bangladesh has recently accepted India's proposal to set up a Joint Task Force to deal with militancy and other anti-national elements. But modalities of the Joint Task Force are yet to be evolved. Dhaka is also showing its desire to sign several agreements with India and the US on the formation of a "South Asian Anti-Terrorism Taskforce" (SAAT), the purpose and modality of which is not clearly known to the public. It should be noted that efforts towards joint anti-terrorist or security operations between India and Bangladesh started soon after Sheikh Hasina came to power. In this regard, a joint counter-terrorist military exercise took place in Jorhat, Assam and West Bengal's Jalpaiguri in February-March 2009 despite February 2009

Mutiny by the BDR. These developments are cornerstones for re-building strong regional ties and trust between the two countries.

However, Bangladesh's opposition leader Begum Khaleda Zia has strongly opposed the setting up of the task force to combat terrorism, alleging that Prime Minister Hasina was using it as an excuse to bring foreign troops into the country. Begum Zia asserted at a rally in the month of May, rally that "there is no militancy in Bangladesh" and claimed that her government (2001-06) had successfully eliminated it.

The Jamaat and fundamentalists have been successful in managing the support of the people in their acts against the secular intellectuals, Non-Government Organisations (NGO) and in their aggressive policies against women emancipation which forced many women to commit suicide. However, despite organized efforts of the Jamaat-e-Islami against women emancipation it is important to note that among Bangladesh's most powerful people are two women who held the post of Prime Minister of Bangladesh, i.e., Begum Khaleda Zia and Sheikh Hasina Wajed. Additionally, due to the long history of moderate Islamic culture, there is a large section of the population that is not inclined towards fundamentalist bigotry.

Endnotes

1. Kanchan Lakshman, Islamist Extremist Mobilization in Bangladesh, *Terrorism Monitor*, Volume: 3 Issue: 12,17/6/2005, http://www.jamestown.org/single/?no_ cache=1&tx_ttnews%5Btt_news%5D=507, 7/10/2008
2. Main aim to replace to the present state of Bangladesh with an Islamic state based on Sharia (Islamic Principles), Oppose democracy, Strict regulation of women, Banning of activities like movies, television, videos, music, dancing etc., Aggressive enforcement of its regulations particularly the use of armed, "religious police". M J Gohari, The Taliban: Ascent to Power, (Oxford University Press), 2001, pp, 26-27.
3. Jamaat-ul Mujahedeen took the responsibility for the blasts. Jamaat-ul-Mujahedeen is a sister organization of the Jamaat-e-Islami, which was the coalition partner of the government between 2001-2006 (Sashanka S. Banerjee) p.158.

4. B Raman, Bangladesh & Jihadi Terrorism—An Update, *South Asian Analysis Group*, Paper No.887, 7/1/2004, http://www.southasiaanalysis.org/papers9/ paper887.html, 12/1/2009
5. Bangladesh: Attacks on Members of the Hindu Minority, *Amnesty International:* London, December 2001
6. International links of ICS include links with Rohingiyas Solidarity Organization, World Assembly of Muslim Youth and International Islamic Federation of Students Organization
7. During Begum Khalida Zia's reign approximately 45,000 Islamic madrassas all over the land, feeding the supply chain of the militants and the suicide bombers, were established in Bangladesh. (Sashanka S.Banerjee, India's Security Dilemmas: Pakistan & Bangladesh, Anthem Press: New York, London, 2006, pp.156-57.
8. For details see, Jama'atul Mujahedeen Bangladesh, South Asian Portal, http://www. satp.org/satporgtp/countries/bangladesh/terroristoutfits/JMB.htm;Terrorism:A Tragic Tale of Continued Denials, New Age, 27 September 2005; Julfikar Ali Manik, 'Bangla Bhai active for 6 years, The Daily Star,Vol.4, No.338, 13/5/2004, http://thedailystar.net/2004/05/13/d4051301022.htm
9. The Times of India, New Delhi, 1 October 1984, cited in Krishna Gopal, Islamic Fundamentalism in Bangladesh and its role in north-east insurgency, in Depanker Sengupta and Sudhir Kumar Singh, Insurgency in North-East India: Role of Bangladesh, Authors Press: New Delhi, p.18
10. NSCN (IM) had their bases at Maudaung (NOM), Nghalphum, Sumsong, Salopi, Pantmapara, villages Nandari and Po-Longia in the district of Maulvi Bazar and at Ujjainpara in Bandarban area. ULFA had its camps at Maijdi, Mymensingh, Rangpur, Mohangaon, Bhairab Bazar, Pulchari, Adampur, Banugashi, Jyantipur, Jaydevpur, Shrimangal and Cox's Bazar. The two Tripura groups, ATTF and NLTF, have preferred Bandarban Khagrachari districts contiguous to Agartala. PLA had a small Manipuri settlements scattered over CHT. It had its base in Sylhet and Chittagong as well. Cited in Krishna Gopal, Islamic Fundamentalism in Bangladesh and its role in north-east insurgency, in Depanker Sengupta and Sudhir Kumar Singh, Insurgency in North-East India: Role of Bangladesh, Authors Press: New Delhi, p.186

11. ISI activities in Assam, Statement laid on the table of the house of the Assam Legislative Assembly under item No.12 dated April 6,2000 by the Chief Minister of Assam, cited in Rammohan, p.10

12. Anil Bhat, ISI's eastward operations-old links in North-East India and new ones in South-East Asia, in Depanker Sengupta and Sudhir Kumar Singh, Insurgency in North-East India: Role of Bangladesh, Authors Press: New Delhi, p.24

13. "By the early mid-1990s, Pakistan Army, ever ready to cause trouble for India, decided to establish and promote liaison with the Bangladesh military, the police and the other security forces. The justification for such an alliance was: (1) Islamic solidarity (2) Past history (3) Promoting enmity with India and destabilize it, a common objective for both. Gradually a firm alliance took shape between Pakistan ISI and the entire gamut of the security services in Bangladesh. It was during this period that a whole lot of separatist militant outfits fighting India in its north-eastern region began setting up their bases on the soil of Bangladesh, aided and abetted by Pakistan's ISI, who had already established itself as a significant force." Sashanka S.Banerjee, India's Security Dilemmas: Pakistan and Bangladesh, Anthem Press: London, New York, 2006 pp.153-15

14. It is reported that one Kuwait-based organization named "Islamic Heritage Society of Kuwait" and "Revival of Islamic Societies" with branches in Saudi Arabia, Kuwait, Qatar and United Arab Emirates are the funding sources from where the Islamic militants secure huge grants to 'promote Islam'. "Jongira Taka Pai Kothai?" (Where from the militants get money?), Sangbad, 20/8/2005, cited in Abu Nasar Saied Ahmed, p.13

References

"Bangladesh Today," 2006. *International Crisis Group Report,* No. 121. "Bangladesh: Human Rights under Threat as Election Tensions Intensify," 2007, *Amnesty International.*

"Captures Fail to Halt Bangladesh Militants,"2006, *Janes Information Group*. "Indian Police Catch two Suspected Militants in Delhi," Reuters, 17 Jan. 2007. "Indo-Bangla Border Fencing to Complete Soon," 2007, *The Economic Times*. ADAMS Brad. 2006. "Bangladesh: Elite Force Tortures, Kills Detainees," *Human Rights Watch*.

Ahmad Rashid, 2002, *Taliban: The Story of the Afghan Warlords*, London, Pan Books

Ahmed, Khaled, 2005, "Bangladesh: Pakistan's blowback in a looking-glass", *The Friday Times*, Lahore

Boustany, Nora, 2007, "Bangladesh Military Accused of Stalling on Elections," *The Washington Post.*

Chakrabarti, Sumon K, Bangladesh: The Shift in the Balance of Terror in South Asia, *International Assessment and Strategy Centre*,13/3/2006, http://www. strategycenter. net/research/pubID.96/pub_detail.asp#

Country Reports on Terrorism 2004, 2005, *U.S. Department of State.*

Datta, Sreeradha,2004, *Bangladesh a Fragile Democracy*, Shipra Publications, Delhi, Eaton, Richard M, 2001, "Who are the Bengal Muslims? Conversion and Islamization in Bengal," in R. Ahmed Ed., *Understanding the Bengal Muslims: Interpretative Essays*, New Delhi, Oxford University Press

Foster, Peter, 2006, "Bangladesh at Risk of Falling to Extremists," *The Daily Telegraph* Gurr, Ted Robert, 1970, *Why Men Rebel*, Princeton, New Jersey, Princeton University Press

Hashmi, Arshi Saleem, 2009, "Religious Parties and Militant Groups in Bangladeshi Politics: A Case Study", *Institute of Regional Studies In Islamabad,* December Juergensmeyer, Mark, 1993, *Religious Nationalism Confronts the Secular State*, Delhi, Oxford University Press

Kabir, Muhammad Ghulam, 1994, *Changing Face of Nationalism: The Case of Bangladesh*, New Delhi, South Asian Publishers

Kalam, Abul 2006, *The challenges of terrorism: Bangladesh response*, in S.D.Muni (ed.), Manohar Publishers & Distributors.

Karlekar, Hiranmay, 2005, *Bangladesh: The Next Afghanistan*, Sage Publication. New Delhi Lakshman, Kanchan, 2005, Islamist Extremist Mobilization in Bangladesh, *Terrorism Monitor*, Volume, 3 Issue

Lawrence, Bruce B, Howarth James. 2005. (Ed.), *Messages to the World: The Statements of Osama Bin Laden,* New York, Verso

Lintner, Bertil, "Bangladesh Extremist Islamist Consolidation, *Faultline*, Vol.14, The Institute of Conflict and Management, New Delhi, 2003

Lintner, Bertil, "Championing Islamist Extremism", *South Asia Intelligence Review*, vol. 1, no. 9, 16 September 2002; South Asia Terrorism Portal; www.satp.org/ satporgtp/sair/ Archives/I_9.htm, accessed on 17/3/2009

Lintner, Bertil, 2002, "Beware of Bangladesh—Bangladesh: A Cocoon of Terror," *Far Eastern Economic Review.*

Lintner, Bertil, 2002, "Is religious extremism on the rise in Bangladesh?" *Jane's Intelligence Review.*

Majid, Farida (2009), WB Report on the goodness of Qoumi Madrassas, *Mukto Mona*, 6/6/2009, http://muktomona.com/wordpress/?p=328, accessed on 6/6/2009

Milan, William, 2007, "Bangladesh at the Crossroads," *Daily Times* (Pakistan) Muni, S D, 2006, *Responding to terrorism in South Asia,* The University of Michigan, Manohar Publishers & Distributors

Patterns of Global Terrorism 2002, 2003, *U.S. Department of State.* Prakash, Ved, *Encyclopedia of Northeast India*, Vol. 2, Atlantic, New Delhi

Raman B, Bangladesh & Jihadi Terrorism—An Update, *South Asian Analysis Group*, Paper No.887, 7/1/2004, http://www.southasiaanalysis.org/papers9/paper887. html, 12/1/2009

Raman, B, 2005, "Goons or terrorists? Bangladesh decides", *Asia Times Online* Riaz, Ali, 2008, *Islamist Militancy in Bangladesh: A Complex Web*, Rutledge, London, New York

Runciman, Walter G, 1966, *Relative Deprivation and Social Justice*, Berkeley and London, University of California Press

Sattar, Abdus, 2004, Bangladesh madrassas shikhkha o samaj jibone tar provab (Madrassas education in Bangladesh and indications in social life), Dhaka, Islamic Foundation.

Sengupta, Depanker and Sudhir Kumar Singh (eds.), 2005, *Insurgency in North-East India,* Authors Press, New Delhi,

Shawakat, Ali, A.M.M, 2006, *Faces of Terrorism in Bangladesh*, Dhaka, The University Press Limited

Simon, Denyer, 2008, "Concern mounts over Bangladesh madrassas after bombs" *Daily Times,* 29/9/2005, http://www.dailytimes.com.pk/default. asp?page=story_29-9-2005_pg4_23

Singh, Sudhir Kumar, *Insurgency in North-East India: Role of Bangladesh*, Authors Press, New Delhi

Stern, Jessica, 2003, *Terror in the Name of God: Why Religious Militants Kill*, New York, Harper Collins

Testimony by Dr. Christine Fair, 2005. *Human Rights Watch*, Congressional Human Rights Caucus Hearing on Bangladesh.

Chapter 6

Internal Conflicts in Pakistan

Sanchita Bhattacharya

Abstract

The internal conflicts and domestic crises in Pakistan are mainly the results of the breakdown of state institutions, yet crosscultural relationships among nation-states are being used maliciously to destabilize the other country or countries sometimes politically and sometimes economically. One of the important components of Pakistan's domestic skirmish is the non-state terror actors. The existence of non-state actors (Islamic extremists) associated with Pakistan or working on Pakistan's land with impunity is considered a menace. Over a period of time, Pakistan is in the path of becoming a frail state, and government policies are making it weaker still. Its disastrous economy, exacerbated by a series of corrupt leaders, is at the root of many of its internal problems. Due to ramshackle economic growth, the country has to deal with the hovering presence of American donations and the larger risk of its 'own' interest in Central and South Asia. Balochistan issue is also one of the major irritants in the domestic sphere of Pakistan. Significantly, the ethnic imbroglio of Balochistan has been infamous for 'kill-and-dump' operations. The US factor and the War on Terror fought over a decade caused overall strain and mass resentment and an easy pretext for terror groups with global Islamic agenda to validate their claims. The War has brought the havoc of drone attacks in the tribal belt of the country, causing massive internal dislocation of people within Pakistan, and increase in violent incidents amongst various ethnic populace in urban areas.

Introduction

Pakistan's short history as a country has been very turbulent. It oscillates between military rule and democratically elected governments, between secular policies and financial backing as a "frontline" state during the Cold War and the war against terrorism. Contemporary Pakistan is engrossed with a number of crises. Most of the issues are due to incompetence on the part of political leadership. In a way, the fabric of the country is threatened by internal threats causing illiteracy, internal population displacement, gender violence, corruption, sectarian adversities, militancy, rural-urban divide, etc. To make the argument more precise, one can state that Pakistan's political instability today is in large measure due to the struggle between three major actors—the civilian wing of the state, the military, and the Islamists (Waseem 2011: iv). The entire country is under attack from within itself.

Since its inception, Pakistan has been continually challenged by diverse groups on the basis of nationalism, regional separatism, religious doctrine and political dogma. This instability has been unfortunately reflected in domestic politics where pluralistic traditions have been regularly diluted by incompetent leadership or interrupted by periods of military rule. Causes like demographic alterations; economic disproportion; scarce and uneven distribution of resources; economic disparity, etc have more or less shaped the ethnic map of Pakistan in an ominous manner.

The first decade of the 21st century witnessed Pakistan as a harsh yet true face of 'collateral damage' in the war waged by the US and its coalition forces. In Pakistan, the battle lines were drawn immediately after 9/11. Pervez Musharraf was asked to decide whether he was with or against America. While the foreign allegiance put Pakistan in the camp of the 'good' with regard to the West, it created an impossible problem on the domestic front (Lall 2010: 99). Today, Pakistan stands at the juncture of an intense battle between two opposing visions of the country's future: one enforces a narrow and radical interpretation of Sharia law and Islam; the other seeks to preserve the modern, liberal, and tolerant face of Pakistan that was the vision of the country at the dawn of independence in 1947 (ICAN 2014: 2). The state is oscillating amid pro and anti liberal ideologies.

The internal conflicts and domestic crises in Pakistan are mainly the results of the breakdown of state institutions, yet crosscultural relationships among nation-states are being used maliciously to destabilize the other country or countries sometimes politically and sometimes economically. One of the important components of Pakistan's domestic skirmish is the non-state terror actors. The existence of non-state actors (Islamic extremists) associated with Pakistan or working on Pakistan's land with impunity is considered a menace. Over a period of time, Pakistan is in the path of becoming a frail state, and government policies are making it weaker still. Its disastrous economy, exacerbated by a series of corrupt leaders, is at the root of many of its internal problems. Due to ramshackle economic growth, the country has to deal with the hovering presence of American donations and the larger risk of its 'own' interest in Central and South Asia. Balochistan issue is also one of the major irritants in the domestic sphere of Pakistan. Significantly, the ethnic imbroglio of Balochistan has been infamous for 'kill-and-dump' operations. US factor and the War on Terror fought over a decade caused overall strain and mass resentment and an easy pretext for terror groups with global Islamic agenda to validate their claims. The War has brought the havoc of drone attacks in the tribal belt of the country, causing massive internal dislocation of people within Pakistan and increase in violent incidents amongst various ethnic populaces in urban areas. In retaliation, both civilian and military establishments are repeatedly attacked by the militants causing severe fatalities.

The sectarian conflict has caused tensions in the southern part of Punjab, Balochistan and also in the urban centre of Karachi and Quetta. The politics of sectarian exclusiveness is also becoming mainstream in Pakistan. Rampant violence and killing in the name of diverse religious sects has become a somewhat trend. Like the sectarian politics, ethnic variations in the country sources more evil than any good. Pakistan does project itself as a 'multi-ethnic' country, although the reality is far away from the acknowledgement of such ethnic multiplicity. The perennial problem has been domination of Punjabis over other ethnicities. The situation is worsened due to frustrating realities of Baloch people, denial of Sindhi identity and negligence of the tribal areas.

Militancy

For almost last one decade the phenomena of terrorism is perceived as an onslaught that drastically changed not only the face of world peace, security, economics and politics but, has put up a challenge for the survival of Pakistan. The role of Pakistan as a frontline state has not only shattered the economy but also suffered countless human casualties and a feeling of insecurity among the masses (Ahmad, Muhammad Ijaz et al. 2011). The economy is virtually in ruins. The ever increasing inflation has pushed more millions below the poverty line. Pakistani society has suffered huge irreparable losses in terms of human lives. It is estimated that Pakistani people have sacrificed over 40,000 persons including 5,000 security staff in US war on terror. The distressing and puzzling aspect of all these sacrifices by the people of Pakistan is that there seems to be no end to terrorism (Javaid and Ali 2013: 53-54). It won't be wrong to state that over period of a decade Pakistan has become a killing field. The absence of the rule of law and the impotency of the courts has made Pakistan a killing field where militants (the Taliban and Islamic fundamentalists among others), and the security forces operate with impunity. Neither these factions nor the civilian rulers have any sense of dignity, respect for life, or desire for justice. Innocent Pakistanis are seen as mere cannon fodder; the right to life has lost all meaning in the ruling political circles elected by the people they are now failing to protect (Asian Human Rights Commission 2013: 5).

Pakistan is confronted with two broad categories of terrorism namely internal and external which can be further classified. It is facing the twin menaces of religious extremism and ethnic strife. The real threat to security primarily comes from "within." The internal terror is caused by banned organisations with strong ethnic and sectarian bias. Areas like, Kuram, Para Chinar, Dera Ismail Khan, and southern Punjab are affected by this kind of terrorism. Suicide attacks and attacks on infrastructure, schools, banks, railway tracks and gas pipelines etc. are some other examples of home-grown terrorism. The international acts are like attacks on high value targets in Pakistan as President, Prime Minister, Marriot Hotel, Sri Lankan Cricket Team, Army GHQ, PNS Mehran Base, Police Stations, drone attacks and FC training centers etc. come in this category. These acts are sponsored by state agents as a tool of state policy (Irshad 2011: 227).

The multi-layered instability within the country, caused by numerous terror and militant outfits has a complex and overbearing impact on the country. The process of Talibanization has changed the course of Pakistan's history for worse. The first stage was characterized by the Pakistan Army's support of the Taliban as a pro-Pakistan group in Afghanistan (1987-1992). The rise of the Taliban and their rule in Afghanistan from 1996 until 2001 was the creation of Pakistani backing (Wasim 2011: 9). In the second stage post 9/11, the Taliban fugitives following US operations entered into the tribal areas of FATA, especially in the Swat region bringing the War into Pakistani soil. The third phase started in 2007 with Jamia Hafsa incident and the Pakistani Army offensive launched in FATA, resulting in increased fatality in the area. A new breed of suicide attackers cropped up in the country leading to rampant incidents of such attacks. The full-scale extremist movement in Pakistan, especially in the tribal belt of KP and FATA is trying to overthrow the government and establish a *Sharia*-based theocratic government. After 2002, as the militants relocated to the Af-Pak border the war has practically entered into Pakistan's terrain. The US backed military operations in Waziristan area has started an ongoing process of engaging in series of 'Operations' for cleaning the area of Taliban.

Apart from the northern tribal belt, also, there are many pro-Taliban groups active inside of Pakistan. Haqqani Network, Jundullah, TTP, LeT-JuD etc are known for being anti-establishment and continuing their course of violence with absolute impunity. The terror outreach in Pakistan, has spread to other parts to the interior, in southern parts of Punjab and also in Karachi. To many scholars one of the reasons for spread of militancy in southern Punjab is linked with proliferation of madrasas in the rural areas of south Punjab. Because of poverty, madrasas in southern Punjab are more important than in the northern part of the province, where the state education system has a bigger presence, and these madrasas have long been a key recruiting ground for the militant groups (Lieven 2011: 291).

The situation in Karachi is worse as the city has become a melting pot of various types of linguistic and ethnic populace. Moreover, the commercial affluence also generates the vast amount of resources into the terror networks along with mafia and criminal gangs operating freely. Even during the Afghan war, Karachi became a transit point for *Mujahideen* on their way to various training camps in Afghanistan. The ISI also actively participated in funding the Mohajir movement of Altaf Hussain and also uniting the drug trade with criminal syndicates of the city. Post 9/11 Karachi has become a major city with substantial al Qaeda presence. Several hundred such terrorists are hiding in various quarters of the city, even in places like the posh areas of Defence Housing Society, and in ghettos of Korangi, where they enjoy enormous support (John 2003: 77-78). Karachi is the hub of organized crime and target for Taliban insurgents. Militants in Karachi have started using the same *modus operandi*, the one they use in the tribal areas by targeting military and police convoys. They also engage in bank robberies, extortion, narco-trading for funding the outfits. The peculiar feature in Karachi is the active presence of insurgents, funded by various political parties. These groups also orchestrate various violent attacks on each other. The crux of the situation in Karachi is precarious, as no one is safe in the city, whether Police, Army, Ranger, or even common civilian.

The footprint of Islamic State (IS) in Pakistan is further causing internal turmoil in the country. The recent attack of IS on the Lal Shahbaz Qalandar sufi shrine in Sehwan town of south Sindh in February, 2017 claimed 88 lives. There is no doubt that the IS influence is increasing inside the country. Pamphlets praising the group were seen in Peshawar and Pak-Afghan border areas in mid-2014. Reports of graffiti supporting the IS were also seen in Lahore, Peshawar, Karachi and tribal area of Bannu. The Balochistan government reports a growing IS footprint in the province and confirmation by the banned terrorist group Jundullah that an IS delegation visited the province to unite various militant groups are major indications of IS interest in Pakistan (Rana 2015: 1).

The political inconsistency of Pakistan and lack of legitimate Government often provide ample scope for terror groups and their parent radical organizations in asserting domination and taking political mileage (Bhattacharya 2016: 102).

Sectarian Conflict

Sectarian violence is among the grave threats to Pakistan's internal security and stability. The escalation of sectarian conflicts in Pakistan can be traced back to the time of Zia-ul-Haq. The initial imposition of Zakat on the entire Pakistani population was severely opposed by the Shias. It was considered as a move in direct reaction to the Iranian Revolution of 1979. The Revolution definitely raised a religious consciousness among the Shiite community of Pakistan. Although, Zia, later on, exempted the Shias from Zakat, the first seeds of sectarian conflict between Sunni and Shia had been sown (Schmidt 2012: 63). The Tehrik-e-Nifaz-e-Fiqh Jafaria (TNFJ), formed in 1979, provided a platform for Shias to express their political viewpoint in Pakistan. The US-funded Afghan War to thwart the Soviets also gave a new impetus in the sectarian conflict within Pakistan, due to the vast amount of fund received from the Middle Eastern countries in the name of Afghan relief. These funds were majorly used in financing various sectarian activities.

The Sunni counterweight to TNFJ was formed in the year 1985, as Sipah-s-Sahaba Pakistan (SSP), by a mullah named Haq Nawaz Jhangvi in the Seraiki belt of Punjab Province. The SSP sought to demonise the Shiite community. It could gain traction in the Seraiki belt primarily due to the strong hostility faced by the majority Sunni population toward the wealthy Shiite feudal landowners who dominated politics and economy of the region (Schmidt 2012: 75). The southern part of Punjab has evolved into a hotbed of Sectarian conflict in the country. Soon after its formation, the SSP began to attack local Shia targets, in the name of declaring Pakistan an officially Sunni state and declaring Shia as non-Muslims. In a disturbing way over the years, SSP's activities have spread to other areas of the country where old Shia-Sunni tensions have been latent, like in Quetta, Peshawar and Kurram Agency of FATA. Lately, SSP and its more radical offshoot, LeJ have started attacking Christians and Ahmedis (Lieven 2011: 293). The more radical group was formed by Shias of Thokar Niaz Beg, Lahore in the name of Sipah-e-Muhammad Pakistan (SMP) (Rana 2004: 415).

The violent anti-Shia riots in Lahore of 1986, followed by 1987 murder of Allama Ehsan Elahi Zaheer, a Saudi backed Sunni cleric and 1988 assassination of Shia leader Arif Hussaini sealed the future of sectarian conflicts in Pakistan. The situation became more violent in mid-1990s with the formation of LeJ in 1996. The recruits of LeJ came from the rural unemployed youth of southern Punjab. In the next decade, in 2003 the US State Department added LeJ to its list of terrorist organisations (Hussain 2007: 94 and 97). In Pakistan, both Sunnis and Shias have ordered themselves as political parties, the former as the Jamiat-ul-Ulema-e-Islam (JUI) and SSP and the latter as TNFJ and SMP. Furthermore, the Shia-Sunni aversion and disapprobation has revolved into armed conflicts that claimed thousands of precious lives (Shah 2014: 445).

The SSP now operating under the name Ahl-e Sunnat Wal Jamaat (ASWJ), forged initial training linkages with al-Qaeda in the 1980s. The bonds grew deeper during the 1990s when the LeJ operated from a safe haven in Afghanistan from which it planned attacks in Pakistan (Rafiq 2014: 2). Also the escalating conflict in the West Asian region is strengthening the sectarian narrative in Pakistan. While the Pakistani state is tilting toward the Gulf Arab Sunni camp, Pakistan-based militants are increasingly setting their eyes on Iran (Rafiq 2014: 3). In Quetta, Shia Hazaras are repeatedly targeted in the sectarian violence. LeJ has reportedly pledged to exterminate Shias and turn Balochistan into a Shia graveyard. However, in the larger perspective, Lej's mission is to purge Pakistan of the Shia population. In the context of the sectarian conflict, within the country, Pakistan is becoming a proxy in war between Iran and Saudi Arabia.

Balochistan

Balochistan issue is one of the major irritants in the domestic sphere of Pakistan. It is the largest of among four provinces, with an area of 347,190 km. The province has rich natural resources, especially energy resources, including an estimated 19 trillion cubic feet of natural gas and 6 trillion barrels of oil reserves (Alamgir

2013). Balochistan also holds vast deposits of gold and copper at Reko Diq in the district of Chagai. The strategic importance of nearing the Arabian Sea with a coastline of 760 km, has created further problem. The Gwadar port (Pakistan-Iran border) and the NATO supply lines have redefined its importance in terms of Pakistan's policies with US and China.

The arid and mountainous region of Balochistan has been abundant with rich mineral resources, and also has major strategic importance. The ongoing process of insurgency has been a sort of protest movement by the local Baloch people who don't recognise the Federal government of Pakistan. They are also divided into various factions lead by prominent Baloch *Sardaars* (chiefs), who are not ready to acknowledge Pakistani establishment. The story is that of incessant rebellion and oppression.

In the context of Balochistan, it can be said that the Province has already experienced Five Rebellions since 1947. First wave of rebellion occurred in 1948, followed by the second in 1955 after the imposition of 'One-Unit' Plan by Ayub Khan, declaration of Martial Law in 1958, the fourth wave in February 1973 when Balochistan Chief Minister Sardar Attaullah Mengal was dismissed by Zulfikar Ali Bhutto and the fifth and continuing wave of conflict began when tension mounted between the Bugti tribe under the leadership of Nawab Mohammad Akbar Khan Bugti and the Provincial and Federal authorities (Pildat Issue Paper 2012: 14). The Baloch nationalist problem has dual identity on both sides of the Goldsmid Line. The insurgency problem cannot be or should not be explained in a linear manner. Unrest and ethnic disparity are faced by Balochs on both sides of the border. For many Balochs, however, nationalism does not extend beyond specific tribal loyalties. The three principal tribal groups are the Marri, Bugti, and Mengal tribes. Leaders from these tribes are capable of raising large armies and supplies but, at the same time, remain highly doubtful of each other (Kupecz 2012: 97). The story of Balochistan is all about abundant natural resources, scare ethnic population and rampant exploitation by the central government and administration. The Baloch grievances are related with decades of suppression, based on ethnicity and gradual demographic transition with increasing Pashtun population and natural resources not at the disposal of Baloch people.

Baloch insurgents are fighting for an independent country of Balochistan. They don't acknowledge the nation of Pakistan and often question and rebel against the Punjabi domination in resource sharing, politics, administration, military and other areas. The Baloch moan the 'forced' imposition of Pakistan identity on them for rampant resource exploitation. Over last six decades, Baloch rebellion and Pakistan's suppression has claimed thousands of lives.

The ongoing tensions are caused due to influx of Pashtun refugees from Afghanistan, numerically marginalising the Baloch population within their own Province. This influx further caused intrusion of extremist militants (Baloch Liberation Army- BLA, Baloch Republican Army-BRA, Jundullah etc.) along with deployment of Federal Army and Para-military forces (UNPO 2014). The formation of *Quetta Shura* of the Taliban has in a way directly brought the War against terrorism inside Balochistan. Worryingly enough, the conflict prior to 2005 was confined to only 7 percent of the area of Balochistan (parts of Kohlu and Dera Bugti districts) whereas 2006-onwards, it has engulfed more than half the area of Province. This insurgency is manifested in attacks on security forces and non-Baloch settlers (Pildat Issue Paper 2012: 15 and 23). Also, expanded natural gas exploration is another source of conflict. Baloch insurgents have frequently targeted gas pipelines (Kupecz 2012: 103). Tug of war between Pakistani establishment and Baloch *Sardaars* and their militia has resulted in decline of stability in the province. The situation is worsened by violent attacks on pipelines, railway tracks, and other state installations by the insurgents. Balochistan is also a strategic hub in terms of geographical location. Its proximity with the Gulf area through seaways has been a major reason for China's interest in developing the Gwadar port.

Crucially, the ethnic imbroglio of Balochistan has been infamous for 'kill-and-dump' operations. The tension emanated from the course of events during the independence of Pakistan. The forces of nationalism in Balochistan are threats to national integration and federation of Pakistan. Groups like Baloch Liberation Army, Baloch Republican Army, Baloch Liberation Front etc are continuously challenging the establishment. Moreover, since 2009 Balochistan has come under increased scrutiny, with the Americans alleging that Quetta and its environs are a safe haven for the Taliban leadership, including Mullah Omar. The Americans are also keeping a close tab on the Quetta Shura (Siddiqi 2012). Other militant groups like LeJ, Taliban, Jundullah also known as the Iranian People's Resistance Movement, are also active in Balochistan. Interestingly, on 9 February 2012, the Oversight and Investigations Subcommittee of the United States House of Representatives Committee on Foreign Affairs convened a hearing on Balochistan, chaired by Congressman Dana Rohrabacher. The fact that the Balochistan issue has made it to the legislature of the world's most powerful country is no mean development (Siddiqi 2012).

Ethnic Conflict

Pakistan is composed of diverse ethnic groups divided in different regions and presents various regional cultures. These cultures neither can be recognised as Islamic nor as un-Islamic (Akbar 2015: 26). There are plentiful reasons responsible for ethnic skirmishes in Pakistan. The common observation within Pakistan is that the state is not ethnically neutral and the dominant linguistic group is the Punjabi. The key institution where this preponderance is most clearly apparent is the army bureaucracy particularly at the highest level (Samad 2013: 5). The reason for Punjabis' relative ease is that they have been overwhelmingly over-represented in the state apparatus and non-representative institutions like military and civil bureaucracy as well as in sectors like the business, commerce and industry. Moreover, the regions constituting Sindh, KP, FATA and Balochistan are facing the ethnic brunt and confused identity due to colonial policies of demarcating international borders without taking into account the local perspective and ground realities. The partition of the sub-continent also contributed its own share to the ethnic politics of Pakistan, with emigrants from mainland India, claiming a respective share in Sindh (Bhattacharya 2015: 251).

As mentioned above, not only Balochistan but, other areas of the country also experience ethnic skirmishes. Being the commercial hub of the country, Karachi is often considered as a cauldron for numerous ethnic groups, settling in the city in search of food and housing. Therefore, the conflict has taken a sort of urban shape in case of Mohajirs fighting with Pashtuns and Sindhis. Violence and insecurity related to ethnic conflicts have gravely disrupted economic activities in urban Sindh where there has been evidence of flight of capital to other regions and shyness on the part of foreign capital to invest, besides billions of rupees lost each year due to recurrent strikes (Ahmed 1996: 631). The heart of the turf war- Karachi, over a period of time has been experiencing gradual migration of Pashtuns and their dominance in the privately owned transport sector (Mushtaq 2009: 283). It can be said that, since 1947, Karachi experienced four major waves of migration: Mohajirs (1940s-50s), Punjabis and Pathans (1960s-80s), Sindhis (1970s-90s) and foreigners including Afghans, Iranians, Iraqis, Ethiopians, Sri Lankans, Bangladeshis, Burmese, Thais and Philipinos among others (1980s-90s) (Waseem 1996: 623). The influx of multi-ethnic migrants into the city, caused linguistic and cultural marginalisation of the Sindhi population in Karachi. Worse, internal migration (mostly from Punjab and KP), the number of Punjabi and Pushto speakers also increased in Karachi, making Balochi and Sindhi minority languages in the city (Budhani et al. 2010: 12). As a result, one can note that the largest city in the country is bitterly divided by ethnic differences and ravaged by violence and gang wars which are criminalising the society at large.

Ethnic violence among youth is common in Karachi and Quetta. There are indiscriminate target killings of members of the different ethnicities and these violent incidents are carried out by the youth cadre of these parties. For example, the MQM, the Awami National Party (ANP), the Pakistan People's Party (PPP), students' wings and the Sindhi nationalists fight in Karachi and in interior Sindh. In Balochistan, Baloch nationalist students and youth wings of the nationalist political parties target the non-Baloch population (Zaman and Sabir 2013: 16).

The ethnic question has also emerged in the tribal areas of the northern part of Pakistan. Also, the military action in FATA by the predominantly Punjabi Pakistan armed forces, and by US Predator aircraft, has a profound political impact. The newly-politicised and radicalised FATA Pashtuns now see themselves as political brethren of the Pashtuns in KP and northern Balochistan. More dangerously by arousing a Pashtun sense of victimisation at the hands of outside forces strengthened the jihadi forces. It has enabled Taliban, with its leadership base in the Ghilzai Pashtun tribes, to pose as the champion of both Islam and of Pashtun nationalism (Harrison 2009: 19). The Swat campaign of 2009, launched by Islamabad introduced a fresh dimension into Pakistan's troubled ethnic relations. It essentially pitched the country's Punjabi-dominated army against the predominantly Pashtun people of the region. It once again reminded the Pashtuns of the Punjabi political and military supremacy (Saikal 2010: 11).

Internal Displacement/ Migration

Since 2008, the conflict between the Pakistani establishment and extremists of the tribal areas in FATA and KP has displaced millions of Pakistanis. Moreover, Pakistan has also hosted Afghan refugees for nearly 40 years, and more than 1.3 million Afghans holding Government of Pakistan issues PoR cards were residing in Pakistan as of October 2016. Since 2002, UNHCR has facilitated the return of more than 4 million refugees from Pakistan to Afghanistan. Protracted conflict between Pakistani Government forces and militant groups has generated displacement and ongoing humanitarian needs in FATA and KP. An estimated 74,830 households remained displaced in FATA and KP as of December 2016, according to the UN estimates (USAID 2017).

As explained in the earlier sections, mass migration and displacement from the northern areas of the country, and also from neighbouring Afghanistan, have resulted in severe resource crunch in urban areas and also caused internal conflicts and violence. In Karachi, 600,000 Afghan refugees eventually settled; the majority of these refugees are ethnically Pashtun, and their migration to Karachi has quickly challenged the socio-political balance of power (Anwar 2014: 13). The perpetual political tussle between MQM and ANP, with respective youth wing has only intensified the level of violence in Karachi. The disparity in economic opportunity also causes internal migration of people towards urban areas of the country. For rural migrants, a possible explanation is that most migration out of rural areas in Pakistan is aggravated by economic concern rather than a desire to seek improved access to these facilities. Evidently, migrants going towards urban districts of the country are motivated by the better access to economic opportunities accessible rather than the amount of access to health facilities and education (Mahmud et. al. 2010: 600).

For 'solving' the Afghan refugee problem, Pakistan is pushing back the refugees into Afghanistan. In the second half of 2016, a toxic combination of deportation threats and police abuses pushed out nearly 365,000 of Pakistan's 1.5 million registered Afghan refugees, as well as just over 200,000 of the country's estimated 1 million undocumented Afghans. The mass departure amounts to the world's largest unlawful mass forced return of refugees in recent times (Human Rights Watch 2017: 1).

The inhabitants of Balochistan also suffer from state induced migration. Pakistani state violence (in the form of aerial bombardments, raids, and collective abductions) against the Baloch has led to hundreds of thousands of Baloch migrating inside and outside Balochistan. Mass migration due to military operations began in the 1970s. The current military operation in Balochistan started in early 2004 resulted in the vast number of displaced people. According to UN estimates, by 2006, there were 84000 IDPs (Internally Displaced Persons) in Balochistan including 26000 women and 33000 children. HRCP (Human

Rights Commission of Pakistan) believes that 50000 more have become IDPs since 2006 (Baloch 2016).

Conclusion

In Pakistani society, collective or group violence is common due to political, ethnic, religious, gender and sectarian segregation. The resultant violent culture of the country generates a brutal cycle of problems, victimizing the core of the nation. In particular, the youth becomes prone to accelerating violence. In the contemporary world, some particular violent and extremists groups identifying themselves as the representatives of Islam surfaced as a serious threat to Pakistan's sovereignty, security, peace and integrity. Although these fundamentalist groups are not true representatives of Islam and the mainstream of population in Pakistan not only reject their claim but also called their thinking completely against and contrary to the Islamic ideology and Islamic teachings. However, these groups had some sympathies and support within the society but these supporters are fewer and as well disliked by the common Pakistani (Akbar 2015: 33). However, unfortunately, the religion has taken the society and population as the hostage.

Pakistan also needs to restrain continuation of ethnic differences and violence to acknowledge pluralistic traditions with alteration in society and culture, eventually leading to political stability. Transparency in the democratic process might bring solace and confidence among people who view Federal Government as tyrannical agent or force. The state needs to recognise the reality of divergent people not only on papers but also in reality and practice. Regrettably, the pre-requisites of democracy never truly existed in Pakistan's polity, which eventually created the vacuum for ethnic grouping. In Pakistan, the accurate and workable democratic system thus has not taken root.

Also, various social evils like poverty, illiteracy, gender discrimination, feudalism, enhance violence and extremism in the country. The sectarian conflicts are never resolved by the leaders of various religious sects. They show less concern to resolve their disagreed issues. Extreme association with a particular sect and the efforts of the leaders to keep away their followers from the teachings, writings and history of the other sects are great hurdles in the way of harmony and reconciliation. Sectarianism has made the whole society disturbed, confused and afraid of target killing (Razi 2014: 69). Sadly, sectarianism has become a part of the political mainstream in Pakistan.

Pakistan nation and state cannot realize stability unless the various fighting factions seek peace. Both the federal and provincial government needs to acknowledge the actual situation and try to devise a workable policy for forging unity in the country. The genuine grievances of people are to be addressed. Until such positive steps are taken, situation can never be rectified and the country can never be redeemed.

References

Ahmad, Muhammad Ijaz et al. (2011), "Pakistani Press and War Against Terrorism in Democratic Era", *Berkeley Journal of Social Science*, 1 (5).

Ahmed, Feroz (1996), "Pakistan: Ethnic Fragmentation or National Integration?", *The Pakistan Development Review*, 35(4) Part II: 631-645.

Akbar, Muqarrab (2015), "Pakistan: An Islamic State or a State for Muslims? A Critical Appraisal of Islam's Role in Pakistan", *Pakistan Journal of Islamic Research*, Vol. 15: 25-38.

Anwar, Nausheen H. (2014), "Urbanization, Gender & Violence in Millennial Karachi: A Scoping Study", [Online: web] Accessed 11 Jul. 2017 URL: http://research.iba. edu. pk/News/Karachi_ScopingStudy.pdf

Asian Human Rights Commission (2013), "Pakistan Country has Turned into a Killing Field", [Online: web] Accessed 10 Aug. 2014 URL: http://reliefweb.int/ sites/ reliefweb.int/files/resources/AHRC-SPR-005-2013-HRRpt-Pakistan.pdf.

Baloch, Meerain (2016), "The Displacement of the Baloch", [Online: web] Accessed 11 Jul. 2017 URL: http://www.nakedpunch.com/articles/250

Bhattacharya, Sanchita (2016), "Pakistan's Socio-Political Disorder Threatening India's Security Scenario", in Shivendra Shahi and Amar Singh (eds.) *Perspectives on India's National Security Challenges: External and Internal Dimensions*, New Delhi: Pentagon Press.

Bhattacharya, Sanchita (2015), "Pakistan's Ethnic Entanglement", *The Journal of Social, Political and Economic Studies*, 40(3): 231-262.

Budhani et al. (2010), "The Open City: Social Networks and Violence in Karachi", [Online: web] Accessed 16 Mar. 2014 URL: http://eprints.lse.ac.uk/28471/1/WP70.2.pdf.

Harrison, Seling S. (2009), "Pakistan the State of the Union", [Online: web] Accessed 19 Mar. 2014 URL: http://www.ciponline.org/images/uploads/publications/ pakistan_the_state_of_the_union.pdf.

Human Rights Watch (2017), "Pakistan Coercion, UN Complicity: The Mass Forced Return of Afghan Refugees", [Online: web] Accessed 15 June 2017 URL: http:// www.refworld.org/docid/58a195374.html

Hussain, Zahid (2007), *Frontline Pakistan*, New Delhi: Penguin Books.

ICAN (2014), *Reclaiming the Progressive Past: Pakistani women's struggle against violence & extremism*, New York.

Irshad, Muhammad (2011), "Terrorism in Pakistan: Causes & Remedies", *The Dialogue*, VI (3): 224-241.

Javaid, Umbreen and Zulfiqar Ali (2013), "War on Terror Partnership: Problems and Prospects for Pakistan", *Journal of Political Studies*, 20 (1): 51-66.

John, Wilson (2003), *Karachi A Terror Capital in the Making*, New Delhi: Rupa Co.

Kupecz, Mikey (2012), "Pakistan's Baloch Insurgency: History, Conflict Drivers, and Regional Implications", *International Affairs Review*, XX (3): 95-110.

Lall, Marie (2010), "What Role for Islam Today? The Political Islamisation of Pakistani Society", in Stephen Lyon and Iain R. Edgar (eds.) *Shaping a Nation an Examination of Education in Pakistan*, Karachi: Oxford University Press.

Lieven, Anatol (2011), *Pakistan A Hard Country*, London: Penguin Books.

Mahmud et.al. (2010), "Internal Migration Patterns in Pakistan-The Case for Fiscal Decentralisation", *The Pakistan Development Review*, 49: (4) Part II: 593–607.

Mushtaq, Muhammad (2009), "Managing Ethnic Diversity and Federalism in Pakistan", *European Journal of Scientific Research,* 33(2): 279-294.

Pildat Issue Paper (2012), "Balochistan Civil-Military Relations", [Online: web] Accessed 12 Mar. 2014 URL: http://www.pildat.org/publications/publication/balochistanconflict/IssuePaperBalochistanConflictCMR.pdf.

Rafiq, Arif (2014), "Pakistan's Resurgent Sectarian War", [Online: web] Accessed 29 June. 2017 URL: https://www.usip.org/sites/default/files/PB180-Pakistan-Resurgent-Sectarian-War.pdf

Rana, Muhammad Aamir (2015), "The impact of the Islamic State on Pakistan", URL: https://www.files.ethz.ch/isn/186949/049ee274000481e510fd0414ba61d63b.pdf Rana, Muhammad Aamir (2004), *A to Z of Jehadi Organizations in Pakistan*, Lahore: Mashal Books.

Razi, Naseem (2014), "Theological Extremism and its Effects: Pakistan Perspective", *Journal of Social Science for Policy Implications,* 2(4): 59-72.

Saikal, Amin (2010), "Afghanistan and Pakistan: The Question of Pashtun Nationalism?", *Journal of Muslim Minority Affairs,* 30 (1): 5-17.

Samad, Yunas (2013), "Managing Diversity in Pakistan: Going Beyond Federalism", [Online: web] Accessed 12 Mar. 2014 URL: http://www.sdpi.org/publications/files/Managing%20Diversity%20in%20Pakistan%20Going%20Beyond%20Federalism%20(W-131).pdf.

Schmidt, John R. (2012), *The Unravelling Pakistan in the Age of Jihad*, London: Macmillan.

Shah, Muhammad Nadeem (2014), "Evolution of Sectarianism in Pakistan: A Threat to the State and Society", *South Asian Studies*, 29 (2): 441-459.

UNPO (2014), "The Plight of the Baloch", [Online: web] Accessed 17 Mar. 2014 URL: http://webcache.googleusercontent.com/search?q=cache:http://www.unpo. org/downloads/822.pdf.

USAID (2017), "Pakistan- Complex Emergency", [Online: web] Accessed 21 Jun. 2017 URL: https://www.usaid.gov/sites/default/files/documents/1866/pakistan_ ce_fs01_01-06-2017.pdf

Waseem, Mohammad (2011), "Pattern of Conflict in Pakistan: Implications for Policy", [Online: web] Accessed 18 May. 2017 URL: http://www.brookings.edu/~/media/research/files/ papers/2011/3/01%20pakistan%20waseem/01_pakistan_waseem.pdf

Waseem, Mohammad (1996), "Ethnic Conflict in Pakistan: The Case of MQM", *The Pakistan Development Review,* 35 (4): 617-629.

Zaman, Muhammad and Imran Sabir (2013), "Youth Violence in Pakistan: The Social Structure and Culture of Violence", *Profilaktyka Społeczna i Resocjalizacja*, Vol. 21: 7-24.

CHAPTER 7

Bangladesh's Recent Economic Performance: Hopes for a Peaceful Future Ahead?

Monica Verma and Karnika Jain

Abstract

Bangladesh's recent economic performance has revived hopes of a stable future for the country. The growth has been led by its textile exports, external remittances and advances in the agriculture sector. The growing economy of Bangladesh has evinced interest of external investors as well with inwards FDI witnessing a jump of more than 44 percent. However, Bangladesh's economic growth and the external investment that it can attract are further dependent on political stability in the country. The threat of Islamic extremism looms large with factors both internal and external to the country aggravating the security situation. This paper seeks to understand if these dynamics are undergoing any change in the country? Can the economic performance put the country on a trajectory of peace and prosperity?

Recent Economic Performance: Hopes for a Peaceful Future Ahead?

Bangladesh, today as a nation reflects a radically different scenario from the eve of its independence. The country had started its journey with a parliamentary democracy but has since turned into a place filled with conflicts, strikes, tensions, and instability. The governance has remained sluggish, centralised and politics dominates a far-reaching aspect of the society. Violence is a part of mainstream politics even as a rising Islamic extremism threatens to send the country into a spiral of conflict. However, the recent performance of Bangladesh's economy has shown hopes for improvement in the political sphere of the country as well.

In the FY 2015-2016, the country has experienced a GDP growth rate of 6.6 percent (World Bank 2016).This is a significant achievement if compared to the times when the average GDP growth rate of Bangladesh was 2.3 percent in the 1970s, that increased to 4.8 percent during the 1980s and 1990s (Aslam Chaudhary, Shirazi and Choudhary 2007).The increase in GDP growth rate has emboldened the country to set ambitious target for the future. As Bangladesh would mark its 50th anniversary of independence in 2021, the government has set the year as a deadline to attain middle income country status by that time. The vision 2021 as articulated in the "Perspective Plan of Bangladesh (2010-2021): Making Vision 2021 a Reality" is a step taken to achieve a stable democracy and prosperous economy. Accordingly, the Perspective Plan has targeted annual real GDP growth rate to rise to 8.0 percent by 2015, and further to 10.0 per cent by 2021 (Bangladesh Government 2012). Though 2015 target could not be achieved but country is trying hard to achieve 2021 goal.

Setting to achieve an annual GDP growth rate of 10 percent is quite ambitious of a country like Bangladesh which is crippled with poor governance, frequent confrontations, strikes, boycotts and political violence. The rising Islamic militancy also contributes to the political instability in the country further creating an inconducive environment for external investments. The lack of productive avenues due to the problem of unemployment is also a hindrance in achieving economic growth and prosperity. There are other serious issues such as hunger, disease, inadequate nutrition, mass illiteracy, lack of educational resources that haunt Bangladesh.

Despite all these problems, Bangladesh as an economy has continued to demonstrate a fairly robust pace of economic development. Agricultural and aqua cultural production, ship building initiatives, continued strong growth in ready-made garment exports, and generous remittances from Bangladeshi expatriates abroad have all contributed to this dynamic performance. In order to maintain this economic performance and ensure that the vision 2021 becomes a reality, the country should focus on the contributing factors of this growth. The problems of political uncertainty and instability remain a major challenge in achieving economic development and need urgent attention. State-sponsored Islamization also needs to be stopped and rights of minorities need to be ensured as well.

This chapter looks at a brief history of Bangladesh's politics followed by discussing the problems of political violence and militant extremism in the country. It argues that the recent economic performance of Bangladesh has raised hopes for a peaceful future for Bangladesh where the drivers of this growth can place the country on a trajectory of peace and prosperity.

This is possible due to the need for investment by the Bangladeshi economy to sustain and increase this economic growth. In order to attract external investments, country's investment climate needs to be improved. That again requires political stability and curbing of political violence. Besides, economic performance is also linked with job creation and delivery of key public goods such as education by the state. The role of the religious institutions in delivering key goods such as education is questionable due to the radical nature of the lessons imparted. Similarly, jobless youth is also susceptible to choose violence because it does not have a comfortable and peaceful lifestyle to lose. The improved economic performance of Bangladeshi economy has created an impetus for prosperity and peace. The efforts undertaken to maintain this growth can ensure that the level of violence and extremism in Bangladesh are also kept under a strict check.

Bangladesh came into existence in 1971 through a war of liberation from Pakistan. It was a product of Bengali nationalism which had secular Bengali identity as its base. The country made progress towards being a politically moderate and democratic country but stagnated due to "a combination of political violence, weak governance, poverty, corruption and rising Islamic militancy" (Ahsan and Banavar 2011). The Constitution adopted in 1972 under the regime of Awami League invoked nationalism, democracy, secularism and socialism as key principles of statecraft (Siddiqi 2011). However, in less than three years later, the country underwent changes and the institution of parliamentary democracy[1] was replaced with a one-party rule. The word 'secularism' was also replaced with "the principles of absolute trust and faith in the Almighty Allah", by amendment article 8 (1) of the constitution. The secular character of Bangladesh's polity was further dented by the Fifth Amendment of the constitution that modified "Bengali nationalism" and adopted "Bangladeshi nationalism" that had religion Islam as an instrumental factor in politics (F. Jahan 2015).[2]

Military dictatorships have dominated the political surface of the country and have actively tried to transform Bengali culture on Islamic religious lines. Weaknesses in addressing the physical challenges, including poor governance, service delivery and security oversight, as well as unresolved questions on an intellectual level regarding a national narrative and identity, have created a basis for violence in Bangladesh (Fink 2010). The axis of violence in Bangladesh are many that majorly includes political violence and a rising militant extremism.

Forms of Political Violence in Bangladesh

Political violence can be described as "acts carried out by individuals or groups with an explicit desire of accomplishing a particular political objective or directed at the party in power to secure political concessions or compromises that are otherwise not possible" (Datta 2005). Violence has become a significant part of the Bangladeshi political landscape. A series of nationwide bomb blasts happened on 17 August 2005 followed by suicide bombings a couple of months later. Such incidents make us aware of the existence of a section of people who dislike the prevailing political system and use extra-constitutional means to show their anger and change the political scenario (Datta 2007).

Violence driven by extremist ideology began soon after the war of liberation in 1971. In recent years, with an increase in the number of Islamist militant groups, it has taken a new turn. This is also connected to a larger than life role that religion plays in mainstream Bangladeshi politics and society. At the same time that politicians in the country have increasingly become autocratic in behaviour. The key institutions including the civil administration, judiciary etc. have been politicized and their autonomy has been suppressed. The rule of law has eroded leading to a spate in instances of violence (R. Jahan 2008).

Rising violence poses a serious threat to democracy and political stability. It traces its roots to rising Islamization of Bangladeshi politics which started with General HM. Ershad (1982-1990) declaring Islam as a state religion at the cost of a secular identity of Bangladeshi politics. This alienated the minority groups and led to forcing of a hegemonic cultural national identity through Islamization on them. The two main political parties- Awami League and Bangladesh Nationalist Party (BNP) started looking to forge alliance with Islamic parties in order to secure power. Thus, gradually, the Islamist political parties also got a strong foothold in the country's politics. Under the patronage of political power, they also started spreading violence and a radical variant of Islam began to emerge (Islam 2011). This was not limited to the top rung of power alone as radical Islamic ideology penetrated the society, education system and even popular culture of the country. Islami Chattra Shibir representing the student wing of Islamist political party Jamaat-E-Islami has contributed to the politicization of academics and has created an intimidating environment for many teachers and students on university campuses. Fundamentalist forces have begun to occupy political space with spill over in the neighbouring countries as well. Illegal madrasas in the border area of Bangladesh have led to the Talibanisation of the society (Bhardwaj 2014). The nexus between politics and religious violence is such that during the caretaker government (2007 to 2009), the incidents of political violence were low because of the ban on political activities.

Street agitations, strikes, violent protests, assassinations, bomb blasts and attacks on civilians and bloggers routinely occur in Bangladesh. *Hartal*, a form of general strike is one of the most pronounced forms of political violence. From 2002 to 2013, 369 *hartal*-days were recorded (Suykens and Islam 2015). They not just cause destruction and political disturbance within the country but they also interfere with the economic activities and hence hamper the rate of economic growth.

Another kind of violence includes the acts of violence against women and minorities particularly against Hindus, Buddhists and ethnic minorities such as Chakmas. Bangladesh is predominantly a Muslim country and 89.52 percent of the country's population is Muslim, and the remaining 10.48 percent consists of religious and ethnic minorities (Ahmmed 2014). The construction of a homogenised society by taking Islam as the state religion has led to the exclusion of minority groups. Promises made by the political parties to improve their condition have faced failures and their situation remains the same. The incidents such as the destruction of 10 Hindu temples and several homes in the Brahmanbaria district on 30 October 2016 and sustained attacks on the indigenous Santals in Gaibandha district shows the level of communal violence in the country (I. Ahmed 2016). There are problems of ethnic conflict with Buddhists in the Chittagong Hill Tracts facing persecution. There is a denial of human rights and identity; whereas cases of harassment, rapes, and physical threats have also been seen. The issue of integrating different racial groups into the nation is still incomplete in Bangladesh.

Issues related to political ideology further aggravate this tension. Political differences exist in every country but in the case of Bangladesh, political differences manifest in street violence. The ruling faction between Awami League and BNP presents a formidable conundrum. Awami League continues to foster Bengali nationalist, is culturally-charged and remains committed to eradicating anti-liberation elements such as Jamaat-e-Islam. On the other hand, BNP, that has its roots in a military coup, cultivates Islamic majoritarian sentiments (M. Hussain 2015). This ideological difference with their respective religious propensities is becoming increasingly complicated with time. Boycott of elections by the losing party is a regular occurrence in Bangladesh's politics.

Weak political institutions is another instrumental factor in worsening situation of political violence in the country. These institutions became the centre of political conflict during the parliamentary era. The domination of political power by one man or one party prevents the separation of key institutions. One such institution is Election Commission (EC). The ruling parties have failed to make the institution an independent body and manipulate issues in favour of its party politics (Moniruzzaman 2009). The multiple forms of political violence as discussed continue to project an image of a politically unstable and conflict-ridden Bangladesh that further takes a toll on its international standing.

Militant Groups: The Funding and Ideology

Islamic militant groups in Bangladesh that began to appear on the political scene in the early 1990s have undergone several transformations. Originally, they were returnees of the Afghan war that forged links with a Pakistani Islamist organization called Harkat-ul-Jihad-al-Islami and formed its Bangladeshi chapter, Harkat-ul Jihad-al-Islami Bangladesh (HuJIB, Movement of Islamic Holy War).However, with time, they have evolved to become a part of the mission of establishing a global 'khilafat' by joining IS in Syria and Iraq. Its funding comes from various international Muslim NGOs and other Bangladeshi terrorist groups (Country Reports on Terrorism 2014).There has been a significant increase in militant activities in Bangladesh, particularly in 2015. One of the main reasons behind the increase in the number of youth joining militant forces is unemployment. Each year, at least 2.2 million individuals enter the job market while only 700 thousand get jobs. 47 percent of youth with graduate and post-graduate degrees are unemployed in the country (Esha 2016).

Both Al Qaeda in the Indian Subcontinent (AQIS) and the Islamic State (IS) have claimed their presence in the country. Bangladeshi Islamist militants show diverse characteristics. Majority of them come from middle class or upper middle class and some of them are even educated (Riaz 2016). People have even started wondering if 'Talibanization' of Bangladesh is underway (Karlekar 2005). Members of the AQIS and IS have also started founding their own local organizations like Shaheed Hamza Brigade (SHB) and the Bangladesh Jihad Group (BJG). The government has arrested three Supreme Court lawyers and an

RMG businessman for their involvement in funding the organizations (Hasan and Rahaman 2016).

Jamaatul Mujahideen Bangladesh (JMB) is another militant group working to establish 'Islamic law in Bangladesh' through armed struggle. The group and its affiliate Jagrata Muslim Janata Bangladesh (JMJB), established a reign of terror in the north-western part of Bangladesh. The JMB has also received asignificant al-Qaida assistance in training and finance (Ahsan and Banavar 2011). Despite the ban on JMB and JMJB in 2006, they have continued to reorganize. A new group called Ansarullah Bangla Team (ABT) surfaced in 2007 under the name of Jamaat-ul Muslemin. The group was funded by external sources and it ceased to operate when funding ended (Riaz 2016). In addition to these groups, there are some lesser-known groups such as Shadat-e Al-Hiqma, Jaish-e-Muhammad and Jahid al Qaeda. However, they are not active post scrutiny in 2007.

Militant groups such as HuJI-B, aims to establish Islamic rule in the country by waging war. It has drawn inspiration from Osama bin Laden and the Taliban. At one point, it raised a slogan, Amra Sobai Hobo Taliban, Bangla Hobe Afghanistan (We all become Taliban and we will turn Bangladesh into Afghanistan) (South Asian Terrorism Portal 2014). The dominance of Middle Eastern Islam (Hanabli) has contributed to the ideas of intolerance among the Muslims of Bangladesh (Bhardwaj 2010). Militants and their patrons have forged a new popular culture by appropriating traditional Bangladeshi cultural practices in effort to glorify and promote jihad and other Islamist militant ideas (Riaz 2008).

Government Inaction: Political Patronage to Extremist Activities

The increase in the number of Islamic political parties in Bangladesh has been an important causal factor in rising militancy and violence in the country. The ultimate objective of these parties is the establishment of an Islamic state. Jamaat-e-Islami is one of the main Islamic political parties that use Madrasas to increase its influence in Bangladeshi society.[3] In the aftermath of countrywide bomb blasts of 2005, seven members of the Jama'atul Mujahideen were arrested and all had been members of either the Jamaat or its student wing, the Islami Chhatra Shibir (Kumar 2009). The Islami Chhatra Shibir (ICS) was founded in 1941. It is a part of a larger Islamist extremist network of the HUJI, Jamaat-e-Islami and Islami Oikyo Jote. It is also been reported to have close links with ISI.[4] The terrorist groups in South Asia and particularly in Afghanistan carry out their activities in Bangladesh through the ICS (South Asia Terrorism Portal 2014).

Since 1991, the governments led by the BNP and Awami League have paid less attention to the rise of Islamic militancy. The most compelling cause of militant Islam in Bangladesh is the state's failure to address unemployment, poverty, environmental degradation and political order (Ganguly 2006). The concern for rising terror was bolstered further by the 2001 elections when BNP came to power in alliance with Jamaat-e-Islami. Islamist parties became the kingmakers in Bangladesh's 'first past the post' system, with both parties vying for Islamist parties' support (Riaz 2008). When the Awami Leaguewas elected to office in late 2008, it adopted a Counterterrorism strategy and banned an Islamist organization in 2009 and blacklisted a number of other suspected organizations (Sarkar 2013).[5] Between 2007 and 2014, 478 members of the Jamaatul Mujahideen Bangladesh (JMB), one of the proscribed organizations, were tried in 177 cases. Of them, 51 top leaders of JMB have been sentenced to death, 178 were given life terms and 245 jailed for different terms (*Daily Star* 2015). Though these groups are banned, they re-organize themselves under different names and then operate and indulge in violent crimes and create nuisance in the country. The rising level of political violence and Islamic extremism has created an environment of political instability in the country. However, the recent economic performance of Bangladesh has created an air of optimism regarding an improvement in the political atmosphere as well. The next section explores this link in detail.

Link between Economic Performance and Political Stability

To make the claim that economically difficult times often spell trouble for peace will not be an overstatement. The fact is that peace and prosperity are interdependent and history is a witness to this. Economic downturn faced by the world during the Great Depression proved to be a fertile ground for the First World War (Strauss-Kahn 2009). The absence of economic development can fuel conflicts both within and among the nations. This is particularly true for developing countries as Dumas (2006) notes that more than 120 wars have been fought since the Second World War. Most of these wars involved developing countries. Even within the nations, the lack of economic development hampers peace. In the wake of poverty and economic marginalization, people are more susceptible to take the risk of violent disruption as against in the case of widespread and inclusive development. This is because economic development raises stakes by taking away the material appeal of the breaking cycle of poverty and marginalization through violent means (J. Dumas 2006). Religious extremism, when reflected in political choices, has a direct effect on the growth rate of the economy as well. A study by Grüner and Brückner estimates a roughly one-percent-point decline in growth when there is a one-percent-point gain in the vote share of right-wing or nationalist parties (Grüner and Brückner 2010). Along with a lack of economic development, the degree of inequality in terms of the distribution of economic gains also has a determining effect on extremist violence. "In a highly unequal country, in terms of increasing relative poverty; unequal distribution of income; and social entitlement may increase the support for far-right parties or extremist groups in the long run", notes Shahab Enam Khan (2017, 196).

Economic reforms have led to stability and growth in Bangladesh but institutional reforms, especially in the face of weakening of institutions of political and economic governance, are needed else democratic consolidation may be hindered and serious economic disruption may be caused (Ahluwalia and Mahmud 2004). An analysis of Bangladesh's political economy highlights the promise economic development holds for the cause of peace and political stability. The role of the political economy of a country is crucial in a manner that it can harden political and economic concerns into political action and even violence (Khan 2017: 197). The dynamics of economic growth can bring in the required stability and eliminate extremism by operating at two levels. At the level of the government, economic growth can be sustained in the long term only if the country's investment climate improves. At the same time, economic growth can prove to be an agent of peace if it enables the state to deliver welfare goods such as employment and education. The following analysis looks at the two main rationales of economic performance leading to peace and prosperity in Bangladesh. The first one looks at the role of improving investment climate followed by delivery of welfare goods such as employment and education by the state.

Rationale Behind Improving the Investment Climate

One of the ways in which economic growth can be a driver for peace and political stability in Bangladesh is by improving the investment climate in order to attract external investments. There has been considerable economic growth and social gains in Bangladesh despite the lack of a perfect democracy and weak administrative government which is also quite often termed as the Bangladesh development puzzle or Bangladesh development surprise surprise (Sen 2014; Mahmud, Ahmed and Mahajan 2008).

The future course of the Bangladeshi economy is now dependent on political stability, improved governance and a check on religious extremism. The dependency of the country on external aid has come down but to consolidate economic stabilization into growth requires the country to improve in many areas including overall investment environment (Ahluwalia and Mahmud 2004). There are various challenges to investment environment in Bangladesh such as political violence, criminalization of politics, rent seeking behaviour of the establishment and *hartals* (strikes). Of these challenges, political violence remains a significant threat to the consolidation of democracy in the country (Islam 2011: 28). Political violence includes the clashes between the police and the activists, political rivals, violence against women and minorities, violence by extremist groups and by state in the form of extra-judicial killings (Islam 2011: 28). Due to the nexus between politicians and violent elements political violence is a crucial factor in creating inhibition in the international business community while making investment decisions related to Bangladesh (Islam 2011: 41).

While political violence has tarnished the image of Bangladesh as an unsafe place, *hartals* are also responsible for causing direct monetary loss. For instance, during 1990-2000, the average loss suffered by the economy due to *hartals* was 3-4 percent of the GDP. Nasreen Khundker (2005) notes, "these costs include foregone earnings and lost employment and output, as well as long-term impacts due to reduced savings, indebtedness, capital losses and reduced profitability for businesses" (Khundker 2005: 33).

The country's political and economic landscape is undergoing transformation. These changes include a decreasing dependency on aid and a rise in economic growth. Besides, the key drivers of growth in the economy are also ripe to receive and utilize external investment. The aspirations of the country are also undergoing transformation with Bangladesh aiming to register its entry in the middle-income countries' club. These factors have made improving the country's investment climate imperative. A serious attempt at improving the investment climate in view of the factors as discussed below would entail improving governance, law and order, checking corruption and political violence as well as religious extremism in the country.

Securing External Investments, Decreasing Donor Dependency

Official development aid's importance as a significant source of foreign exchange has come down for Bangladesh as exports and remittances have picked up in the country. Hence, flow of aid as a proportion of GDP or percent of investment has also declined over time. This means that the component of aid that once constituted 2.9 percent of GDP in 1995-2004 has now come down to 1.9 percent of GDP in 2014 (Rahman 2015). In view of a better economic performance driven by the export industry and external remittances, donor dependency has reduced in the country. At the same time, the prospects for receiving foreign aid like in the older times are also increasingly turning gloomy. This is because, in addition to the traditional recipients, demand for foreign aid is increasing in conflict and post-conflict countries. This diminishing trend in aid-flow calls for effective utilization of the existing aid by the country (Hasan 2011). Especially, because the contribution of aid is still significant to different development projects such as health, education and physical infrastructure in the country (Hasan 2011).

The reduced availability of aid and a reduced dependency on aid in view of exemplary economic performance presents a compelling case for enacting measures of good governance in Bangladesh. This is further aggravated by structural factors such as high population density combined with the ecological vulnerability that makes the country a less popular choice from the investment point of view (Sen 2014: 205). Thus, seeking investment remains a crucial aspect of the economy as Sen (2014) also identifies two key challenges to Bangladesh's economic growth. These include a low overall investment rate in the economy particularly due to a lack of improvements in governance conditions and a virtual stagnation in the overall domestic savings rate in Bangladesh's economy (Sen 2014: 202). According to him, there exists a considerable room for boosting investment to finance additional growth in Bangladesh (Sen 2014: 203).

Bangladesh has tried to seek external investment for the economy, however, it has achieved only a limited success so far (Mahmud, Ahmed and Mahajan 2008: 25). The reasons include a lack of political governance, institutional reforms, political risk and violence and other political factors such as corruption, terrorism etc. The lack of political governance costs Bangladesh in terms of unfavourable contract terms that potential investors put during negotiation. A redressal of the lack of political governance along with institutional reforms will be able to attract crucial investments for facilitating technology transfer and meeting resource gap in the country (Mahmud, Ahmed and Mahajan 2008: 26-27). The relationship between political violence and FDI inflows is also very strong. There is a negative effect of political risk and macroeconomic policy uncertainty on FDI inflows (Azam, Khan and Iqbal 2012). Potential investors consider political factors such as the change of government, attitude of the opposition, transparency in bureaucracy, degree of nationalism, corruption and terrorism etc. during pre-investment decision making (Mian and Alam 2006). It seems that the only way Bangladesh can attract anymore foreign aid and investment in the country is by proactively making efforts to allay the fears of potential investors and donors.

Need for Foreign Investment in Readymade Garments

Since 1990s, readymade garments (RMG) sector has emerged as a key driver of Bangladesh's export-oriented growth (Mahmud, Ahmed and Mahajan 2008: 19). It has also been identified as a key driver of planned growth acceleration under the 6th plan. However, any increase in labour-intensive exports such as readymade garments is dependent on investment on a large scale in sectors such as power, natural gas and water (Sen 2014: 206-207). Bangladesh's textile industry is right now facing both opportunities and threats. Due to a rising labour cost in East Asian countries, Bangladesh has emerged to be a popular source for readymade garments exports (Lopez-Acevedo, Medvedev and Palmade 2017). But at the same, time labour productivity remains a challenge as there is a dearth of investment in manpower as well. Labour productivity is much lower in Bangladesh as compared to that of Sri Lanka, South Korea and Hong Kong (Chowdhury, Ahmed and Yasmin 2014). The law and order situation also needs to be improved else RMG sector may lose its edge as the key driver of economic growth. Finished products have to be sometimes shipped via air in order to make up for the lost time even as frequent general strikes and political unrest raise the cost of production (*ibid.*). The sorry state of law and order also interferes with the seeking of investment for the low-cost export oriented sectors including RMG. Around 95 percent of the textile industry is domestically-owned as the RGM sector as well as energy and infrastructure sector is bereft of FDI due to intra-party strife, pervasive corruption and policy instability (A. Ahmed 2011).

The textile industry has emerged to be a strong driver for the economic growth in Bangladesh that can be used to build a well-entrenched ecosystem for further growth. More than 80 percent of the country's export basket consists of low end readymade garments. If the country focuses on developing an investment ecosystem around these priority sectors then only it will be able to sustain and increase the current level of growth (World Bank 2016). This requires the country to set its house in order by checking political violence and extremism even as it tries to maintain law and order and control strikes and strife in the country. If the country can bring more investments to the RMG sector and a strong positive reformation continues, the sector would be able to deliver the expected growth (Akter 2017).

Vision to Become an Upper-Middle Income Country

Bangladesh has averaged a growth rate of 5-6 percent annually since the 1980s (World Bank 2016). This has helped the country in securing a place in the club of middle-income countries. But it now wants to outdo this performance by posting a 7.5-8 percent rate of economic growth in order to register its presence in the club of upper-middle-income countries (Asian Development Bank 2016). However, the policies followed by the country will prove to be insufficient in the medium term to deliver the required growth rate if it does not actively court potential investors (ibid). Bangladesh has successfully covered the first phase of structural transformation by targeting low-cost export markets but to go further a new strategy is needed that broadens its horizon to include critical investment in education and infrastructure and building and strengthening of institutions and rule of law (ADB 2016). In order to secure its place in the upper-middle income group, country needs to ensure a growth rate of 7.5 percent to 8 percent. GDP growth rate is linked to investment as investment improves productivity that further raises income. Investment in infrastructure triggers a virtuous cycle of growth where better infrastructure improves productivity that in turn makes exports more competitive. Competitive exports attract FDI which further lead to an increase in productivity (Z. Hussain 2013). In order to 'warm up' for the upper-middle income status, Bangladesh needs to attract FDI as a prerequisite for rapid development as besides increasing productivity FDI inflow can also facilitate job creation, infrastructural development, increase efficiency of the local labour force and bring in necessary modern technology (Chakraborty and Vasanthagopal 2015). Bangladesh has covered significant ground from being a basket case to a lower-middle income country. The country has been historically dependent on aid from developed countries and international organizations but in order to make a successful transition to a middle-income state, foreign investment is crucial (A. Ahmed 2011).

Energy Sector: Need for Foreign Investment

In the case of Bangladesh, there is a clear causal relationship between energy utilization and GDP growth. This relationship also extends to FDI and energy sector. The resources and technology required by the energy sector in Bangladesh make seeking foreign direct investment imperative. Only then the requisite GDP growth is possible (Khatun and Ahamad 2013).

But according to a report by the Asian Development Bank, low FDI is a great cause of concern. This low degree of FDI is a result of poor infrastructure, disorderly urbanization, uncertainty about property rights and their enforcement. This is especially true in the case of oil and gas sectors, where the investors are not convinced that Bangladesh is an attractive place to establish business, despite the presence of a hard-working and low-skilled labour (ADB 2016). As a result, the country is undergoing a power and energy crisis and its manifestations include costly and erratic power supply (Wiig and Kolstad 2014). In order to meet its future energy objectives, Bangladesh needs to attract FDI in substantial measure (Wiig and Kolstad 2014: 4).

This entails improving the investment climate by checking the level of political violence in the country. Bangladesh's liberal policy regime regarding FDI inflows alone has not proved to be a sufficient condition to attract FDI. Policymakers must focus on removing barriers such as political instability, delay in decision making, inefficiency of human resources, corruption and lack of governance (Khatun and Ahamad 2013: 21). This also means that the two major political parties must bury the hatchet in order to improve Bangladesh's image as a country that means business. Bangladesh has a huge energy potential but in order to prosper and utilize this fruitfully, the inter-party rivalry has to end (A. Ahmed 2011).

The need for foreign investment by Bangladesh to sustain and increase its economic growth in long-term needs the country to improve the investment climate by ensuring political stability, a strict check on religious extremism and improved law and order. The measures taken to ensure economic growth stays will also put the country on a trajectory of peace. What remains to be seen is intent and efforts on the country's part to realize this link between prosperity and peace.

Economic Growth to Provide Welfare Goods

On one hand, Bangladesh needs to improve the investment climate in order to sustain its current rate of economic growth and achieve the target of 7.5-8 percent growth. On the other hand, as a result of the current economic growth, the state in Bangladesh is better-placed to provide welfare goods such as education and employment to its people. There is a causal link between extremism and lack of education and employment. This is particularly true for a young country like Bangladesh. Around 47.6 million or 30 percent of the total 158.5 million people in the country are young with a larger share of the working population to the non-working population (Ahmed and Alam 2016). While the young population presents an opportunity in the terms of demographic dividend, the same section has also been a major victim of the process of radicalization and extremism because of a lack of access to satisfactory levels of education, health and well-being, employment, political and civic participation (Khan 2017: 196). If Bangladesh is able to provide these goods to the young population, they will be lesser inclined to join the cause of extremists.

Job Creation to Keep Youth Occupied

The level of extreme poverty and unemployment in Bangladesh encourages people to engage in violent activities. The stakes are quite low for such people unlike those who have a better standard of living and stable jobs. Unemployed youth can be easily motivated by the extremist groups to join their cause. However, economic growth has led to significant job creation in the economy. As a result of trade liberalization and economic deregulation, employment opportunities have been generated on a large scale in the labour-intensive and export-oriented readymade garments sector along with shrimp production sector. The shrimp sector employs over half a million-rural poor in various stages of processing and shrimp culture and is the second largest export industry after readymade garments (Ahmed and Sattar 2004). This has also led to pro-poor growth in the country as the resultant employment has stimulated other parts of the economy as well.

Despite this, the country needs to focus on increasing this economic growth in view of a large section of youth that needs jobs in Bangladesh. Over two million youths enter the job market every year making job creation through increased economic activity even more necessary (Lopez-Acevedo , Medvedev and Palmade 2017). Job creation is also a crucial factor if Bangladesh has to realize its vision of becoming a middle-income country. The World Bank Group has also identified job creation as the country's top development priority, a prerequisite for reaching the middle-income country status by 2021 (World Bank 2016).

Quality Education to Discourage Extremism

The government's inability to provide quality education has increased the popularity of the Madrassah education in Bangladesh. It is a cheaper, accessible and a more Islamic alternative to education (Riaz 2011). Currently, as a 'weak state' Bangladesh also attracts a significant share of largesse from Saudi Arabia in the education sector along with other weak states such as Yemen, Sudan, Nigeria, Somalia and Afghanistan. These institutions are allegedly involved in spreading militant ideology in these countries, however, at the same time, this link cannot be overplayed for the want of abetter evidence (Graff 2010). However, still, Islamic extremism has penetrated the education system in Bangladesh. There are serious allegations against the Islami Chhatra Shibir, a student wing of Jamaat-e-Islami for using violence against Bangaldesh Chatra League (a student wing of Awami League) and also carrying out violence outside the campus. News reports also suggest its alleged link with militants (Ahsan and Banavar 2011). Jamaat owns 6 universities and a think-tank in Dhaka while it also has a preference for appointing party-cadres as university professors when in power (Kumar 2012: 85-86). Absence of state in a key sector such as education is an important factor responsible for the rise of militant Islam besides other factors such as a favourable socio-political environment, criminalization of politics etc. (Riaz 2008: 44-60). Here the rise of Hefazat-e-Islam, an organization that opposes any move to reform quomi madrassah education is notable. These madrassas that were once considered as "abode of the poor and neglected" have now developed into a potent political force (Griffiths and Hasan 2015). An increased growth in the economy can enable the state in Bangladesh to fund welfare goods such as education. Currently, government spending on education is around 2 percent of the GDP which is the second lowest in South Asia and lower than other countries in the world that are at a similar level of development (World Bank 2016c). However, a rise in economic fortune can ensure that the government makes provision for education in the country so that this crucial need is not left to be fulfilled by extremists.

Bangladesh is currently witnessing an interesting turn in its fortunes. From a country that used to be a basket case, it has now become a lower-middle income country. The resilience shown by the economy even in the face of a grim political situation is exemplary. However, the catch is that the conditions required to sustain this performance demand political stability and peace. The country can be well-placed on the trajectory of peace and prosperity but the way is still fraught with dangers such as rising militant Islamism and political violence.

End Notes

1. The Awami League's Sheikh Mujibur Rahman pushed through the fourth amendment to the constitution.
2. They both are been scrapped and declared illegal during the current rule of Sheikh Hasina. 5th constitutional amendment was declared illegal as it was made by army government and not by elected government. There was declaration of secular principles by Article 12 and 'Absolute faith and trust in Allah' was removed from the Constitution.
3. There are two types of madarsas- Aliya and Quami. Unlike Aliya madarsas, Quami madarsas are outside the government and provide only religious education. Jamaat uses this kind of platform to spread Islam in the country.
4. Inter Service Intelligence, Pakistan's external intelligence agency.
5. Hizb-ut-Tahrir was banned on October 22, 2009. Later seven other organizations Hizb-ut-Tawhid, Islami Samaj, Ulema Anjuman al Baiyinaat, Islamic Democratic Party, Tawhid Trust, Tamir ud-Deen and Alla'r Dal were blacklisted for their suspected involvement in militant activities.

References

ADB. (2016). *Bangladesh Consolidating Export-led Growth: Country Diagnostic Study.* Washington: Asian Development Bank.

Ahluwalia, I., & Mahmud, W. (2004). Economic Transformation and Social Development in Bangladesh. *Economic and Political Weekly*, 4009-4011.

Ahmad, A. (2013). Bangladesh in 2012 Economic Growth, Political Under-development. *Asian Survey*, *53* (1), 73-83.

Ahmed, A. (2011). Potential for Progress: Opportunities for Economic Growth in Bangladesh. *Harvard International Review*, *33* (3), 28-31.

Ahmed, I. (2016, November 21). *Attacks on Hindus, indigenous people expose Bangladesh's growing intolerance.* Retrieved June 22, 2017, from Scroll.in: https://scroll.in/article/821554/attacks-on-hindus-indigenous-people-expose-bangladeshs-growing-intolerance

Ahmed, S. D., & Alam, O. (2016). Demographic Dividend in Bangladesh: Opportunities and Challenges. *Asian Journal of Multidisciplinary Studies*, *4* (4), 108-116.

Ahmed, S., & Sattar, Z. (2004). Impact of Trade Liberalisation: Looking at the Evidence. *Economic and Political Weekly*, 4059-4067.

Ahmmed, M. M. (2014). Violence against the minorities in Bangladesh. *Himalayan Journal of Sociology and Anthropology*, *6*, 112-118.

Ahsan, Z., & Banavar, P. (2011). Who are the militants? In A. R. Fair, *Political Islam and Governance in Bangladesh* (pp. 71-91). Routledge.

Ahsan, Z., & Banavar, P. (2011). Who are the militants? In A. Riaz, & C. Fair, *Political Islam and Governance in Bangladesh* (pp. 71-90). Oxon: Routledge.

Akter, A. (2017, February 15). *An overview of Bangladesh RMG 2016.* Retrieved June 4, 2017, from Textile Today: http://www.textiletoday.com.bd/overview-bangladesh-rmg-2016/

Asian Development Bank. (2016, October 11). *Bangladesh: Challenges and Opportunities in Moving to Upper Middle Income Status.* Retrieved May 18, 2017, from Asian Development Bank: https://www.adb.org/news/features/bangladesh-challenges-and-opportunities-moving-upper-middle-income-status

Aslam Chaudhary, M., Shirazi, N., & Choudhary, M. A. (2007). Trade Policy and Economic Growth in Bangladesh: A Revisit. *Pakistan Economic and Social Review*, *45* (1), 1-26.

Azam, M., Khan, M., & Iqbal, N. (2012). Impact of political risk and uncertainty on FDI in South Asia. *Transition Studies Review*, *19* (1), 59-77.

Bangladesh Government. (2012, April). *Perspective Plan Of Bangladesh 2010-2021: Making Vision 2021 A Reality.* Retrieved May 2017, from http://bangladesh.gov.bd/sites/default/files/files/bangladesh.gov.bd/page/6dca6a2a_9857_4656_bce6_139584b7f160/Perspective-Plan-of-Bangladesh.pdf

Bhardwaj, S. (2010). Contesting Identities in Bangladesh: A study of secular and religious frontiers. *LSE Asia Research Centre*, 27.

Bhardwaj, S. (2014). Illegal Bangladeshi migration: Evaluating India Bangladesh Approaches. *CLAWS* (Winter), 59-76.

Chakraborty, R., & Vasanthagopal, R. (2015). Warming –up of Bangladesh for a Middle Income Country Status by 2021: Achievements Challenges and Actions. *International Journal of Commerce, Business and Management*, *4* (5), 614-617.

Chowdhury, M., Ahmed, R., & Yasmin, M. (2014). Prospects and Problems of RMG Industry: A study on Bangladesh. *Research Journal of Finance and Accounting*, *5* (7), 103-118.

Country Reports on Terrorism. (2014). *Foreign Terrorist Organizations.* US Department of State.

Daily Star. (2015, March 28). *Militants spreading wings.* Retrieved June 20, 2017, from Daily Star: http://www.thedailystar.net/city/jmb-targets-cops-politicians-74176

Datta, S. (2007). Islamic Militancy in Bangladesh: The Threat from Within. *South Asia: Journal of South Asian Studies, 30* (1), 145-170.

Datta, S. (2005). Political Violence in Bangladesh:Trends and Causes. *Strategic Analysis, 29* (3), 427-447.

Esha, R. I. (2016, July 30). *Understanding youth militancy in Bangladesh*. Retrieved June 21, 2017, from Dhaka Tribune : http://www.dhakatribune.com/bangladesh/2016/07/30/understanding-youth-militancy-bangladesh/

Fink, N. C. (2010). On the borderlines: Politics, religion and violence in Bangladesh. *United Nations University Press*, 91-111.

Ganguly, S. (2006). *The Rise of Islamic Militancy in Bangladesh.* Washington, DC: United States Institue of Peace.

Graff, C. (2010). Poverty, Development, and Violent Extremism in Weak States. In S. Rice, C. Graff, & C. Pascual, *Confronting Poverty: Weak States and U.S. National Security* (pp. 42-89). Washington: Brookings Institution Press.

Griffiths, M., & Hasan, M. (2015). Playing with Fire: Islamism and Politics in Bangladesh. *Asian Journal of Political Science, 23* (2), 226-241.

Grüner, H. P., & Brückner, M. (2010, May 16). *The OECD's growth prospects and political extremism.* Retrieved May 18, 2017, from Vox: http://voxeu.org/article/global-crisis-and-political-extremism

Hasan, K., & Rahaman, F. M. (2016, October 12). *Businessman held for financing Hamza Brigade.* Retrieved June 22, 2017, from Dhaka Tribune: http://www.dhakatribune.com/bangladesh/2016/10/12/businessman-held-financing-hamza-brigade/

Hasan, M. D. (2011). Foreign Aid Dependency of Bangladesh: An Evaluation. *The Chittagong University Journal of Business Administration, 26*, 281-294.

Hussain, M. (2015). Political Violence in Bangladesh Today. *Economic and Political Weekly, 50* (11).

Hussain, Z. (2013, September 1). *What will it take for Bangladesh to become a Middle Income Country?* Retrieved April 12, 2017, from The World Bank: http://blogs.worldbank.org/endpovertyinsouthasia/what-will-it-take-bangladesh-become-middle-income-country

Islam, M. (2015, March 8). *Prospects and challenges of garment industry.* Retrieved June 3, 2017, from The Daily Star: http://www.thedailystar.net/prospects-and-challenges-of-garment-industry-21008

Islam, S. (2011). Political Violence in Bangladesh. In A. Riaz, & C. Fair, *Political Islam and Governance in Bangladesh* (pp. 27-45). London and New York: Routledge.

J. Dumas, L. (2006). Development and Peace: A Virtuous Circle? *Tenth Annual Conference on Economics and Security.* Greece: City College, Thessaloniki.

Jahan, F. (2015). *Indigeneous identity disputes in democractic Bangladesh.* Buenos Aires: CLACSO.

Jahan, R. (2008). The Challenges of Institutionalising Democracy in Bangladesh. *Institute of South Asian Studies , 39.*

Karim, L. (2013). NGOs-Modern Landlords with a Global Vision. In M. Guhathakurta, & W. V. Schendel, *The Bangladesh Reader: History, Culture, Politics.* Durham and London: Duke University Press.

Karlekar, H. (2005). *Bangladesh:The next Afghanistan ?* New Delhi: SAGE .

Khan, S. E. (2017). Bangladesh: The Changing Dynamics of Violent Extremism and the Response of the State. *Small Wars & Insurgencies , 28* (1), 191-217.

Khatun, F., & Ahamad, M. G. (2013). *FDI in the Energy and Power Sector and Economic Growth in Bangladesh.* Dhaka and Bergen: Chr. Michelsen Institute and Centre for Policy Dialogue.

Khundker, N. (2005). *Beyond Hartals - Towards Democratic Dialogue in Bangladesh.* United Nations Development Programme.

Kumar, A. (2012). *Bangladesh's Fight Against Terrorism.* New Delhi: Institute for Defence Studies and Analyses.

Kumar, A. (2009). Jamaat and its agenda of Islamic state in Bangladesh. *Strategic Analysis , 33* (4).

Lewis, D. (2011). *Bangladesh: Politics, Economy and Civil Society.* New Delhi: Cambridge University Press.

Lopez-Acevedo , G., Medvedev, D., & Palmade, V. (2017). *South Asia's Turn: Policies to Boost Competitiveness and Create the Next Export Powerhouse.* Washington: World Bank.

Mahmud, W., Ahmed, S., & Mahajan , S. (2008). *Economic Reforms, Growth, and Governance: The Political Economy Aspects of Bangladesh's Development Surprise.* Washington: World Bank Commission on Growth and Development.

Mian, M., & Alam, Q. (2006). Foreign direct investment and development: The Bangladesh scenario. *Monash Business Review , 2* (1), 1-9.

Moniruzzaman, M. (2009). Party politics and political violence in bangladesh: issues, manifestation and consequences. *South Asian Survey , 16* (1), 81-99.

Rahman, S. (2015, November 15). *Bangladesh moves into crisis of aid utilisation.* Retrieved June 3, 2017, from http://www.thedailystar.net/business/bangladesh-moves-crisis-aid-utilisation-172582

Riaz, A. (2008). *Islamist Militancy in Bangladesh: A Complex Web.* New Delhi: Routledge.

Riaz, A. (2008). *Islamist Militancy in Bangladesh:A complex web.* New Delhi: Routledge.

Riaz, A. (2011). Islamist Politics and Education. In A. Riaz, & C. Fair, *Political Islam and Governance in Bangladesh* (pp. 115-135). Oxon: Routledge.

Riaz, A. (2016). Who are the Bangladeshi 'Islamist Militants' ? *Perspectives on Terrorism , 10* (1), 2-18.

Sarkar, K. (2013, August 21). *Ten Islamist outfits to face ban.* Retrieved June 20, 2017, from Dhaka Tribune: http://archive.dhakatribune.com/law-amp-rights/2013/aug/21/government-mulls-banning-10-islamist-outfits

Sen, B. (2014). Beyond Minimalism of Growth with Safety Net: Is Development 'Inclusive' in Bangladesh? In A. Hussain, & M. Dubey, *Democracy, Sustainable Development and Peace: New Perpestives on South Asia* (pp. 197-218). New Delhi: Oxford University Press.

Siddiqi, D. M. (2011). Political Culture in contemporary Bangladesh: Histories, Ruptures and Contradictions. In C. F. Ali Riaz, *Political Islam and Governance in Bangladesh* (pp. 7-27). Routledge.

South Asia Terrorism Portal . (2014). *Islami Chhatra Shibir (ICS).* Retrieved June 18, 2017, from South Asia Terrorism Portal: http://www.satp.org/satporgtp/countries/bangladesh/terroristoutfits/ics.htm

South Asian Terrorism Portal. (2014). *Harkat-ul-Jihad-al-Islami (HuJI).* Retrieved June 23, 2017, from South Asian Terrorism Portal website: http://www.satp.org/satporgtp/countries/india/states/jandk/terrorist_outfits/HuJI.htm

Strauss-Kahn, D. (2009, October 23). *Economic Stability, Economic Cooperation, and Peace—the Role of the IMF.* Retrieved May 24, 2017, from International Monetary Fund: https://www.imf.org/en/News/Articles/2015/09/28/04/53/sp102309

Suykens, B., & Islam, A. (2015). *The distribution of Political Violence in Bangladesh (2002-2013).* Belgium: Conflict Research Group.

Wiig, A., & Kolstad, I. (2014). *Expanding foreign investment in the energy sector Challenges and risks for Bangladesh?* Bergen: Chr. Michelsen Institute.

World Bank. (2016c, October 13). *Bangladesh: Ensuring Education for All Bangladeshis.* Retrieved June 6, 2017, from World Bank: http://www.worldbank.org/en/results/2016/10/07/ensuring-education-for-all-bangladeshis

World Bank. (2016). *GDP Growth Rate.* Retrieved 2017, from The World Bank: http://data.worldbank.org/country/bangladesh

World Bank. (2016, April 7). *Helping Bangladesh Reach Middle Income Country Status.* Retrieved May 21, 2017, from World Bank: http://www.worldbank.org/en/news/feature/2016/04/07/World_Bank_Group_s_New_Country_Partnership_Framework_helps_Bangladesh_Reach_Middle_Income_Country_Status

World Bank. (2016, November 14). *With Reforms and Investments, Bangladesh can Become an Export Powerhouse.* Retrieved June 5, 2017, from The World Bank: http://www.worldbank.org/en/news/feature/2016/11/14/reforms-investments-bangladesh-come-export-powerhouse

CHAPTER 8

The Sri Lankan Insurgency and Future Prospects

B.D. Mowell

Abstract

The Sri Lankan civil war was the culmination of several decades of ethnic and religious tensions. An increasingly disenfranchised and alienated Tamil minority fueled support for a separatist agenda and an initially diverse range of militant groups, out of which the Liberation Tigers of Tamil Eelam (LTTE), more commonly known as the Tamil Tigers, emerged as dominant. The ensuing 26-year civil war engulfed the country, resulting in an estimated 100,000 deaths and economic stagnation. Elements among both the Sinhalese Hindumajority and the Tamil Buddhist minority were victims as well as perpetrators of brutality and internal conflict among factions within each group was common. The LTTE gained international attention for widespread suicide bombings, assassinations and other acts of violence that led the EU, the United States and many other foreign powers to ultimately label them as a terrorist organization. The latter designation factored heavily into the international community largely turning a blind eye to the brutality of counterinsurgency efforts on the part of government forces, which militarily defeated the last remnants of the LTTE in 2009.

To date, transnational actors including the UN have been largely unsuccessful in pursuing accountability for claims of genocide and other human rights violations which both sides have levied against each other. In addition to unresolved tensions lingering from the war years, many of the underlying issues which facilitated the conflict remain---chiefly the marginalization of the Tamil minority. With the support of Sinhalese nationalists, the Sri Lankan government has also become increasingly authoritarian since the war, one of many factors which may indicate temporary dormancy rather than permanent resolution of the conflict.

Introduction

The Sri Lankan Civil War did not receive the full attention of many western countries in part due to being overshadowed by other international crises in the era and perhaps also due to the perception that the conflict was of limited direct significance to the west. However, in many respects, the Sri Lankan insurgency was one of the most significant conflicts of the late 20th and early 21st centuries. The Liberation Tigers of Tamil Eelam (LTTE), commonly referenced in media outlets as the Tamil Tigers, would serve as a pattern for many unrelated insurgent movements and militant groups around the globe. LTTE tactics such as high-explosive suicide vests/belts and the use of women in the execution of attacks were uncommon practices internationally at the time, but have since been adopted as routine operational tactics by many of the world's most infamous terrorist organizations including the Al Aqsa Martyrs Brigade, Boko Haram, Chechen militants, and ISIL. The conflict was also significant in terms of the magnitude of violence and the degree of brutality often perpetrated by both sides. The destruction of the last bastion of organized LTTE resistance in 2009 marked the official end of the Sri Lankan Civil War but many of the underlying centrifugal forces and other circumstances which precipitated the original conflict remain. This chapter provides an overview of the war, its aftermath and explores the potential for the conflict to reignite.

Historical Context

Armed conflicts customarily have deep-seated roots and the Sri Lankan Civil War was no exception. The country's two largest ethnicities, Sinhalese and Tamils, have been indigenous to the island for well over two thousand years, both thought to have originally migrated to the island from the Indian mainland (Mahadevan 2002). While genetic research has shown them to be distant relatives and possibly branches of the same ancestral origin, distinct religious and other cultural traditions characterized the Sinhalese majority and Tamil minority over the centuries. The Sinhalese comprise some 74 percent of Sri Lanka's population, are primarily Buddhist and speak Sinhala, whereas Sri Lankan Tamils constitute around 12 percent of the national population, are mostly Hindu and speak Tamil. The British also brought as many as one million Indian Tamil (ethnically and culturally related to Sri Lankan Tamils but geographically located in South India) laborers to the island's rapidly expanding network of commercial plantations and today Indian Tamils comprise approximately 4 percent of the country's population. During the era of British colonial rule, tensions between the groups began to rise as a perception existed among the Sinhalese majority that Tamils commonly collaborated with the British and in exchange received preferential status in business, education, civil service appointments and other spheres.

The degree of discrimination felt by many Sinhalese under British rule contributed to Sinhalese political nationalism and an associated Buddhist cultural/religious revival wherein beginning in the 19th century, emphasis was placed upon organizing schools, temples and other institutions to unite and rekindle pride in the traditions of the island's majority group and to oppose colonial and minority control. As one element of the larger post-WWII unravelling of British colonial rule around the world, independence was ultimately attained in 1948. Both in the last years of colonialism and in initially charting a path for the newly independent nation, some effort was made to bring about an atmosphere supportive of reconciliation, political pluralism and egalitarian representation of Sri Lanka's many ethnicities. However, the voices that ultimately prevailed in the new national government were those of a largely unified Sinhalese Buddhist nationalist movement which sought to right real or perceived wrongs experienced by the country's majority under generations of colonial rule and minority privilege.

A range of policies were implemented behind the latter goal, among the most significant of which were new language requirements enacted in 1956. An initial agreement to establish both Sinhala and Tamil as dual official languages of the new country was abandoned in favor of only the former. English was widely spoken as a second language among the Tamil minority (as well as the Sinhalese upper class) but as English was also removed as an official language, the Tamil population---among whom Sinhala was not widely spoken---was to a great degree disenfranchised from many opportunities including government jobs and university seats. Due principally to the Sinhala language requirement, the country's Tamil minority was soon underrepresented relative to its share of the national population with regard to civil service positions held and also in terms of the number of students in the state educational system (Abeysekera 1979).

Other actions on the part of the Sinhalese-dominated national government also marginalized and alienated the Tamil minority. For example, citizenship laws enacted soon after independence recognized two forms of citizenship: by ancestry and by registration. However, both required documentation as proof which disqualified most Indian Tamils as the majority were illiterate, and later legislation officially designated Indian Tamils as aliens rather than Sri Lankan nationals (Wickramasinghe 2009). Reclamation projects initiated by the British toward the end of colonial rule and continuing into statehood witnessed public funds used to repopulate and farmland mostly in Tamil-majority areas that had reverted to wilderness after having formerly been used in plantation agriculture. Resettlement efforts brought mostly ethnic Sinhalese from the island's most crowded population centers in the south and west to historically Tamil regions in the north and east, causing concern among Tamils that their numbers were being watered down in their own heartland. It was also not insignificant that the Sinhalese majority government established Buddhism as the official national religion in the new constitution---this following decades of sporadic religious intolerance in which Hinduism was denounced by many Sinhalese nationalists as paganism. The small Christian (many of whom were ethnic Tamils who converted under British colonial rule) and Muslim communities were also subject to periodic persecution and inflammatory rhetoric. Within a generation of independence, either via language requirements or other forms of discriminatory actions, alienation and fear had facilitated the rise of strong nationalist sentiment among many within the Tamil minority.

Amid a deteriorating climate in which cross-cultural intolerance, acts of vandalism and violent clashes were increasingly common, a Tamil separatist movement had emerged by the 1970s. Many Tamil nationalists no longer saw functional coexistence with the Sinhalese majority within a single multi-ethnic state as a realistic option. Pro-independence elements demanded autonomy for the roughly one-third of the island nation's territory in which Tamils were the majority, principally the northern and eastern coastal areas. Many Tamil leaders sought to achieve independence through democratic and legal means, but growing numbers of militants saw armed conflict as the only means of securing autonomy. Many such groups existed by the 1970s, most little more than local gangs of alienated youth often competing internally with each other for power, but one would emerge as dominant and through the continued escalation of hostilities, place the country on the path to a ruinous 26-year civil war.

The LTTE and the Civil War

In 1975, a young disaffected Tamil separatist, Velupillai Prabhakaran, assassinated the politically-moderate Tamil mayor of Jaffna, the most important urban area in Tamil-majority territory. Prabhakaran had helped establish a small militant group dubbed the Tamil New Tigers three years earlier and through his rhetoric and the notoriety he achieved via the assassination, he attracted militants to his cause and soon founded a more violent splinter group, the Liberation Tigers of Tamil Eelam (LTTE), with the latter two words the Tamil language reference for their territory in Sri Lanka. For the next several years, the LTTE pursued a campaign of violent resistance to Sinhalese rule and competed with other Tamil separatist groups for influence. In July 1983 following a Tamil ambush which killed 13 government soldiers, mobs of Sinhalese nationalists directed their anger toward Tamil civilians in weeklong violent rioting that resulted in up to 3,000 Tamil deaths, countless assaults and the destruction or looting of thousands of homes and businesses. The riots and the realization that government security forces generally made no effort to quell the violence being directed against them facilitated a mass exodus of several hundred thousand Tamils from Sinhalese-majority areas to Tamil lands in the north and east. The riots also served to galvanize Tamil anger, driving many to support the push for autonomy by armed conflict if necessary and cementing the status of the militant LTTE as the dominant voice among Tamil separatists. Accordingly, the July 1983 riots are generally regarded as the beginning of the Sri Lankan Civil War. The 1983 riots and ensuing civil war also created a mass exodus of Tamils who fled abroad, many of whom organized themselves as diaspora communities to politically and financially support LTTE efforts (Smith 2010).

Multiple neutral observers including Amnesty International and Human Rights Watch allege that during the course of the conflict both sides committed and were also targets of human rights violations including torture, summary execution, use of child soldiers and deliberate targeting of civilians by military forces and both sides levied claims of genocide against each other (Bhattacharji 2009; Bajoria 2009). A range of abuses was perpetrated by the Sri Lankan government during the war, a pattern that escalated following the collapse of a 2001 ceasefire agreement. Arbitrary and mass arrests of civilians were commonplace. Tamils including civilians and the injured were denied access to media and international organizations, and all foreign NGOs were eventually ordered out of the country. Government forces were also accused of blocking access to potable water, food and medicines from Tamils including civilians interred in displaced person camps---conditions in which former UN Secretary-General Ban Ki-moon described as "appalling" upon being given brief access (Suntharalingham 2009). Among the more widely-condemned actions of government forces was the practice wherein the military declared localized safe zones for Tamil civilians near front lines which were then shelled by Sri Lankan forces. Government representatives have long insisted that reasonable effort was made to ensure the safety of civilians and that such effort were frustrated by Tamil fighters who used civilians as shields and hid among civilian ranks to launch military strikes, claims that are not entirely without foundation (Dimanno 2013). Widespread allegations have also been levied that government troops often shot Tamils attempting to surrender or summarily executed them after taking them prisoner (Anand and Bastians 2016). The government has downplayed the frequency of such occurrences and noted that such events reflect the confusion and chaos of battle and also that LTTE suicide bombers were often purposefully blended in with groups about to be taken prisoner, meaning frontline government troops---often young men with limited training and experience---feared for their lives when taking prisoners (Anderson 2011).

The brutality of the LTTE received more notoriety in international media outlets in part due to their official designation as a terrorist organization. Labelled "deadly extremists" by the governments of the US and many other nations, the LTTE exhibited many characteristics of a terrorist organization including inventing the suicide belt and perfecting the use of suicide bombers---designated as "Black Tigers", pioneering the use of women in suicide attacks, attacking civilian targets and assassinating thousands perceived to be their enemies including two world leaders, Rajiv Gandhi, former Indian PM assassinated in 1991 and Ranasinghe Premadasa, Sri Lankan President assassinated in 1993 (FBI 2008). Supporters of the insurgency and many neutral international observers reject labelling the LTTE as a terrorist group, noting the existence of oftentimes equivalent brutality on the part of government forces during the war and also stressing that the war stemmed from decades of Sinhalese nationalism which led to structural inequalities and institutionalized repression of the Tamil minority (Kaushik 2015). Such perspectives also note that the national and to a great degree international media narrative concerning the war was controlled by the Sri Lankan government which sought to delegitimize the LTTE and the Tamil separatist agenda.

However, many actions of the LTTE served to validate government claims that they were a terrorist group including attacks targeting a civilian airliner, commuter trains and buses, religious/cultural centers and other public places in which scores of civilians including Tamils and foreign travelers were killed and wounded over the course of the conflict. Attacks upon non-military targets usually focused upon Sinhalese Buddhists and the LTTE customarily avoided targeting foreign/westerners for fear of international reprisals, the bombing of a Sri Lankan Air flight containing mostly tourists in 1986 being a notable exception. The arguments of the LTTE and their supporters that they were a political insurgency rather than a terrorist group were further undermined by the adoption of many of their methods by notorious international terrorist organizations including Al Qaeda. Ultimately, nearly 40 countries officially designated the LTTE as a terrorist organization including India, the UK and the US as did many international organizations including the European Union, which in turn significantly complicated LTTE efforts to raise funds and garner support internationally.

Many states and other international actors altered their positions concerning the LTTE as the war progressed. As a case study, the evolving position of India throughout the conflict is a very telling indicator of the nature of LTTE and how the international community's perception of the group deteriorated over time. Sympathetic to the marginalized status of Tamils and their desire for self-determination, the Indian government is believed to have provided surreptitious support including arms and training to the LTTE in the earliest years of the conflict (Dixit 2003; dos Santos 2007). However, when Rajiv Gandhi came to power following the assassination of his mother by Militant Sikh nationalists, India began pursuing a neutral conflict-management stance, halted military aid to the LTTE and worked to mediate a diplomatic solution to the conflict (Rao 1988). With the failure of negotiations, India imposed a ceasefire in 1987 and deployed up to 100,000 peace-keepers (Indian Peace Keeping Forces or IPKF) at peak strength in an effort to maintain the truce and disarm the LTTE. The LTTE had not agreed to elements of the ceasefire including their own disarmament and soon fighting erupted between the IPKF and LTTE, resulting in around 1,200 fatalities among Indian forces over the next three years before they ultimately withdrew. In retaliation for India's policies, the LTTE assassinated Rajiv Gandhi in 1991, resulting in the organization being officially classified as a terrorist group by India, among the first countries to do so. Despite being the regional power in

South Asia, India was stung by the assassination and the failure of mediation and peacekeeping efforts and pursued a hands-off strategy in the Sri Lankan conflict for the next several years. However, in the final years of the civil war, India supported the efforts of the Sri Lankan government to quell the LTTE, though tacitly to avoid antagonizing India's own Tamil minority (Destradi 2012).

No ideological linkages or political partnerships have ever been proven to exist between LTTE and other international terrorist organizations. Yet LTTE is known to have used illicit means to finance its operations (e.g. narcotics, robbery, extortion, etc.) and via efforts to launder money internationally and also purchase weapons on the global market the organization engaged in transactions with international criminal syndicates as well as terrorist groups including Abu Sayyaf, al Qaeda affiliates, PKK, and the Taliban (Jayasekara 2009). Partly due to the latter connections, the LTTE became more ostracized internationally beginning in 2001 as the international security climate following 9/11 facilitated a hardline stance against terrorist organizations and any group or individual associated with them. Many of the tactics employed by LTTE cemented a shift in international opinion concerning the organization and led dozens of other countries to classify the organization as a terrorist group in coming years. For example, prior to the LTTE, suicide bombings were relatively rare and usually reserved for only the most high-value targets, but the LTTE transformed the practice into an almost routine military practice with an assembly-line approach to supplying bombs and bombers. Prior to the insurgency in Iraq, LTTE forces perpetrated more suicide bombings than any group in history, which succeeded in striking fear into the hearts of counter-insurgency forces and serving as symbols of selfless dedication to the cause for its militant supporters while also horrifying much of the world and tempering international views of the organization as a terrorist group (Lewis 2012).

The war was characterized by four distinct phases interspersed with periods of truce which were often violated to varying degrees by both sides before ultimately collapsing. The first phase began in the wake of the 1983 riots and concluded four years later with an accord establishing the withdrawal of government forces from the most Tamil-claimed territory in the north and the implementation of India's ill-fated peacekeeping mission. Peace talks collapsed in 1990 following (1) LTTE executions of as many as 750 police captives which Colombo had ordered to surrender and (2) LTTE attacks and expulsions targeting Muslim minorities in the Tamil-controlled territory (Salter 2015). The brief ceasefire of a few weeks in 1995was shattered by LTTE bombings and missile attacks, precipitating the capture of substantial government-held territory by insurgents and marking the start of the conflict's third phase. After nearly one-third of the country's territory had fallen under LTTE control, and some 150,000 government troops failed to defeat a Tamil separatist force thought to number only around 10,000, what at the time was described as a "permanent" ceasefire was mediated by Norway in 2002 (Rotberg 2010). The terms of the accord were initially promising with the LTTE agreeing to drop demands for regional autonomy in exchange for a guarantee of power sharing in a unified Sri Lanka. Within a year, the truce began to unravel as the LTTE claimed the government was not negotiating in good faith. The 2004 Indian Ocean tsunami and the devastation it inflicted temporarily prevented the total collapse of the truce, but prospects for the accord to facilitate a permanent peace looked increasingly bleak as ceasefire violations on both sides mounted. The LTTE used the relative calm of the final period of ceasefire to consolidate their leadership role over the Tamil population, killing some 200 internal political rivals between 2002-2006 according to human rights groups (Beardsley and McQuinn 2009: 634). Rebels eventually resumed a suicide bombing campaign and in 2006 the Sri Lankan air force began bombing LTTE positions ostensibly to reestablish water supplies for Sinhalese-populated agricultural regions which had been cut off by the insurgency. By January 2008, a new and more hardline government in Colombo had officially abandoned the accords and announced a final push to quell the insurgency militarily.

The fourth and final phase of the civil war was characterized by some of the most intense fighting and the heaviest civilian and military casualties. This stage was also characterized by a shift in the balance of momentum wherein government forces remained largely on the offensive with a beleaguered and weakening LTTE struggling unsuccessfully to defend. One of the most significant obstacles faced by the insurgents in the last years of their campaign was a chronic arms shortage. Never awash in arms, as the war progressed the LTTE became increasingly pressed to supply arms and ammunition to its fighters. The worsening arms shortage reflected (1) the increased isolation of the LTTE internationally stemming from more countries classifying the group as a terror organization and the concomitant increases in scrutiny such a designation brought to criminal organizations or other entities that might have otherwise been suppliers and (2) the success of prolonged efforts on the part of the Sri

Lankan government involving other governments in actively combating the LTTE's international networks of supporters and operatives. The Sri Lankan military had also progressively tightened its grip over LTTE-controlled areas, interdicting more arms shipments and destroying more arms manufacturing facilities locally as the final phase of the war progressed (Smith 2010).

The aggressive government offensive on multiple fronts succeeded in bleeding the LTTE of fighters and resources and in recapturing considerable territory previously under separatist control. After initially having split LTTE-controlled territory into two separate shrinking zones---one in the north and one in the east---by the start of 2009, the guerrillas only controlled a small northern enclave. Oddly, even as indications continued to mount that the Tamil insurgency was in its death throes, many of its supporters remained optimistic, perhaps hoping for yet another ceasefire or internationally-mediated settlement which never came (Mohan 2014). Public sentiment and political rhetoric in Sri Lanka supported the complete destruction of the LTTE and the associated terrorist threat posed by their existence and the war would be prosecuted accordingly. By May, the remnants of the once feared and potent LTTE occupied only a narrow stretch of beach 7 square kilometers in size which was completely overrun by May 16, with Prabhakaran and other LTTE leaders killed while attempting to escape the last rebel-held pocket.

As the final chapter of the insurgency unfolded both sides are believed to have committed large-scale human rights violations against the civilian population, the rebels in refusing to allow large numbers of civilians to flee combat zones and often using them as human shields and the government in indiscriminately shelling areas they designated as safe zones. The precise numbers of casualties are disputed, but most estimates place the number of war deaths at approximately 70,000 prior to the climactic final assault which resulted in 20,000 to 70,000 additional casualties, the majority of which were likely civilians caught between the two forces (*BBC* 2015). While the exact numbers killed may never be known, what is clear is that the scale and nature of the brutality displayed by both sides in the conflict have reinforced deep-seated animosity and mistrust between segments of the country's population and will likely require multigenerational effort on the part of both Sinhalese and Tamils to reconcile.

The Aftermath and Prospects for Resurgence

Prabhakaran had constructed an almost mythical cult of personality around himself while the leader of the LTTE and had exercised near complete control of the organization, micromanaging many aspects of its operations. While fears lingered for several years that the LTTE would soon resume operations, Prabhakaran's death and the final crushing defeat of separatist forces in the field apparently disillusioned surviving supporters who may not have been able to envision a feasible path for the LTTE to regroup. No known political heirs to Prabhakaran or plan of succession in the event of his death or capture had been designated, but as virtually all remaining leaders of the organization had died in the climactic final siege or months leading up to it, such plans would likely not have proven effectual. However, much speculation has been offered concerning the degree to which an important element of the LTTE organization internationally may have survived the conflict at least partly intact.

Nearly one million Sri Lankan Tamils are believed to live abroad as diaspora communities, with most concentrated in wealthy areas including Australia, Canada, and the EU states (Beardsley and McQuinn 2009). Many members of the diaspora communities willingly supported the LTTE, at least prior to designations as a terrorist group being imposed by many of the nations in which they lived. Other donors within the Tamil diaspora community reported being coerced by predatory international rings set up by the LTTE and its supporters into regularly contributing portions of their earnings to finance the organization, likely generating a larger cash flow than would have been derived via voluntary donations (Byman et al 2001; Becker 2006). In any case, foreign sources were more important than locally-raised funds for several reasons: (1) the sheer volume and purchasing power of funds raised from the Tamil minority in developed countries was greater than funds raised within Sri Lanka; (2) funds raised abroad were simply a higher return on investment as nothing was provided in exchange; and (3) funds raised internationally came with fewer strings attached and were devoid of the social contract often implied with locally raised monies such as taxes levied in LTTE-controlled areas in exchange for provision of a range of state services (Beardsley and McQuinn 2009: 633, Stokke 2006).

At the conclusion of the war, the international fundraising network upon which the LTTE had relied for fundraising and also political support remained at least partially intact and concerns existed that it may be used in an effort to revive the insurgency. The government of Sri Lanka publicly claimed in 2011, two years after the civil war ended, that such international networks were looking for opportunities to rebuild the organization (Stanford 2015). Thus far, the consensus among international intelligence agencies is that such a revival does not appear to be imminent, perhaps in part due to cautious optimism on the part of many Tamils that the post-war climate in Sri Lanka may yet improve.

In the aftermath of the war a range of conciliatory gestures were made by the Sri Lankan government toward the Tamil minority, some of which were more symbolic than utilitarian. The government of President Rajapaksa publicly promoted the vision of a less ethnically and regionally divided nation in favor of a commonly-shared identity and patriotism as Sri Lankans. Such advocacy of reconciliation among the country's ethnic groups supplanted calls for investigations into war crimes potentially committed by government forces. In fact the regime's persistent refusal to pursue accountability including investigations into human rights violations during the conflict soured relations with many western nations including the US and effectively helped drive the Rajapaksa regime increasingly into the foreign affairs orbit of China (DeVotta 2015: 106). Examples of substantive post-war efforts to reconcile with the Tamil minority in the years following the insurgency do exist. Recent initiatives have targeted rebuilding and economic development in many of the areas most affected by the war. At least some effort has been made to attract investment and create jobs in war-torn areas and government subsidies have been made available to assist affected persons in war zones in the rebuilding of their homes and businesses (Anand and Bastians 2016).

Critics note that the rule of President Rajapaksa, who presided over the LTTE's defeat and the first years of post-war recovery,has also been characterized by regime consolidation efforts in which democratic traditions were eroded in favor of an increasingly authoritarian political climate. In elections held following the end of the civil war both the President and the ruling party, the United People's Freedom Alliance (UPFA), won decisive victories which they interpreted as a popular mandate to amass more control. Various actions taken to consolidate power following the elections included arresting opposition political leaders, abolishing presidential term limits and eroding the division of power between branches of government to allow more authority to be vested in the executive, actions which were criticized by opposition parties and by many in the international community including the US (Miwa 2013). With regard to the Tamil minority, the Rajapaksa regime was also seen as antithetical to democratic normalization as it drew its support from Sinhalese-Buddhist nationalism, supported continued militarization of Tamil-majority areas and opposed investigation and prosecution of human rights abuses that had occurred during the war and its aftermath. For many years following the civil war little government effort was made to assist hundreds of thousands displaced by the conflict, most of whom were Tamils.

In 2015 elections, following several years of rampant corruption, nepotism, and executive overreach as well as economic stagnation, opposition candidate Maithripala Sirisena defeated the incumbent president amid high voter turnout and despite initial threats by the outgoing regime to invalidate the voting results, a peaceful succession occurred (DeVotta 2015). The Sirisena government has moved at least somewhat away from the authoritarian trends of its predecessor and made a number of conciliatory overtures since assuming office. For example, the government has promised internal investigations into human rights violations by the military although it has thus far refused to allow the judicial participation of the international community in the process, possibly for fear current and former government leaders would be implicated (Sriskanda-Rajah 2017: 160). Soon after taking office Sirisena instituted constitutional reforms to curtail presidential powers including reinstating terms limits and has also promised to ensure press freedom and facilitate power sharing and otherwise pursue reconciliation with the country's minorities including the Tamils, though at the time of writing no clear path to achieving the latter goals had been formulated (Palgrave-MacMillan 2016). Also of concern to the Tamil population is the retention of the policy wherein during a national emergency---as determined by the government---the president can assume extraconstitutional powers and essentially govern by degree.At present no clear indication exists that LTTE is reformulating but with the continuing specter of authoritarianism, ethnic/religious nationalism, and the marginalization of Tamils and other minorities inadequately resolved, the conditions may exist for new strains of the insurgency to eventually emerge.

Concluding Thoughts - The Limits of International Engagement

Perhaps the greatest lesson derived from the conflict is that international engagement and regional security regimes are as yet not a consistently effective means of resolving armed conflict or even minimizing their severity. For India to have played a more effective role as a regional hegemon in brokering a resolution to the conflict and serving in a potent peacekeeping capacity it would have likely needed to be regarded with greater trust and credibility from both sides. With Indian-Sri Lankan relations at a low point during much of the civil war and Tamil separatists perceiving the Indian government as having betrayed them, India's capability as mediator and peacekeeper was undermined from the outset. India presently has a range of pressing regional security concerns related to neighboring states that are potentially unstable and/ or sources of terrorist activity including Afghanistan and Pakistan, and also expanding Chinese influence in South Asia (Sood 2016). Fortunately, among a range of concerns related to regional security and stability the Indian government appears to have prioritized improving bilateral relations with Sri Lanka in recent years. For example, while previously voting in support of UNHRC resolutions condemning Colombo, India abstained from the voting on the annual resolution beginning in 2014 in an effort to forge better ties with the Sri Lankan government and as a means of acknowledging the at least limited concessions the latter made in response to some Indian diplomatic efforts regarding reconciliation including allowing provincial council elections in certain Tamil-majority areas (Kumar 2016: 123). While points of contention remain including Sri Lanka's increasingly cordial relations with China, bilateral relations between India and Sri Lanka are largely favorable and potentially strengthen India's influence as a source of regional peace and stability.

The Sri Lankan Civil War also serves as a case study with regard to the often limited capacity of the international community to broker peaceful resolutions to disputes if both sides are intransigent in their positions and unwilling to make substantive compromise in order to achieve peace. In this case with the government claiming the separatists were not committed to sincere negotiations and the LTTE claiming that no meaningful solutions were being offered by the state (Matthews 2010). Over the 26-year course of the war numerous negotiations were attempted including six attempts at formal peace talks at the behest of various states and international organizations with none yielding more than fleeting periods of lull in the conflict. Also, both during and after the civil war many countries as well as the United Nations Human Rights Commission (UNHRC) have publicly and repeatedly condemned the both the Sri Lankan government and the LTTE for the conduct of their military forces and called for formal and open investigations into war crimes and human rights violations as well as improvements in the post-war human rights climate, largely to no avail thus far. If the underlying ethnic and regional tensions and other centrifugal forces that triggered the original conflict are to be sufficiently addressed, it will most likely occur through the willingness of all parties to reconcile and forge a shared, peaceful future path rather than via international engagement.

References

Abeysekera, C. (1979). "Ethnic Representation in the Higher State Services." In Social Science Associates (eds.), *Ethnicity and Social Change in Sri Lanka* (pp. 179-195). Colombo, Sri Lanka: Karunaratne and Sons.

Anand, Geeta and Dharisha Bastians (2016)."Rebuilding Lives, and Homes, Shattered by Sri Lanka's Civil War." *The New York Times*. 17 May.

Anderson, Jon (2011). Death of the Tiger: Sri Lanka's Brutal Victory Over its Tamil Insurgents." *The New Yorker*. 17 January.

Bajoria, Jayshree (2009). "The Sri Lankan Conflict."Council on Foreign Relations. https://www.cfr.org/backgrounder/sri-lankan-conflict Accessed on 25 May, 2017.

BBC (2015)."Post-war Sri Lanka."http://www.bbc.com/news/world-south-asia-11393458 Accessed 1 July, 2017.

Beardsley, Kyle and Brian McQuinn (2009). "Rebel Groups as Predatory Organizations: The Political Effects of the 2004 Tsunami in Indonesia and Sri Lanka." *The Journal of Conflict Resolution* 53(4), 624-645.

Becker, Jo (2006). *Funding the "Final War": LTTE Intimidation and Extortion in the Tamil Diaspora*. New York: Human Rights Watch.

Bhattacharji, P. (2009). "Liberation Tigers of Tamil Eelam: Sri Lanka Separatists." Council on Foreign Relations.https://www.cfr.org/backgrounder/liberation-tigers-tamil-eelam-aka-tamil-tigers-sri-lanka-separatistsAccessed on 10 May, 2017.

Byman, Daniel, Peter Chalk, Bruce Hoffman, William Rosenau, and David Branna. (2001). *Trends in Outside Support for Insurgent Movements*. Santa Monica, CA: RAND Corporation.

Destradi, Sandra (2012). "India and Sri Lanka's Civil War: The Failure of Conflict Management in South Asia." *Asian Survey* 52 (3), 595-616.

DeVotta, Neil (2015). *An Introduction to South Asian Politics*. New York: Routledge.

Dimanno, R. (2013). "Sri Lanka's Hidden Genocide." *Toronto Star*. 4 Nov. 2013.

Dixit, Jyotindra (2003). "Sri Lanka." in Dixit, Jyotindra (ed.), *External Affairs: Cross-Border Relations*, New Delhi: Roli Books, 47-96.

Dos Santos, Anne (2007). *Military Intervention and Secession in South Asia: The Cases of Bangladesh, Sri Lanka, Kashmir, and Punjab*, Westport, Conn./London: Praeger

Security International.

Federal Bureau of Investigation.(2008) "Taming the Tamil Tigers from Here in the US." https://archives.fbi.gov/archives/news/stories/2008/january/tamil_ tigers011008 Accessed on 1 June, 2017.

Jayasekara, Shanaka. (2009) "Tamil Tiger Links with Islamist Terrorist Groups."*International Institute for Counter-Terrorism*https://www.ict.org.il/ Article/1023/tamil-tiger-links-with-islamist-terrorist-groups Accessed on 5 May, 2017.

Kaushik, Ambika (2015). "Sri Lankan Civil War: What if the Tamil Tigers Weren't Labelled as 'Terrorists'?" *The Diplomat*. 24 July.

Kumar, Satish (2016). "External Security Situation: Asia, Africa, and Latin America." In *India's National Security: Annual Review 2015–16*. Satish Kumar (ed.), New York: Taylor and Francis, 123.

Lewis, Jeffrey (2012). *The Business of Martyrdom: A History of Suicide Bombing*. Annapolis, MD: Naval Institute Press.

Mahadevan, Iravatham (2002). "Aryan or Dravidian or Neither?– A Study of Recent Attempts to Decipher the Indus Script (1995–2000)."*Electronic Journal of Vedic Studies*.8(1).

Matthews, Bruce (2010). The Limits of International Engagement in Human Rights Situations: the Case of Sri Lanka." *Pacific Affairs* 82 (4), 579.

Miwa, Hiroki (2013). "Strong Presidency and Vulnerable Political System in Sri Lanka."In *Presidents, Assemblies and Policy-Making in Asia*. Yuko Kasuya (ed.). New York: Palgrave-MacMillan.

Mohan, Rohini (2014). *The Seasons of Trouble: Life Amid the Ruins of Sri Lanka's Civil War*. London, UK: Verso Books.

Palgrave MacMillan (2016). *The Statesman's Yearbook 2017: The Politics, Cultures and Economies of the World*. New York: Palgrave MacMillan, 1118.

Rao, P. (1988). "Ethnic Conflict in Sri Lanka: India's Role and Perception."*Asian Survey*, 28 (4), 419-436.

Rotberg, Robert (2010). "Sri Lanka's Civil War: From Mayhem Toward Diplomatic Solution." In *Creating Peace in Sri Lanka: Civil War and Reconciliation*. Robert Rotberg (ed). Washington DC: Brookings Institution Press.

Salter, Mark (2015).*To End a Civil War: Norway's Peace Engagement in Sri Lanka*. Oxford, UK: Oxford University Press, 21.

Smith, Chris (2010). "The Military Dynamics of the Peace Process and its Aftermath." In *Conflict and Peacebuilding in Sri Lanka: Caught in the Peace Trap*? Jonathan Goodhand, BenedicktKorf, and Jonathan Spencer (eds.). New York: Routledge.

Sood, Vikram (2016). "India's Regional Security Concerns." In *India's National Security: Annual Review 2015–16*. Satish Kumar (ed.), New York: Taylor and Francis, 123.

Sriskanda-Rajah, A.R. (2017). *Government and Politics in Sri Lanka: Biopolitics and Security*. New York: Taylor and Francis, 160.

Stanford University (2015)."Mapping Militant Organizations: Liberation Tigers of

Tamil Elam." http://web.stanford.edu/group/mappingmilitants/cgi-bin/groups/view/225 Accessed on 10 June 2017.

Stokke, Kristian (2006). "Building the Tamil Eelam State: Emerging State Institutions and Forms of Governance in LTTE-Controlled Areas in Sri Lanka." *Third World Quarterly* 27 (6), 1021-1040.

Suntharalingham, Shiamala (2009). "Sri Lanka: Health as a Weapon of War?" *BMJ: British Medical Journal.* 338 (7708) (13 June 2009).

Wickramasinghe, Nira (2009). "After the War: A New Patriotism in Sri Lanka?" *The Journal of Asian Studies* 68 (4), 1045-1054.

CHAPTER 9

In the Realm of Transnational Threats: Focusing Human Trafficking of Sri Lankan Refugees and Human Security Threats

Prasanta Kumar Sahu

Abstract

Transnational threats are non-military threats that cross borders and either endangers the political and social integrity of a nation or the well being of that nation's populace. The paper attempts to presume the relation of refugees in the realm of human trafficking, one of the transnational threats. The human security threats cum trafficking risks of refugees includes insecurity, sexual violence, lack of legal protection, socio-economic and political marginalization, social isolation and alienation, severe disruptions in family structure etc. The paper tries to focus on the theoretical perspectives of transnational threats in the realm of refugees with reference to the Sri Lankan refugees and human trafficking issues. It is seen that after civil war, the Sri Lankan Tamil refugees tried to flee to various countries and often trapped in trafficking. So the research paper tries to evaluate the human trafficking of refugees and human security threats confronting the Sri Lankan Tamil refugees mainly from Southern India whom tries to depart illegally to Australia. The paper also tries to analyze the role of international organizations and the need for a global order to resolve the refugee crisis as well as the transnational threats as the subject matters subsist beyond the paradigm of 'boarders and borderlands'.

Introduction

"Transnational threats" were the burgeoning malignancy to the human capabilities, impasses threat to the very existence of a human being and human security in particular. Transnational threats are non-military threats that cross borders and either endanger the political and social integrity of a nation or the well being of that nation's populace. Pumphrey (2000) contend that the transnational threats pigeonholed by their global nature ie., these threats stand astride both domestic and foreign domains. It can be seen that the nature of 'transnational threats' changed in the present day from state being the primary drivers to individual based basically clusters of individual.[1] "Transnational threats" as any transnational (across international borders) activity that threatens the national security includes illicit trafficking of arms, international organized crime mainly human trafficking and smuggling, uncontrolled refugee migration, and environmental damage. In other words, these threats consist of widespread international crime viz., narcotics trafficking, money laundering, corruption, cyber crimes, extreme terrorist activities, arms trafficking, cyber crimes, mass migration, human trafficking and smuggling, movement of infectious diseases, environmental degradation, ethnic and religious hatred. Transnational crimes were known a significant threat to the vulnerable populace viz., refugees or asylum seekers.

The central objectives and research questions of the paper underlines:

1. To focus on the theoretical perspectives of transnational threats in the realm of refugees.
2. To contextualize the human trafficking or smuggling (transnational threats) of Sri Lankan refugees (mainly from Southern India to Australia)
3. Why is Australia being the chosen paradise for Tamil refugees?
4. Does the transition from refugees to illegal migrant cum economic migrants ensuing the Tamil refugees being the victim of human trafficking mafia?
5. To look into the possibilities of international organizations in restoring global order and tacking the problem of 'refugee human trafficking'

Sphere of Transnational Threats or Transnational Crimes: Beyond the paradigm of "Borders and Borderlands"

Transnational threat or transnational organized crime constructs security threats in different level namely at the international, national and human security level. At the international level, transnational crime subverts the international system by weakening institutions and norms which is essential for its functioning. At the national level, it undermines the consistency of the state or the power mechanism and thereby destabilizes the security system of the country. At the individual level, it has an unfathomable impact on human security. The transnational threats are the subject matter subsists beyond the paradigm of 'boarders and borderlands'. Borders imply political territories with appropriated spaces clearly designed by state or society. In other words, Borders or borderlands were spaces of emblematic and material stakes. Border implies having a set of a clear- cut borderline for regulating, controlling, and determining the modes of communication of populace living on both sides of the barrier.[2] Borderlands are inhabited territories located on the margins of a power center, or between power centers, with power understood in the civilization as well as the politico-economic sense.[3] Cedeao (2005) holds that borderlands are soiree places where questions rage, gravely judge the current national and regional policies as a part of grass roots integration and border management. That means, cross-border areas or borderlands were considered as the haven for decision making centers viz. Administrative decentralized authorities and local governments. Besides, borderlands are the spaces of having the socio-culture blending, cohesive living environments with dynamic markets, transportation facilities, and existence of traditional nobilities wherein the inefficient formal mechanism and undesirable procedures to solve disputes (Arragain and Saillot 2005). But the paradigm of borders and borderlands became illogical and annulled in the realm of the concept of Trans nation and the threats or crimes emerging from the international actors. As it can be seen that national security of a nation or human security of a person were threatened highly in international borders than in a country's borderland only. According to the UN Convention, a transnational crime group is one comprising three or more members, organized for a set period of time before and after they act in a coordinated manner to commit a 'serious crime' for the intention of acquiring financial or other benefit. According to security experts, from 1990s, transnational organized crime became the emerging security threat and some defy straight to the state authority and to the well-being of their citizens.

Transnational Crime: Contextualizing Human Trafficking in the Realm of Human Security Threats

Transnational crime or threat runs to counter the government's interest ie., to protect people in violent conflict, defend people from the proliferation of arms, and shore up the security of people on the move, instigate transitions for post-conflict situations. Transnational crime is the direct threat to the individuals in the form of human trafficking and smuggling. Furthermore, in worldwide, Trafficking in persons (TIP)[4] in international borders vestiges the second largest transnational criminal enterprise. TIP is an insidious and vicious abuse of human rights. Trafficking in persons entails the conscription and movement of human beings with the intention of slave-like practices threatens the human security in general. Human security implies safeguarding the prime liberties that is, protecting people from ruthless and extensive threats and crimes, and creating political, social, economic, environmental, military, cultural and peaceful surroundings thereby strengthening aspirations to populace the building blocks of survival. Primarily, the concept of human security constitute two attributes namely freedom from fear and freedom from want. As per United National Development Programmed (UNDP), threats to human security have been positioned in seven categories namely economic security, food security, health security, environmental security, personal security, community security and political security. The human security approach mainly the people centered one limelight on all round human development and, explores the linkages between governance and security to establish the fundamental contributing factors that devise the security of human life.

According to Ashcroft (2003) Trafficking is a transnational criminal enterprise which had no boundaries or borders. Profits from trafficking feed into the reserves of recognized crime and the trafficking is fuelled by other criminal activities such as document fraud, money laundering and migrant smuggling etc. As human trafficking entails no boundaries, refugees or asylum seekers struggling for identity always end up being victims of transnational criminal activities. Crepean (2012:63)[5] pointed out that management of the movement of persons at the border itself is a public security matter which includes both national and international security issue.

Kyle and Koslowski (2001) pointed out "...Trade in humans and migrants is more than a subcategory of global migration...[It] is a subject that intersects contemporary anxieties concerning the global political economy, ethnic and gender stratification, multiculturalism, population growth, political corruption, transnational crime, the Internet, human rights abuse, and the (in)ability of states and global agencies to control effectively...". Refugees cum forced migrants tried to cross borders illegally but most of them end up in human trafficking or smuggling. Trafficking in persons is the third largest criminal activity worldwide generating an estimated USD 9.5 billion in annual revenue. Jordan (2002) contends that due to the denial of the problem of trafficking by states; the objectification of the victims and failure to consider the victims' human rights because states view trafficking as organized criminal activity; the conflation of trafficking in persons with undocumented migration by governments; and the improper definition of the crime of trafficking. This statement is true in case of refugee trafficking victims as they require proper legal documents or permitted to any state entitlements resulting human rights violations. In other words, the refugee trafficking victims were more prone to human security threats.

Article 3 of the UN Protocol clearly defined Trafficking as the recruitment, transportation, transfer, harboring or receipt of persons, by means of the threat or use of force or other forms of coercion, of abduction, of fraud, of deception, of power or of a position of vulnerability or of the giving or receiving of payments or benefits to achieve the consent of person having control over another person, for the purpose of exploitation. United Nations (2001) further clarified that the word 'exploitation' includes exploitation of the prostitution of others or other forms of sexual exploitation, forced labor or services, slavery or practices similar to slavery, servitude or the removal of organs. According to the European parliament, trafficking in human beings as "the illegal action of someone who, directly or indirectly, encourages a citizen from a third country to enter or stay in another country in order to exploit that person by using deceit or any other form of coercion or by abusing that person's vulnerable situation or administrative status" (Rijken 2003). The human trafficking occurring amongst Sri Lankan refugees predominantly come under deceiving and abusing the person's vulnerable position (here illegal migration among stateless refugees) via the middlemen or traffickers.

Trafficking is related to other criminal activities such as terrorism, money laundering, drug trafficking, document forgery and human smuggling (US Department of State 2005). Trafficking has been stated that irreparable loss of human capital on the labor market through depression in wages, fewer people left to care for the increasing elderly population and undereducated generation US Department of State (2005). Article 2 the protocol[6] states: "to prevent and combat trafficking in persons, paying particular attention to women and children; to protect and assist the victims of such trafficking, with full respect for their human rights; and to promote cooperation among State parties in order to meet those objectives" (UN 2001). US Department of State estimated that 600,000 to 800,000 people are trafficked across international borders. According to the United Nations Economic and Social Council (UNESC 2004) over 1.2 million children are trafficked globally every year. ILO figure shows that the regional distribution of the number of forced labor as a result of trafficking. They are as follows: Asia and Pacific 1,360,000; industrialized countries 270,000; Latin America and Caribbean 250000; Middle East and North Africa 230,000; transition countries 200,000; and Sub-Saharan Africa 130,000 (ILO 2005). Broadly, governments and NGOs both agreed that 80 percent of transnational trafficking victims are female and that 50 percent minor children. Furthermore, the majority of the approximately 800,000 victims taken across national borders each year are females trafficked into the sex trades.

Human Trafficking of Refugees and Human Security Threats: The case of Sri Lankan Tamil Refugees

Refugees[7] and internally displaced people are a momentous indication of human insecurity crises. As human security embodies personal belongings, home, family ties, citizenship or entitled to a nation, and significantly peaceful living but refugees are doubly insecure: they (refugees) flee because they are afraid; and in fleeing they start a precarious existence.[8] According to the 1951 convention[9] and the 1967 protocol[10] of United Nations refugee is a person who "owing to a well-founded fear of being persecuted for reasons of race, religion, nationality, membership of a particular social group or political opinion is outside the country of his nationality and is unable towing to such fear is unwilling to avail himself of the protection of that country". Illegal migration is one part of the trafficking process and among the transnational trafficking victims, refugees' play a decisive role as their vulnerability became the key victimized persons.

In 2000, the General Assembly, as part of its United Nations Protocol to prevent, suppress and punish Trafficking in Persons, especially Women and Children (UN Protocol), defined 'Trafficking in Persons' in the subsequent manner.

a. "Trafficking in persons" shall mean the recruitment, transportation, transfer, harboring or receipt of persons, by means of the threat or use of force or other forms of coercion, of abduction, of fraud, of deception, of the abuse of power or of a position of vulnerability or of the giving or receiving of payments or benefits to achieve the consent of a person having control over another person, for the purpose of exploitation. Exploitation shall include, at a minimum, the exploitation of the prostitution of others or other forms of sexual exploitation, forced Labour or services, slavery or practices similar to slavery, servitude or the removal of organs.

b. The consent of a victim of trafficking in persons to the intended exploitation set forth in subparagraph (a) of this article shall be irrelevant where any of the means set forth in subparagraph (a) have been used.

c. The recruitment, transportation, transfer, harboring or receipt of a child for the purpose of exploitation shall be considered "trafficking in persons" even if this does not involve any of the means set forth in subparagraph (a) of this article.

d. "Child" shall mean any person less than 18 years of age."

Further, the United Nations Smuggling Protocol defines Smuggling of migrants as: the procurement, in order to obtain, directly or indirectly a financial or other material benefit, of the illegal entry of a person into a State of which the person is not a national or permanent resident. It is also to be noted that all the migrant smuggling constitutes trafficking, and further smuggling does not require coercive or deceptive means. On the other hand, trafficking requires coercive or deceptive means. A person cannot consent to being trafficked, even where he or she has consented to be smuggled across international borders.

Anne T Gallagher in her work entitled "*The International law of Human trafficking*" examines whether the fear of trafficking or trafficking represent a valid reason for asylum. Gallagher points out that the forms of exploitation inbuilt in the trafficking experience viz., abduction, incarceration, rape; sexual enslavement, enforced prostitution, forced labor and physical beatings represent severe violations of human rights. Furthermore, trafficking of women and girls for purposes of enforced prostitution or sexual exploitation is a form of gender related violence, also comes under the legal definition of 'refugee'. There exists greater probability that the trafficked women and children can particularly vulnerable to retaliation, re-trafficking, isolation and discrimination.

Here, the focus of the paper only takes human trafficking of Sri Lankan refugees as most of them were deceived with false promissory notes that they would be given citizenship by taking huge ransoms or tried to illegally migrate in insecure vessels in which a significant number perished at sea. The human security factors of the Sri Lankan refugees were under threat in the international boundaries. The paper tries to evaluate the human trafficking and human security threats occurring among Sri Lankan Tamil refugees. Here the researcher's main focus will be the human trafficking of Sri Lankan Tamil refugees via illegal migration from Southern India to Australia. At first, the effort will be made to substantiate the political history of Sri Lankan refugee crises and how the Sri Lankan refugees came to Southern parts of India mainly Tamil Nadu, Kerala. In India, the Sri Lankan refugees came both through there partition of Indian origin Tamils due to the ethnic violence and statelessness cum civil war-induced refugees through various phases. The rationale behind why the Sri Lankan refugees came to India can be traced with the following reasons viz., the safety issue i.e., abode in the safe place where no threat and another can be the ethnic similarities where their voices will be heard and can enjoy peace.

The Sri Lankan conflict cum civil war created a colossal refugee crisis both internally and other parts of the world. It is estimated that Sri Lanka's Internally Displaced Personnel (IDPs)[11] in the year 2008 is approximately 250,000 and 450,000 were the evacuated civilians. Among them, there were displaced people both in camp sites and non-camp sites. The noteworthy point is that there were overloaded evacuated civilians in the government camps where severe security challenges were reported. Furthermore, most of the camps were facing serious challenges such as lack of hygiene facilities, proper sanitation, food and medical equipment amenities. The report shows that the number of refugees ranging from 80,000 to100,000 was in the Colombo region only. The foremost problem that the internally displaced refugees were facing is that as their entire livelihood had been destroyed, it demands a novel beginning from the ashes.

Ever since the broke out of Sri Lankan civil war in 1983; Tamil Diaspora have had made European cum neighboring countries as their domicile. Estimates claimed that there were almost 817,000 displaced Sri Lankan Tamils living abroad (UNHCR 2001). The immediate result of these atrocities against Tamils throughout Sri Lanka is that a large number fled the island, and took refuge in the countries namely India, Australia, Canada, the United States, the UK, and many other Western European countries. In fact, according to some estimates, approximately one-quarter of all Sri Lankan Tamils presently live in abroad. This equates to roughly 600,000 to 800,000 Sri Lankan Tamils spread throughout over 40 different countries, with the greatest intensity in Canada and the UK. It is also crystal clear that Sri Lankan refugees were scattered in developing neighboring countries and Western developed countries. The astounding standard of living of

Australia and the proximity from Southern India made many Sri Lankan Tamil refugees to depart illegally and became victims of human trafficking or other human security threats.

Sri Lankan Tamil refugee trafficking is a contemporary phenomenon and their human security threats have been a widely discussed in the current dailies and it being the secondary data, the effort will be made to uncover findings out of it. Besides, the study is also based on expert interview among journalists covering the stories of Sri Lankan Tamil refugee trafficking. The following study tries to contextualize the human trafficking or smuggling (transnational threats) of Sri Lankan refugees (mainly from Southern India to Australia), the reason behind Australia being the chosen paradise for Tamil refugees, whether the transition from refugees to illegal migrant cum economic migrants ensuing the Tamil refugees being the victim of human trafficking mafia and tries to give solution to the problem of refugee human trafficking.

Sri Lankan Tamils sailing from the South Indian coast in wretched boats dreaming of better living in Australia and Canada. In Australia, priinary destinations in Australia were Christmas Island; coco Island etc.[12] Thousands have died in the attempt to illegally migrate while the Human trafficking Mafia made millions.[13] This statement was justified by S.C. Chandrahasan, head of the Organization for Eelam Refugees Rehabilitation (OfERR) quote:"Over 600 Sri Lankan Tamils have perished in the Indian Ocean sailing from the south Indian coast in sea-unworthy boats for greener pastures in Australia and Canada". Most of the recruiting agents and sub-agents mostly held these through Mangalore, Kollam, and Kochi. The preferred launching points for these boats include Mangalore, Munambam (Kochi), Kollam, Kanyakumari, Nagapattinam, Cuddalore, Pondicherry, Chennai and Vizag (Andra Pradesh).[14] Sources in trafficking Mafia revealed that the boats were usually procured in Kochi, Kollam or Kanyakumari (Kerala). The Hindu(edn. Kochi) reported in its news entitled "Suspected human trafficking: 23-member group detained in Thiruvananthapuram" that an international human trafficking racket haulage twenty-three suspected illegal migrants via sea to Australia on the false promise that there was excessive demand for cheap labour.

Daily Mirror in its report[15] entitled "Sri Lankan Tamil refugees being trafficked: India" dated 11th March, 2013 asserted that Sri Lankan Tamil refugees are being the victims of trafficking inthe way of sending them to Australia. The

Home Minister RPN Singh also give anaffirmative statement in the LokSabha that since 2010, almost 1,163 Sri Lankan refugees wereintercepted by the security forces along with 57 Indians and for almost 41 cases wereregistered in the relation to human trafficking of Sri Lankan refugees in India.

The daily "*Fair Observer*" in its article entitled Sri Lankan refugees: Voyages of Uncertainty dated 11th May 2013 asserted the human trafficking of Sri Lankan refugees in the way of faulty promises such as undertaking the voyage to developed countries like Canada, Australia in shabby vessels and exploiting them to give huge random. As per the Human rights groups, the human smugglers charge between £16,000 and £33,000 to traffic refugees and in order to escape from the refugee life, the large number of Sri Lankan Tamils pursued illegal journeys by risking their lives in the recent years.

Recent statistics reveal that more than 60 boats brought more than 5000 refugees to Christmas Island.[16] It is also confirmed that people smugglers are ramping up operations to exploit the continuing political impasse in Australia regarding the most suitable policy to deal with those seeking asylum. The reason behind the booming of human traffickers is that mounting demand for voyage along with the escalating prices in Southern India ensures big chunks of profits. For example, the news like the following captured the headlines every week viz., "5 held for duping Lankan refugees to the tune of Rs. 20 lakh"[17] is one of the instances in which the accused had told the refugees that they would take them to Australia from Kochi in a boat.

Wright (2012) contends that more than 60 boats with more than 5000 asylum seekers arrived in Christmas Island, a place in Australia in the year 2012.[18] Further, more than 1500 Sri Lankan Tamil refugees landed on Cocos Island. Hodge (2012) contends that the number of Sri Lankans paying human smugglers for the voyage to Australia has increased significantly.[19]

Rohan Gunaratna (2012)[20] contends that the operations to smuggle boat people to Australia is indubitably linked to the LTTE international human smuggling network. "The Sri Lankan Human Smuggling enterprise consists of three components, Criminals, Criminals who collaborate with the LTTE and a new class of terrorist-criminals. While the first and the second categories existed during the conflict, the face of human smuggling changed at the end of the conflict. Although the LTTE engaged in human smuggling operations for a longtime, the LTTE became globally known for this illegal trade only after

October 2009. To relocate their leaders, members, helpers and their families in Asia to the West, mostly to Canada but now it has become a lucrative business to smuggle not only Tamils but Muslims and Sinhalese as well".

The Australian Maritime Safety Authority (AMSA) has confirmed 110 people have been rescued from the sea. Western Australia police commissioner Karl O'Callaghan told reporters: "Some of the very early reports suggest that up to 75 people may have drowned, but I do stress that they are unconfirmed at this stage," "We are very concerned for a large number of people who may have drowned," "We know from what we've been hearing from the aircraft that there's not 200 life jackets on board. There has been an increase in refugees fleeing Sri Lanka and attempting the perilous journey across the Indian Ocean to Australia." For all the risk, the threat of jail and the uncertainty of the other side, there is no shortage of young men from Sri Lanka willing to chance the perilous crossing.[21] Doherty (2012) maintained that many Tamil refugees are informed false notion and make believe that they will be granted citizenship on the arrival or their claims are assured when they reach Christmas Island.[22]

With the above-cited various instances regarding human trafficking of Sri Lankan refugees, we can make following conclusions.

1. *Altering Identities*: From Refugees to economic migrants[23] cum illegal migrants? It is the valid rationale behind refugee's being trafficked. A vast number of refugees trapped into the clutches of traffickers mainly because of their over aspiration to have a high standard of living. They want to alter their refugee identity status to economic migrants which transpire the traffickers to trap them. The middlemen try to cerebrally assassin the refugees and make them believe the benefits and charge huge random for voyage. Identities imply collections of information that other people and institutions have about a person, collections that they use to distinguish the individual from other people in their minds or records.[24]
2. *Why is Australia being the chosen paradise for Tamil refugees?* The answer is proximity; developed nation; vast opportunities and above all the traffickers try to believe the refugees regarding their links and promised citizenship there. The Sri Lankan refugees with the intention to have the high standard of living tried to migrate illegally to Australia and other well-developed nations can be seen to alter refugee identity to 'being economic migrants'.

International Organization and Global Order: Role in Resolving Transnational Threats or Crimes

In order to resolve the transnational threats or crimes and maintain global order, dominant international organization is necessary as the nation- state has limitation to curb as it will apprehend other nation's security. So there is a need for establishing a 'human security regime' to protect the categories of extremely vulnerable persons (mostly refugees, migrants and internally displaced) by strengthening the regime in three ways viz., developing norms, strengthening institutions (both national and international) and, operationalising and implementing strategies.[25] Picarelli, John T (2008: 489) in his article entitled "Transnational Organizational Crime"[26] contend that at the international level, a variety of International and regional organizations have formed to coordinate against transnational crime. Further ,institutions of civil society also play a significant role to wipe out transnational crime.[27] McAdam (2008) adds that the international protection regime for refugees and forced migrants progressively more at risk as measures were premeditated to enhance the security of borders, of people, of institutions and of national identity intrude upon human rights.[28] Most of the human trafficking occurs among the refugees because of lack of awareness regarding the possibilities of being trapped, so the individual awareness is given a prime importance. Thus, a multi-layered approach is required as the transnational threats necessitate a collective action from all the countries along with individual awareness. As states cannot fight these groups alone because of the operation of transnational crime groups across borders, strengthening international organizations with a strong head is needed with the cooperation of all the countries. As the criminals change their destination from country to country, need for interlinking all the countries security system to catch these transnational criminals. In short with a powerful international organization blending security systems of all the nations, sturdy civil society, media, and individual awareness can curb the transnational threats or crimes in general.

Conclusion

Transnational threats or crimes after all created by the human beings with the existing loopholes or influential for protection. If the security of every country is stringent with no loopholes to do the crime, there will be no crime or security issues, further no transnational threat. As there are loopholes or high influential to protect these criminals, it continues to exist. Every country protects its citizens but refugees are the exception as they were also treated as troublemakers. So efforts should be made to have humanitarian intervention to protect and help the refugees because of their vulnerable situation, they bend into the clutches of human traffickers. Further, if a person of a country is being trafficked or that country has huge trafficker's mafia, then it should be noted that the country's military force is weak. It is most often seen that every country tries to invest more in their military sector to show their military strength but it is a misconception. On the contrary, if a country is having its citizens trafficked or there exist trafficking mafia, that country can be said to be nominal in protecting national security. In short, there is a need for a stringent International organization (may be an International Police/Military Force) to combat the transnational threats as it harms the peaceful living and human as well as national security (of all countries) in general.

Endnotes

1. Khosla, IP (2009), "*Evolving a theoretical perspective on human security*" in the edited work of Lamprecht, Christian, Todd Hataley & Kim Richard Nossal". "Evolving transnational threats and border security: A new Research Agenda", pp.22
2. Barta, Miroslav (2010),"Borderland Dynamics in the era of the pyramid builders in Egypt". Ed. "*Understanding life in the Border lands: Boundaries in Depth and in motion*" Georgia. University ofGeorgia Press, pp.22
3. Zartman, William I (2010:2), "Identity, Movement and Response in Edited work entitled "*Understanding life in the Border lands: Boundaries in Depth and in motion*" .Georgia.. University ofGeorgia Press, pp.2
4. Trafficking in persons (TIP) involves the use of violence, threats or deception to create a pliant and exploitable work forcetrafficking in persons, unodc/un.gift)
5. Crepean, Francois (2012), "Movement of persons and Border security" in the edited work ofLamprecht, Christian. Todd Hataley& Kim Richard Nossal, "*Evolving Transnational threats andBorder security: A new Research Agenda*". Ontario. Centre for International &DefencePolicy.Queen's University Press, pp.63
6. The protocol supplements the UN Convention Against Transnational Organized Crime

7. 'Refugees' are the people who are uprooted from the land of their own and forced to run away to adifferent place for the safety of their life leaving all their belongings and dreams behind.
8. "Human Security: A Refugee Perspective" – Keynote Speech by Mrs. Sadako Ogata, United NationsHigh Commissioner for Refugees, at the Ministerial Meeting on Human Security Issues of the"Lysoen Process" Group of Governments, Bergen, Norway, 19 May 1999 HC Statements, 19 May1999. Retrieved from: www.unhcr.org/3ae68fc00.html 9/9
9. Convention relating to the status of Refugees adopted on 28th July 1951 by the *United NationsConference of Plenipotentiaries on the Status of Refugees and Stateless persons.*
10. Article I, Protocol relating to the status of Refugees held in New York on 31st January 1967.
11. Internally Displaced Persons (IDPs) are the world's most vulnerable people remain inside theirhome countries as victims of forced displacement. http://www. unhcr.org/pages/49c3646c146.html
12. R.Bhagwan Singh (12 July 2012) "More than 600 Sri Lankan Tamils sailing from South Indian Coast have perished in the Indian Ocean". (Note: Christmas Island and the Cocos (Keeling) islandswere the territories of Australia in the Indian Ocean.)
13. ibid
14. ibid
15. www.dailymirror.lk/news/28808-sri-lankan-tamil-refugees-being-trafficked-india.html
16. R.Bhagwan Singh. (12 July 2012) "*More than 600 Sri Lankan Tamils sailing from South IndianCoast have perished in the Indian Ocean*".
17. The Times of India (9 September 2013), "*5 had for duping Lankan refugees to the tune of Rs. 20lakh*". Coimbatore
18. Wright, Tony. (June 30, 2012), "*On Christmas Island*", Fairfax Media Network, www.theage.com.au/national/on-christmas-island-20120630-219g8.htm
19. Hodge, Amanda (29 July 2012) "*Sri Lankan Navy officials want Australia to deport Lankan Asylumseekers in large numbers*". Colombo. "dbsjeyaraj.com dbsjeyaraj.com/dbsj/archives/8819

20. Head, International Centre for Political Violence and Terrorism Research (ICPVTR), Singaporemakes the remarks on Sri Lankan Tamil refugee trafficking and smuggling to the daily "*The SundayObserver*"
21. Doherty, Ben (23 July 2012), "*The Sri Lankan Tamil village which wants to come to Australia*", dbsjeyaraj.com/dbsj/archives/8448 5/5
22. ibid
23. Economic migrants are primarily triggered by poverty related displacements in their countries oforigin. (Abrar, Chowdhury R (p.138). "*Human security, globalization and migration: The case of temporary migrant workers of South Asia*")
24. Harper, Jim (2006),"*Identity crisis: How identification is over used and misunderstood*".Washington D.C. Cato Institute, PP.63
25. Abrar, Chowdhury R. (2010), "*Human security, Globalization and Migration: The case oftemporary migrant workers of South Asia*", *pp.109*
26. Picarelli, John T (2008) in his article entitled "Transnational Organizational Crime" in the editedwork of Paul D. Williums entitled "*Security Studies: An Introduction*". New York:Routledge.
27. Ibid,pp. 491
28. McAdam, Jane (2008). "*Forced Migration, human rights and Security*",Oregon: Hart Publications, pp.23

References

Abrar, Chowdhury R (2003), "Human security, globalization and migration: the case of temporary migrant workers of South Asia", pp.107-123, In *Human security in South Asia: gender, energy, migration and globalization* /ed. by P.R. Chari and Sonika Gupta- New Delhi: Social Science Press.

Abeysekera, Charles and Newton Gunasinghe (eds.). Facets of Ethnicity in Sri Lanka. (Colombo: Social Scientists' Association 1987).

Ali, M. (2005). Treading along a Treacherous Trail: Research on Trafficking in Persons in South Asia. In F. Laczco and E. Gozdziak (Eds.), Data and Research on Human Trafficking: A Global Survey (pp. 141-164). Geneva: International Organization for Migration.

Arasaratnam, Sinnappah. 1979. "Nationalism in Sri Lanka and the Tamils." In Collective Identities, Nationalism and Protest in Sri Lanka, edited by Michael Roberts, 500–522. Colombo: Marga Institute

Asian Human Rights Commission, INDIA: Police officers run human trafficking cartel. Retrieved on 8 September 2013 from http://www.humanrights.asia/news/ ahrc-news/AHRC-STM-036-2 013

Bose, S. States, Nations, Sovereignty: Sri Lanka, India and the Tamil Eelam Movement. (New Delhi: Sage Publications, 1994).

Barta, Miroslav (2010), "Borderland Dynamics in the era of the pyramid builders in Egypt", Ed. "*Understanding life in the Border lands: Boundaries in Depth and in motion*", pp.22, Georgia: University of Georgia Press.

Convention relating to the status of Refugees adopted on 28th July 1951 by the *United Nations Conference of Plenipotentiaries on the Status of Refugees and Stateless persons.*

Crepean, Francois (2012), "Movement of persons and Border security", pp.63, eds. Lamprecht, Christian, Todd Hataley& Kim Richard Nossal, "*Evolving transnational threats and Bordersecurity: A new Research Agenda*", Ontario: Centre for International & Defense Policy: Queen's University Press.

Department for Economic and Social Affairs (2004) World Economic and Social Survey, Part II: International Migration, New York: UN

Doherty, Ben (23 July 2012). "*The Sri Lankan Tamil village which wants to come to Australia*", dbsjeyaraj.com/dbsj/archives/8448 5/58.

Dwivedi, Manan (2009). "*South Asia Security*". Delhi. Kalpaz Publication. ISBN-978-81-7835-759-1

Doherty, Ben &Patidar, Som (15 June 2012), "*The AGE* India refugee boat racket". Frank Laczko and ElzbietaGozdziak, "Data and Research on Human Trafficking: A Global Survey," Special Issue, International Migration 43, no.1–2 (2005).

F. Laczko, "Human Trafficking: The Need for Better Data", Migration Information Source, (November 2002), 1–6. Available at: http://www.migrationinformation. org/Feature/display.cfm?ID=66 (accessed on 25 August 2008).

Daily Mirror, www.dailymirror.lk/news/28808-sri-lankan-tamil-refugees-being-trafficked-india.html Goldstein, Joshua.S&Pevenhouse, Jon.C (2008), "*International Relations*" (Eighth Edition). Pearson. ISBN- 978-81-317-24795

Goodwin Gill, Guy S. (2008). "Forced Migration: Refugees, Rights and Security" in ed. McAdam, Jane. "*Forced Migration, Human rights and Security*", *Oregon*: Hart Publications

Hodge, Amanda (29 July 2012) "*Sri Lankan Navy officials want Australia to deport Lankan Asylum seekers in large numbers*", *Colombo*, "dbsjeyaraj.comdbsjeyaraj. com/dbsj/archives/8819

Harper, Jim (2006), "*Identity crisis: How identification is over used and misunderstood*". Washington D.C. Cato Institute, pp.15.

International instruments UNHCR, refugees, and asylum Statelessness, Internally displaced persons, Migrants, Human rights (volume 1) *Collection of International instruments and legaltexts Concerning refugees and others of concern to unhcr*, June 2007, Geneva: Division of international Protection Services.

Iredale, R. and Piper, N. (2003) Identification of the Obstacles to the Signing and Ratification of the UN Convention on the Protection of the Rights of All Migrant Workers: The Asia-Pacific Perspective, Paris: UNESCO

Jayatilaka, D. (2010) Research Study on Human Smuggling in Sri Lanka: Windows for Intervention by the International Organization for Migration (IOM).

Karunaratne, C. Existing Legislation on Trafficking in Persons in Sri Lanka [Presentation], ILO.

United Nations High Commissioner for Refugees, http://www.unhcr.org/pages/49c3646c146.html

K. Kangaspunta, "Collecting Data on Human Trafficking: Availability, Reliability and Comparability of Trafficking Data," in Measuring Human Trafficking: Complexities and Pitfalls, ed. E. Savona and S. Stefanizzi (New York: Springer, 2007), 27–37.

Khosla, IP (2009), "Evolving a theoretical perspective on human security", pp. 22, eds. Lamprecht, Christian, Todd Hataley& Kim Richard Nossal, "*Evolving Transnational threats and bordersecurity*: *A new Research Agenda*

Lobasz, J. k. (2010). Beyond Border Security: Feminist Approaches to Human Trafficking. In L. Sjoberg, (Ed.), Gender and International Security: Feminist Perspectives (pp. 214-234). New York: Routledge

McAdam, Jane (2008), "*Forced Migration, human rights and Security*", Oregon: Hart Publications.

Ogata, Sadako (1999), "*Human Security: A Refugee Perspective*", Norway, United Nations High Commissioner for Refugees, at the Ministerial Meeting on Human Security Issues of the "Lysoen Process" Group of Governments, 19 May 1999 HC Statements, 19 May 1999, Retrieved from: www.unhcr.org/3ae68fc00.html 9/9

Phil Williams "Drugs, Human Trafficking, and Fraud as a Security Threat" (presentation, Geneva Centre for Security Policy, 25 June 2007).

Picarelli, John T (2008), "*Transnational Organizational Crime*" edn. Paul D. Williums "Security Studies: An Introduction". New York. Rutledge.

Samaranayake, S. (2010) Sri Lanka and Human Trafficking: Professional's Handbook [Working Draft].

Schrijvers, J.."Fighters, Victims and Survivors: Constructions of Ethncity, Gender and Refugeeness among Tamils in Sri Lanka," *Journal of Refugee Studies*, vol. 12, no.3, 1999.

... "Tamil-Muslim Violence, Gender and Ethnic Relations in Eastern Sri Lanka," *NETHRA*, vol. 2, no.3, April–June 1998.

Shastri, A. "Estate Tamils, The Ceylon Citizenship Act of 1948 and Sri Lankan Politics," *Contemporary South Asia*, vol. 8, no. 1, March 1999.

Skeldon, R. (2003) Migration and migration policy in Asia: a synthesis of selected cases, London: DfID

Shelley, L. (2010). Human Trafficking: A Global Perspective. New York: Cambridge University Press.

Sheldon X. Zhang and Samuel L. Pineda, "Corruption as a Causal Factor in Human Trafficking," in Organized Crime: Culture, Markets and Policies, ed. D. Siegel and H. Nelen (New York: Springer, 2008), Chapter 4.

Singh, R.Bhagwan (12 July 2012), "*More than 600 Sri Lankan Tamils sailing from South Indian Coast have perished in the Indian Ocean*".

Tadjbakhsh, S. and Chenoy, A. M. (2007). Human Security: Concepts and Implications. New York: Routledge.

Tandia, Aboubakr (2005), "*Borders and Borderlands Identities: A Comparative Perspective of Cross-border Governance in the Neighborhoods of Senegal, the Gambia and Guinea Bissau*". Senegal. Grouped detrudes ET de Recherchessur les Migrations

The Times of India. (9 September 2013), "*5 had for duping Lankan refugees to the tune of Rs. 20 lakh*", Coimbatore

Vamadevan, M. *Rehabilitation Of Sri Lankan Repatriates in Tamil Nadu: An Assessment*. (Trivandrum: Center for Development Studies 1987

Wright, Tony (30 June 2012),"*On Christmas Island*", Fairfax Media Network, www. theage. com.au/national/on-christmas-island-20120630-219g8.htm

Zartman, William I (2010), "Identity, Movement and Response", pp:2, (edn.) "*Understanding life in the Border lands: Boundaries in Depth and in motion*", Georgia: University of Georgia Press.

CHAPTER 10

Understanding Present-day Islamic Extremism: Bangladesh Perspective

Taslima Islam

Abstract

Bangladesh, a small country with her large population, has made remarkable economic and social progress. Bangladesh has already met several targets of the Millennium Development Goals (MDGs) and is now preparing to achieve the Sustainable Development Goals (SDGs) too. However, the path of progress is being deterred by the violent activities of Islamic extremists. Extremism is not new in Bangladesh; its seed was sown at the time when secularism was removed from the country's constitution and subsequently, Islam was taken as a state religion. At that time, the homogeneous (88 percent Muslims) as well as underdeveloped society did not take it so negatively, but in course of time, it has made the society vulnerable, which is going to introduce Bangladesh as an extremist country. Terrorist groups do not remain in a geographic area, rather they spread over the developed and semi-developed countries quickly. The present government has made visible strides for stamping out extremism from the society, but the stand of all political parties including the political party who is in power against extremism is questioned. This paper aims to explore the changing features of militant groups and the roles of the political parties against extremism.

Bangladesh has emerged remarkably with its less natural resources and vast manpower as well as upheld its attraction as a potential country to other developing countries. To become a middle-income country, it has already been able to meet most of its economic challenges and is on right track. Despite this rapid success, violent extremism in the name of Islam has been put in an appearance as a cumber of all successes in Bangladesh. The government is determined to overcome the issue; the Islamic militant groups might be controlled, but a question has come to all-Can Bangladesh pull out its root forever? Within a year, the security force conducted 20 operations, and 67 terrorists including 5 women and 6 children were killed. As the questioned role of political parties, Islamic radicalism has got access to politics and society and in continuation, global Islamic terrorist groups have mixed with local Islamic militant groups aims to set up Islamic radical government. Indeed, the mainstream political party such as Awami League (AL) and Bangladesh Nationalist Party (BNP) make coalition with Islamic political parties for sharing vote bank without any shrink, which makes vulnerable Bangladesh today.

In South Asia, Bangladesh has become a new hunting ground and the latest front of the Islamic State for its geographic location and proximity to both targeted country of IS (Islamic State) is India and Myanmar. Sheikh Abu Ibrahim al Hanafi's (real identity unknown)' interview published in the mouthpiece of IS, 'Dabiq' magazine in its 14th edition on April 13, 2016, where he clearly explained that they have organizational base in Bangladesh, from where they have plans to attack India and Myanmar to "avenge the persecution on Muslims.". Claiming the responsibility of killing Cesare Tavella by IS in 28 September 2015, the new chapter of radical Islamic terrorism has opened in Bangladesh. Though Sheikh Hasina, the Prime Minister of Bangladesh, consistently denied the presence of IS or any international terror groups in the country and blamed the homegrown militant for terrorism incidents. The Indian government, on the other hand, claims that there are 50 Islamic militant groups operating in Bangladesh, and has accused Dhaka of harboring 148 arms training centers (Cochrane 2009). However, the root of that militant groups is, this new formed Islamic militant groups are more organized and the intensity is deeper.

Islamic extremism does not boom in a day in Bangladesh. Therefore, to understand present-day violent of Islamic extremism, need to look up how Islam has inserted in politics to fill out the ambition of political leaders and how Islamic militant groups bought up and emerged as the national threat to all. Also, standing out of political parties against Islamic extremist is described.

Rise of 'Political Islam' in Bangladesh: A Historical Preview

Under the umbrella of Islam, the West and East Pakistan could not live together happily and finally, both were separated after 24 years of the creation of Pakistan. East Pakistan earned freedom in 1971 through a nine-month bloodshed war and introduced itself as a new country 'Bangladesh'.

Bangladesh, the youngest country in South Asia, who has boldly introduced itself as a first secular country in South Asia by the constitutional proclaim in 1972, which was adopted on the 4th November, 1972 and effected from the 16th December, 1972 during the period of the first government led by Sheikh Mujibur Rahman, Father of the Nation. The four basic principles of the constitution (nationalism, democracy secularism, and socialism) clearly defined the political, moral and religious values of the newborn country. Moreover, through the Article XII of the constitution, all forms of communalism have been eliminated as well as all Islamic parties and their activities have been banned. Mujibur Rahman always wanted to keep religion aside from politics and that has a reflection on his remarkable speech which he gave in parliament to define the meaning of secularism in Bangladesh "Secularism doesn't mean faithlessness, much less atheism. It is meant to ensure the right of each and every citizen of the country to practice his/her religion....Religion is indeed a very sacred thing, and this must not be used for political gains. Let me reassure you that it (adoption of secularism) has not curtailed people's religious rights. I have only arranged for each and every citizen of the country to practice his/her religion out of his own free will (Mahmud 2011)." Likewise, Sheikh Mujibur Rahman took many breakthrough steps, but the reality was different and tough for Bangladesh as a new country. Except India and Soviet Russia, no country favored the emergence of Bangladesh, even most of the Muslim countries treated Bangladesh in a way as if it hit Islam by being separated from its Muslim brother Pakistan and did not give it either recognition or aid. On the other hand, due to unlimited corruption, nepotism and favoritism, price hike, famine and so on, Mujibur Rahman could not hold his 'precursor of freedom' image among general people. Over and above, Mujib's government did not want to lose the power and started oppressing other political parties to win the 1973 general election anyway. Subsequently, Mujib's government bought the fourth amendment in the parliament and passed it in just thirteen minutes on the 25thJanuary, 1975.Through the most controversial amendment, one-party political system was established so that the democratic character of the constitution vanished, and it actually put the leadership of Mujibur Rahman in question. In the last few years of his rule, Mujibur Rahman took steps to promote Islamic values in social life. One of his well-known steps was re-establishment of Islamic Foundation by the 1975 ordinance, which was abolished in 1972. Also, that government passed Islamic Development Bank Act and encouraged the development of Islamic banking in Bangladesh. Surprisingly, Mujibur Rahman started to pay frequent visits to Islamic gatherings too.

Eight months after the assassination of Sheikh Mujibur Rahman, Major General Ziaur Rahman came into power as the seventh President of Bangladesh and thus the military regime began Later, Ziaur Rahman launched a new political party, Bangladesh Nationalist Party (BNP) on the 1st September, 1978. He tried heart and soul to enhance his acceptance among general people and become a popular leader through his "19-point programme" which was designed to bring rapid socio-economic transformation and reorient foreign policy. To successfully implement that programme and get support from massive people, Ziaur Rahman used "Islam" as a trump card. Therefore, Ziaur Rahman brought significant changes in the constitution, education system, electronic media and everywhere, which made the presence of Islam clearer and more visible. By passing the fifth amendment in 1979, the commitment of 'Secularism' in the constitution was replaced by 'absolute trust and faith in Almighty Allah' through article 8(1) and 8(1A). Moreover, "Bismillahir Rahmanir Rahim" was inserted at the beginning of the constitution, just above the Preamble. The Article 38 was withdrawn, which prohibited religion-based politics and their political activities. Even Ziaur Rahman rehabilitated the war criminals and later those war criminals formed the country's main Islamic party which is the well-known fundamental group, named the 'Bangladesh Jamaat-i-Islami (BJI)'.However, in this period, the Madrassa Education Board was established by the Ordinance No. IX of 1978. A course on Islamic studies was introduced as a compulsory subject for Muslim students and other religious courses started for non-Muslim students at the school from levels I to VIII. The state-controlled electronic media began broadcasting Azan – the call for prayers – five times a day and to carry programs on Islam's role in daily life (Riaz, Faithful Education: Madrassahs in South Asia, 2008). Besides, Ziaur Rahman gave more efforts in strengthening relations with Muslim countries. Article 25(2) was inserted into the constitution and it provided that "the state shall endeavor to consolidate, preserve and strengthen fraternal relations among Muslim countries based on Islamic solidarity".

General Hussain Mohammad Ershad became the President of Bangladesh in 1982 through a bloodless coup and was in power for nearly a decade. General Ershad frequently talked about the "inevitability" of Islam in the state (Kabir K. S. 2013). He wiped out the secular character of the constitution to play a political game. He passed the eighth amendment on June 9, 1988 and declared 'Islam' the State religion. Also, a new clause Article 2A was inserted into the constitution, which clearly said that "the State religion of the Republic is Islam but other religions may be practised in peace and harmony in the Republic." During his period, Islam was stretched in institution as well as in media. On an institutional level, Islam was made a part of everyday life from the transmission of Muslim prayers on state run TV and radio stations to the establishment of various institutions focus on the cultivation of religion, such as the Ministry of Religion, Islamic universities and Madrassa (Hasan & Griffith 2015). Besides, religious education was extended up to class ten in order to make more religious-minded students, and the religious institutions expanded and developed both in quantity and quality.

With a political ambition in mind, General Ershad formed a political party in January 1986, Jatiya Party (JP). Khaleda Zia, wife of Ziaur Rahman and chief of BNP, formed government in 1991 after popular uprising and then came again in power in 2001. Both times, her government made a tie with the cadre based fundamental party, BJI. As the tie of 1991 was not long lasting, BJI made good friendships with the opposition party AL. Consequently, BNP had to contest alone in the general election of 1996 and was defeated. Later on, BNP became more cautious and prepared to win the general election of 2001 and formed a political alliance, named as "Four Party Alliance" in 1999. Interestingly, in that alliance, there were two political parties, Islami Oikkya Jote (IOJ) and BJI which were totally Islam based political parties. Indeed, BJI understood that their friendship with AL would not be cozy and they started to feel afraid that AL would take actions strictly against their top-notch leaders whose activities were controversial in 1971. In 2012, BNP extended their alliance partners and took the new name '18 Party Alliance', in which were one-third Islamist political parties. Notably, one of the central focuses of the BNP's entire electoral campaign was Islam- the need of defending Islam' from the 'un-Islamic' political forces (Kabir N. 2010). In the manifesto of the 2001 general election, BNP clearly expressed that if BNP government came in power, they would not enact any law contrary to Islam. During the second term of BNP-led government, BJI won 17 seats in the general election of 2001 and also got another 4 women's reserved seats. BNP's government highly pleased BJI by giving two ministerial posts to Maulana Motiur Rahman Nizami as Minister of Agriculture and Ali Ahsan Muhammad Mojaheed as Minister of Social Welfare. However, BNPled government also promoted Islamic education through primary education where the first objective was among 22 objectives "To create confidence and belief on almighty Allah on every learner so that they can build up the same belief and confidence and also be inspired the same in their thinking and practical activities and help them to develop their spiritual, moral, social and human evaluations" (Khaleduzzaman, Role of Education Commission in development of Primary Education in Bangladesh 2014).

Sheikh Hasina, the eldest daughter of Sheikh Mujibur Rahman, won the general elections of 1996, 2008 and 2014 and led the governments. In 1996, AL formed the government with the support of Ershad's leading political party, JP and in 2008 AL shaped a well-known alliance 'The Grand Alliance' with another 13 political parties. However, by the mid-1990s. Islamic symbols and idioms had become part of everyday political vocabulary (Siddiqi 2010).The Awami League's election poster depicted a hijab-clad Sheikh Hasina praying to Allah. The leader of AL, Sheikh Hasina used to wear hijab (Yasmin, Politics of Secularism in Bangladesh 2010). Also, she was seen to use rosary. In the manifesto of 2001, AL announced "no law will be enacted, which will be inconsistent with the dictates of the Quran and Hadiith." Moreover, AL approved education commission reported that 'the madrassa education an integral part of the national education system' (Report of the Education Commission 1998). Even, AL did not move back to make coalition with Islamist political party such as the electoral pact in 2006 with Bangladesh Khelafat Majlish, a radical orthodox party. Subsequently, AL maintains a good relationship with the fundamental group, Hefajat-e-Islam to win the next election. Indeed, AL wants to hold both in a parallel way-secularism image and nearness of Islamic vicinity. After assuming power in 2008, AL government tried to make a balance between secularism and Islam in the constitution through the fifteenth amendment in 2011. By this amendment, 'absolute faith and trust in Allah' was removed from the constitution and revived article 12 to restore secularism and freedom of religion.

However, since 1990s, using Islam in politics with the motto of gaining favour from the general people has become a common feature of the country's mainstream political parties. During the 1996 election campaign, each of the main political parties appealed to Islam for votes, and have done so in every subsequent election campaign (Hasan & Griffith 2015).The reasons behind the use of Islam in politics are almost same. Let's look at the following explanations:

Firstly, when a government feel that they have formed a government without maintaining the country's constitutional rule, they believe mass people will not tolerate them easily for a long time. In these circumstances, the government use religion to look for the room in common people's mind. In Bangladesh, Islam has always become a tool to legitimatize the authoritarian characterized government either that is a military or democratic government. For example, Mujibur Rahman's government declared an emergency in 1974 and switched to one party political system instead of the multi-party system. As a result, Mujibur Rahman would have enjoyed absolute power as the President, which was totally contradictory tothe constitution. Mujibur Rahman introduced patronizing Islam and he himself started using Islamic phrases 'Inshallah' in publicly and banned many things which seemed un-Islamic as well. Then two military rulers, Ziaur Rahman and General Ershad came into power through the military coups, which marked the decline of democracy. Both Ershad and Zia invoked Islam to secure political legitimacy (Siddiqi 2010). General Ershad frequently visited various shrines and mosques as well as made weekly trips to Atroshi Pir (a religious person who used to live in Atroshi) by helicopter.He did not take 'Islam' as a religion; rather he took it to show off his personal attitude as a pious man. After winning the election of 2014 without contest, AL government themselves put their democratic behavior into question. In these circumstances, AL has taken 'Islam' as an umbrella where any Islamic political party can take shelter without any hesitation except BJI. It will provide a positive appearance of AL to the Muslim voters. On the other hand, AL government have taken initiatives to restore the constitution of 1972, where the main principle was secularism, but AL did not disagree on reaffirming 'Islam as the state religion' by the high court. In the roundtable organized by SAARC Cultural Society, Abdur Razzaq, the party's Presidium Member and former minister said, "Islam has been kept as the state religion for strategic reasons". Anyway, AL does not want to disappoint the Muslim majority people.

Secondly, there is no friend or foe in politics to share the vote bank. The ultimate goal of all the mainstream political parties is assuming state power for alongtime. For example, to gain the highest number of seats in parliament, BNP is always backed up by the Islamic political parties since its inception in 1978 as BNP's organizational constitution does not contradict to ally with an Islamic political party. On the contrary, AL always speaks about secularism and the fundamental principle of its constitution says 'Secularism or in other words ensuring freedom of all religions as well as non-communal politics'. Surprisingly, AL, BNP and BJI joined together the uprising against General Ershad's government, and again AL allied with BJI against BNP Government in 1994. They altogether made a series of street protests and joined several meetings. Recently AL has allied with the conservative Islamic political party Hefajat-e-Islam, agreeing with their ideologies and met some of their demands for gaining their vote bank of over one core voters. As a result of this sweet relationship, the education ministry of Bangladesh has removed 17 poems and stories from school textbooks just because the authors seem atheists and the statue of Lady Justice was also removed from in front of the Supreme Court at late night of 25 May 2017. Also, AL government recognized Dawra Hadith degree under the Qawmi Madrasa Education Board in 2017 through an ordinance. The policy makers of AL claimed that the relation with Hefajat-e-Islam is a strategic relation. But the question of how could AL who claimed as a secular party makes relation with an orthodox party is unsolved.

Changing Features of the Islamic Fundamentalist Groups

Since 1990 in Bangladesh, the tension between secularism and Islamization has increased which spreads animosity among different sects of Islam and against other religions with a view to occupying political and state power. In consequence, radical Islamism made a stronghold to dismantle political system and social progress. Also, it is easier to cajole general people in the name of Islam in Bangladesh. Therefore, local militant groups have got an opportunity to mingle with International Islamic militant groups. The Afghanistan war, in particular, connected the local militant groups with international Islamic militant groups. Around 3000 Bangladeshis participated as volunteer mujahedeen in the Afghanistan War and many of them received training in Pakistan as well. After returning from the war, they kept in touch with those Islamic militant groups as they were hoping to make Bangladesh a Sharia law based Islamic state through jihad.

In Bangladesh, the majority of Muslims are Sunnis who mainly follow the thought of Hanafi Madhab. There are other sects of Islam such as Shia, Ahle Hadith, Ahmadiyya community etc. in the country. The followers of Hanafi Madhab consider 'Sahih Muslims' the second most authentic hadith collection, and they follow the teachings of Jihad as mentioned in its 1840 no. hadith of volume 5 explained by Al-Nawawi, a hadith scholar-"As for rebelling against the ruler and fighting him, it is forbidden by consensus of the Muslims even if he is sinful and oppressive". Under Sunni, there is another thought of school which is called Hanbali Madhab. This Madhab was adopted and nurtured by Abd al-Wahhab; then it is widely known as 'Wahhabism'. Sunni critics find Wahhabism as similar as 'Salafism' because most of the Salafists follow the thought of Hanbil Madhab although Salafists are divided into groups in terms of their beliefs and practice of Madhab. However, in the mid-nineteenth century, Ahle Hadith emerged in Northern India and has championed Salafism in recent times. They believe in the 'Takfiri' doctrine which permits violence against the leaders and Muslims who deviate from the true path. Takfir is a pronouncement to declare any (non-practicing Muslim), to be an unbeliever (*Takfir*), apostate, (*Murtad*) hence liable to be killed (Faith Forum, 2010). By the by, after being found to have links with a series of recent terrorist activities in Bangladesh, they have become the center of controversy. Around 27.5 million followers of Ahle Hadith live across the country (PROBE News Magazine, 2010). This community lives mainly in the Northern and Southern parts of Bangladesh. However, Dr Asadullah Al Galib, Shaykh Abdur Rahman and Siddique ul-Islam are the followers of Ahle Hadith, and they had a dream to turn Bangladesh into an Islamic state where everything would be governed by Sharia law.

Harkat-ul-Jihad-Al-Islami Bangladesh (Huji-B) as a branch of International Islamic militant group launched in 1992, led by Abdur Rahman Faruqui. This group maintained a close tie with Al-Qaeda. They have received financial assistance from Pakistan, Saudi Arabia and Afghanistan and training from the Talibans directly.In the first four years Huji-B's activities were largely restricted to the Southeastern hills closed to the border with Myanmar, suggesting that their initial objective was to use Bangladeshi as a launching pad to influence the Rohingya movement inside Myanmar (Economist 2015). Then Huji-B was split into two groups on the issue of establishing Sharia law at first in Bangladesh or Myanmar. One group which was led by Mufti Abdul Hanan had a major objective to establish Islamic rule in Bangladesh at first. For this purpose, Huji-B targeted intellectual people who want a secular Bangladesh. Huji-B was responsible for at least 14 attacks in the country, in which over 100 people died. Several times Huji-B invaded AL's rally and made assassination attempts to Sheikh Hasina and in various cultural functions. However, the known leader Mufti Abdul Hannan was arrested in 2005 and sentenced to death on 12 April 2017.

Jamaatul Mujahedeen Bangladesh (JMB) was formed by Shaykh Abdur Rahman in April 1998. This Islamic militant group believes in the 'Salafism' sect and aimed to establish Sharia law in Bangladesh. JMB follows the ideal of Jihad of the Taliban of Afghanistan.JMB was funded from Saudi Arabia, Kuwait, Qatar, Brunei, Sudan, Pakistan and various Islamic foundations. To establish Islamic rule, they targeted the country's present judiciary system and opposed democracy. By detonating 500 bombs in 63 districts among 64 districts, attacking court areas and killing judges, JMB was shaking Bangladesh. In four and a half years (September 2001-December 2005), JMB carried out 26 attacks in the country. A total of 73 persons were killed and about 800 injured in these incidents (Sultan 2016).The International Crisis Group estimates that JMB had approximately 2000 members with 50 women groups of about 500 women. However, JMB was banned in 2005 and later Abdur Rahman was executed to death in 2007.

Jagrata Muslim Janata Bangladesh (JMJB) led by commander Siddique ul-Islam known as Bangla Bhai. This militant group launched in 1998 and the objective was as same as JMB, and even both worked together as both groups' leaders were highly influenced by the Afghan war. Their half-baked ideas on Islamic revolutions are contained in few pamphlets-some of them are not even four pages long-that were being clandestinely circulated in mosques around the country during 2004-2005 (Ahmad 2007). Bangla Bhai claims the outfit has 30,000 activists and about 10,000 thousand full-time activists across the country (Ahsan 2005).

Hizbut-Tahrir (HT), started operating in Bangladesh in 2001. HT aimed to establish caliphate and so they opposed democracy, women's involvement in politics, capitalism and so on. The party is known to have a strong base in North South University and Dhaka University, including among female undergraduate students and some of the teaching staff (Harrison 2013). HT's student wing used to tempt university students. A significant phenomenon about HTB is that it is 'becoming popular among teachers and students of secular universities in the country (Hasan M. , Historical Developments of Political Islam with Reference to Bangladesh 2011). However, this group was banned in 2009.

Ansarullah Bangla Team (ABT), the new dimension of Islamic militant groups, which was reorganized by Huji-B and JMB. Inspired by Anwar al Awalki and led by local Mufti Jashimuddin Rahmani, ABT began to attract new recruits in 2012 when its presence in cyberspace became prominent (Anarullah Bangla Team, 2013). Later, ABT took the new name as Ansar al-Islam and worked as the Bangladesh chapter of Al-Qaeda in the Indian sub-continent (AQIS). This group supports the armed jihadi ideology of terrorist groups such as al-Qaeda and Islamic State (IS) to wage holy war in Bangladesh and abroad (Wolf 2016). ABT aimed to set up radical Islamism in youths' mind and allure them to participate in local Jihad. Therefore, ABT used to be active in social media to promote jihadist ideology and training manuals to guide terror attacks, even ABT translated al-Qaeda's works into Bengali for their local audience. At first, this militant groups used the website of 'Ansar al-Mujahideen English Forum' (AAMEF) and Al-Qaeda then started to use 'bab-ul-islam.net' website which rudiments in Pakistan. This group came into limelight after killing secular bloggers such as Ahmed Rajib Haider, Avijit Roy, Washiqur Rahman, Ananta Bijoy Das, Niloy Chakrabarti, Faisal Arefin Dipan and AKM Shafiul Islam. The leader of ABT, Mufti Jasimuddin Rahmani was arrested in 2013 along with 30 members. ABT terrorists arrested by Bangladeshi sleuths have admitted that they have been trained, as outlined in the 79-page manual, How to Kill Secretly, written by Master Hei Long, a US-based martial arts expert (Guha 2015). However, ABT was banned under anti-terrorism laws on 25 May 2015.

Immediately after the controversial Islamic militant groups being banned and their notorious leadersbeing arrested for trial, Neo-JMB emerged, which stormed Bangladesh once again. Intelligence officials say that the JMB had split into several factions and one of it has re-surfaced as 'Neo-JMB' (*The Asian Age*, 27 June 2017). That group's major leaders and operatives did not accept the leadership of Saidur Rahman, who once headed JMB. Other groups such as ABT and HT have merged with the Neo-JMB and this extremist group follow the ideology of the Middle East-based Islamic State (IS). Tamim Ahmed Chowdhury, a Canadian-Bangladeshi coordinated this group with the assistance of a top JMB leader, AbulKashem alias Boro Huzur. Writers, online activists, publishers, Hindu and Christian priests, foreigners and members of Shia community have been attacked by the group since 2014. Subsequently, the most touchable incident happened in a café called Holey Artisan Bakery, Gulshan, Dhaka on 1 July 2016, where 20 people including 17 foreigners were brutally butchered.

In addition to the Islamic militant groups mentioned above, there are several groups who are active in Bangladesh such as Ahle Hadith Andolon Bangladesh

(AHAB) by Dr Asadullah Al Galib; Islami Biplobi Parishad (IBP) by Moulana Abdul Jabber; Hizbut Towhid (HT) by Mohammad BayezidKhan Ponni and so on. All the major Islamist militant groups are interlinked with each other. All of them have the same route education-madrassa education, past political involvement with BJI and jihadi experience in Afghanistan, which has eventually given them opportunities to come closer. Shaykh Abdur Rahman's role to organize them and his assistance in these groups were impeccable. Some media reports claim that JMJB is an outgrowth of the JMB, others as a youth front of HUJI (Rahman & Kashem 2011). Therefore, the characteristics of these Islamic groups are almost same. To build a society based on Islamic model which would practice the Holy Quran and Hadith, they invaded those which deemed anti-Islamic such as cinema hall, cultural events, fairs, meetings, rallies, etc. Therefore, they targeted to abolish the thought of secularism by killing intellectual and secular persons as well as the present judiciary system what was influenced by the British judicial system. However, through madrassa and on a small scale of secular educational institutions, these militant groups tried to make a network across the country. Even some fanatic youths from through Mosques, religious gatherings, etc. were allured to join those radical groups.

Neo-JMB is quite different than previous Islamic militant groups in terms of recruitment and operational tactics. This group is made up of both types of members- upper middle or rich class with education in elite schools and high-level knowledge on modern technology and poor class with madrassa background. They prefer to recruit IT related engineering background students for using advanced technology in making grenades, hand bomb and so on. As usual, it was believed that almost all Islamic extremists would be from poor socioeconomic and educational backgrounds and being radicalized in madrassa. Now it is proven wrong! Surprisingly, a few converted Muslims, high officials, army officers and women are found to be involved in Neo-JMB. They have changed operational tactics too. In previous invasions, police, judiciary, government, minorities and cultural events were victims but Neo-JMB started assassination of targeted scholars, secular writers, bloggers or teachers, minorities and foreigners. During attack of neo-JMB, jihadists used to carry sharp weapons, machetes and small arms to assassinate meticulously, whereas previous groups' members used grenade or bomb. Moreover, IS affiliated websites or magazine or infographic claims the responsibility for the killing and provide photos, videos, interviews etc. When Neo-JMB attacked Holey Artisan Bakery, IS's news agency 'Amaq' claimed the responsibility for attacking Holey Artisan Bakery and released the cafe's inside photos of the repulsive incident. However, when the country's security forces are repressing radical terrorism, this group is trying to stand again and again under new commanders. According to media, till now the leadership of Neo-JMB has changed four times after the killing of Tamim Chowdhury. The security forces try to find out missing young boys and make a digital database of about three thousand terrorists. But it is shocking that the preparation of militant activities cannot be uprooted as they actively work on internet by promoting views of Anwar al Awalaki and Jasimuddin Rahmani.

Role of Political Parties against Islamic Extremism

As a Muslim populated country, Islamic values are nurtured in the social life of Bangladesh, but in politics, this practice was abandoned till 1976, and afterwards religion mainly Islam based political party has become a precious attachment of all mainstream political parties to gain state power. Interestingly, Islamic political parties are considered a kingmaker since 1990s. As a result, Islamization has entered smoothly and spread in politics and society. However, the mainstream political parties, AL and BNP play a dual role on the one hand, when in state power, they strongly stride for stamping out Islamic extremism from society, and on the other hand, when as an opposition party, they do not back out to make coalition or friendship relations with those Islamic political parties. Let's look at the instances.

BNP government officially outlawed the Islamic militant radical groups, Shahadat-e-al Hikma, JMB, JMJB and Huji-B, but a paradox is that Huji-B enjoyed the full-fledged patronage of BNP and its coalition partner BJI. For sharing vote bank, they also made a coalition with Islami OikyoJote (IOJ) whose group Amir was Shaykh Ul Hadith Allamah AzizulHaque was one of the leading founders of Huji-B. Moreover, Huji-B' operations commander Mufti Hannan claimed the law enforcers were not supposed to arrest him since some influential ministers of the BNP-led government had assured him that he would be exempted from the August 21 grenade attack case(Liton & Islam, 2016). The former home and then the commerce minister of BNP led government, Altaf Hossain Choudhury's name came in the front line. Ruhul QuddusTalukder, deputy minister for land, allegedly helped through the rise of militant kingpin Siddiqul Islam Bangla Bhai, the commander of JMJB. One of the most troubling aspects of the Jamaat's presence in parliament is its link with various radical

Islamist organizations (Ganguly, The Rise of Islamist Militancy in Bangladesh 2006). Though BJI always denied any links with the Hujior any Islamic militant groups and also claimed that finding links with those groups is a rumor and propaganda against them. But the speech of Maulana Matiur Rahman Nizami, minister of agriculture of BNP led government claimed that there was no one by the name of `Bangla Bhai' and that he was a creation of the media. Moreover, it is also true in 2000s BJI became moderate, some of them especially the student wing of BJI, Chhatra Shibir joinedthe militant groups such as Harkatul Jihad and JMJB to pursue violent jihad. Subsequently, BNP also supported and wanted to assist to Hefazat leaders when they gathered this group in the Shapla Squire, Motijheel for a rally.

AL, however, is a symbol of secularism in politics of Bangladesh. AL-led government has taken an outstanding step to establish secularism through passing the fifteenth amendment of the constitution in 2011. In addition, AL governmentsuppres Islamism firmly. Moreover, the top leaders of BJI were jailed and hanged to death for crime against humanity committed during the 1971 war. Furthermore, AL, as a political party, plays an active role to process the Islamization in politics. Even Sheikh Hasina, head of the AL, began to express her and her party's alignment with Islam (Hasan M. 2015). Showing indomitable faith in Islam and use Islamic phrases in publicly, praises sentences of Allah in banner and festoons and so on. Actually, AL is confused to choose between the discourse of secularism and Islamization to get the state power. For instance, AL government banned ABT and HT as well as faced several worse attacks from Huji-B, but at present, AL makes woo with Hefazat-e-Islam, whose leader is Ahmed Safi. He said "Huji is a dedicated-truly-Islamic organization and has been serving and protecting the national and international Muslim community through brave jihad for eight years. I fully support this organization and prayed for them from my heart. Everyone should help and support them. As a true Muslim, it is a holy responsibility to work with Huji. May Allah bless them"(Shuvo, 2017). Habibur, one of the key organizers of Hefajat said in his interview "Only the establishment of a Khilafat (pan-Islamic movement)-based state following the Taliban ideology can change the lot of the nation."Furthermore, when atheists and bloggers were killed by fanatic members of extremist groups, AL government curiously urged the bloggers to maintain 'a limit' in their writings so that the peoples' religious sentiments are not hurt.

AL's blind support to Hefajat is in question. It seems AL become polite with Hefajat and other smaller Islamic political parties to gain the support of their voters in the upcoming general election. There are around one crore voters in the vote bank of Hefajat and its allies, the vast majority of whom are from Qur'anic schools. To please them, AL-led government acknowledged the certificate of Quranic schools. Kazi Jaforullah, presidium member of AL said, "There is no meaning to discuss Quomi and Hefajat too much. The students of Quomi school are people of this country". He added that it would be a great step to prevent militants by bringing them into the mainstream political parties. In fact, AL has allied with Hefajat, on the one hand, for vote bank, and on the other hand, AL wants to keep Hefajata way from BNP. The present situation seems AL wants that Hefajat will be standing out as a kingmaker in the next election instead of BJI. After the starting of tribunal of war criminals, BJI became weaker and were also banned by the Election Commission of Bangladesh. However, AL should not forget that Hefajat is a madrassa based party and these madrassas [illegible]alesced under Hefajat. Also, this Hefajat threated armed resistance on [illegible]ssue of state religion, even their 13-points charter is irrational and baseless [illegible]hich could turn Bangladesh into an Islamic state. Both Jamaat and Hefazat-e-Islam may have different names but they remain steadfastly united in pursuit of their goals to make Bangladesh an Islamic state (Mukharji 2017). On the other hand, Gulf countries, mainly Saudi Arabia, UAE and Qatar fund money to promote Wahhabism in Quomi madrassas.

Hefazat-e-Islam, a fundamentalist group, wants to play roles as a pressure group, which must be a threat to the country's democracy. The 13 points of the Islamist group Hefajat-e Islam may be the last thirteen nails in the coffin of Bangladesh Democracy as experts think too ominous"(IndiaFacts 2015). Moreover,the AL is being criticized to intimate with Hefajat-i- Islam. "The fact that [the Awami League] will not hear of an interim government may mean that it thinks it is going to lose. You may win without the support of the Islamists, but you cannot win against them," warns a Dhaka academic (Bouissou 2013).

References

Ahmad, M. (2007). Islam, State and Society in Bangladesh. In J. V. John L. Esposito, *Asian Islam in the 21st Century* (pp. 49-80). New York: Oxford University Press.

Ahmed, S. (2004). *Bangladesh: Past and Present.* New Delhi: APH Publishing Corporation.

Bennett, C. (2010). *Muslim Women of Power: Gender, Politics and Culture in Islam.* London: A&C Black.

Bhattacharjee, J. (2011). Bangladesh: Political Trends and Key Players. *Strategic Trends: South Asia Series*, 1-38.

Bhonsle, R. K. (2007). *South Asia Security Trends.* New Delhi: Atlantic Publishers & Distributors (P) LTD.

Gain, B. (2015). Islamization Under the Democratic Government: An Overview of Bangladesh. *Indian Journal of Applied Research*, 28-29.

Ganguly, S. (2006). *The Rise of islamist Militancy in Bangladesh.* Washington: United States Institute of Peace.

Harrison, F. (2013). *Poilitaical Islam & the Elections in Bangladesh.* London: New Millennium.

Hasan, M. (2011). Democracy and Political Islam in Bangladesh. *South Asia Research 31(2)*, 97-117.

Hashmi, T. (2006, July 11). *Countercurrents.org.* Retrieved from Countercurrents.org: https://www.countercurrents.org/hashmi110706.htm

Hashmi, T. I. (2004). Islamic Resurgence in Bangladesh: Genesis, Dynamics and Implications. In S. P. Limaye, *Religious Radicalism and Security in South Asia* (pp. 35-72). Hawaii: Asia-Pacific Center for Security Studies.

Islam, D. M. (2014). The Politics behind the Passage of Fourth Amendme[...] Constitution of the People's Republic of Bangladesh and Its Provisions: [...] Analysis. *Public Policy and Administration Research 4(9)*, 55-66.

Islam, D. M. (2016). Military Take over by General Ershad and Constitutional A[...] in Bangladesh: A Modest Politico-Legal Study. *Journal of Law,* [...] *Globalization* , 1-11.

Islam, M. D., & Huda, F. (2016). Religion and Politics: Bangladesh Perspective. *International Journal of Management and Humanities*, 1-5.

Islam, M. S. (2011). "Minority Islam" in Muslim Majority Bangladesh: The Violent Road to a New Brand. *Journal of Muslim Minority Affairs 31(1)*, 125-141.

Kabir, K. S. (2013). Islam as a Symbol of Ligitimization: The Islamization. *Asian Journal of Social Sciences & Humanities 2(3)*, 261-269.

Khaleduzzaman, D. M. (2014). Role of Education Commission in development of Primary Education in Bangladesh. *IOSR Journal of Research & Method in Education*, 37-50.

Khondker, H. H. (2010). State and Secularism in Bangladesh. In T. C. Michael Heng Siam-Heng, *State and Secularism: Perspectives from Asia* (pp. 213-234). Singapore: World Scientific.

Lintner, B. (2004). Religious Extremism and Nationalism in Bangladesh. In S. P. Limaye, *Religious Radicalism and Security in South Asia* (pp. 413-436). Hawaii : Asia-Pacific Center for Security Studies.

Mitra, S. K., Enskat, M., & Spiess, C. (2004). *Political Parties in South Asia.* New York: Praeger Publishers.

'Neo JMB' evolves (2016, August 18), *The Asian Age.* Retrieved fromhttps://dailyasianage.com

Rahman, M. A., & Kashem, M. B. (2011). *Understanding Religious Militancy and Terrorism in Bangladesh.* Dhaka: Institute of Cultural Affairs.

Riaz, A. (2008). *Faithful Education: Madrassahs in South Asia.* U.S.A: Rutgers University Press.

Riaz, A. (2012). *Islamist Militancy in Bangladesh: A Complex Web.* Routledge. Riaz. A. (2015). Bangladesh. In N. DeVotta, *An Introduction to South Asian Politics* (pp. 58-82). New york: Routledge.

Riaz, A., & Rahman, M. S. (2016). *Routledge Handbook of Contemporary Bangladesh.* New York: Routledge.

Siddiqi, D. M. (2010). Political Culture in Contemporary Bangladesh: Histories, Ruptures and Contradictions. In A. Riaz, & C. C. Fair, *Political Islam and Governance in Bangladesh* (p. 12). Routledge.

Sultan, T. (2016, August 16). Salafi ideology behind JMB's rise. Dhaka, Bangladesh.

Totten, S. (2012). *Centuries of Genocide: Essays and Eyewitness Accounts.* Routledge.

Yasmin, L. (2010). Politics of Secularism in Bangladesh. In A. Riaz, *Peace and Justice* (pp. 46-54). New Delhi: Pearson Education.

CHAPTER 11

Financing of Terrorism in a Globalised World: A Case Study of Pakistan

Monoj Das

Abstract

Money is the lifeblood of terrorism if radical ideology and extremism are at the heart of it. The terrorist organisations need money to terrorise and perpetrate their operations. Though the problem of terrorism/insurgency in Pakistan is rooted in its very formation, the actual origin of it could be traced back to the Soviet military intervention in Afghanistan in 1979 and the decade-long civil war (1979-1989) followed by it. With this, the trend of state sponsorship of terrorism started in Pakistan, as the state provided all the financial and material assistance to the 'mujahideen' groups to cater the state's vested interests. However, the end of the Cold War and the onset of globalisation have transformed the nature, quality and support structure of terrorist groups.

This paper would at first focus on the historical origin of terrorism in Pakistan. Following that the complex security situation of Pakistan with an emphasis on the existing terrorist groups would be discussed. In the next section, the paper would make a conscious effort to identify and assess the significance of the funding sources adopted by the terrorist groups in Pakistan in the globalised world providing ample opportunities to them. In the final section, an emphasis will be given in assessing the role of the Pakistani state in addressing the problem of terrorism/insurgency and countering terrorist financing.

Introduction

Money is considered as the "lifeblood of terrorism," if radical ideology and extremism are at the heart of it. The terrorist organisations require funding not merely to finance their violent operations, but to meet their organisational costs and to create a congenial environment necessary for sustaining their activities (Financial Action Task Force 2008: 4). Money helps in meeting their material expenses and activities like propaganda, recruitment of cadre members, infrastructure, and maintenance. Therefore, it is vital for the terrorist organisations to mobilise and generate a large amount of monetary assets to sustain their organisations and meet the political mandate they are intended to achieve. It serves as an accelerating force for transforming the nascent militants into sophisticated and lethal terrorist movements capable of inflicting global attacks and security threat (Acharya et al 2009: 95). James Adams has very precisely noted that in the transformation of emerging organisations motivated by radical ideologies to full-fledged recognised terrorists, it is crucial for all these groups to acquire a sufficient amount of money to finance their activities and inflict violence in the society or among the people (Adams 1986: 53).

In the initial phases of terrorism, particularly during the Cold War period, the terrorist organisations and their financial and material requirements were financed mostly by the legitimate governments or sovereign states popularly known as the "state-sponsored terrorism." During this phase of the history of terrorism, the state-sponsored terrorist organisations often carried their operations as proxies for sovereign nations in a covert manner to inflict harm on enemy nations or to instigate conflict. The radical regimes used it as an instrument to pursue their foreign policy agendas. The state-sponsored terrorism can achieve strategic objectives when the use of regular or conventional forces is not feasible. During the Cold War, the Soviet Union and many of its Eastern European allied states operated as patrons of many Western European terrorist groups, Marxist guerrillas in Central and South America and numerous Middle Eastern organisations (Aubrey 2004: 44). However, the onset of globalisation and the end of Cold War changed the business environment for most of the governments and organisations, likewise for the terrorist organisations. Similar to any other organisation (especially political organisation), terrorist groups, criminal or non-criminal, also required varied source of funding for their activities. The disintegration of the Soviet Union resulted in a relative decline of state sponsorship, though did not put a complete end to it. Many terrorist organisations had to look for other sources of material and logistic support which was made even tougher with the launch of the "War on Terror" as a reaction to the 11 September 2001 terrorist attack in the United States (Jenks and Fuller 2017:142). Nevertheless, terrorist groups have learned to take advantage of the prevailing political and economic conditions. The opportunities provided by globalisation in the form of easing of trans-border mobility, advances in communication technologies and a global financial system networked through information technology have empowered the terrorists to raise and move money for their activities around the globe (Biersteker 2002: 75).

Like the global scenario, Pakistan's support to the terrorists declined considerably with the coming of it as a frontline state in the United States led 'Global War on Terror' following the 9/11 terrorist attacks. Pakistan-based terrorist groups use a wide variety of fundraising means including, among other things the manipulation of hawala, money laundering, abuse of the charitable sector, narco-finance, and abduction for ransom and globalisation has been an enabling force in developing this new economy of terror. Many terrorist groups (more particularly the Al-Qaeda and the Tehrik-e-Taliban Pakistan) having their 'safe havens' in the tribal areas of Pakistan have been operating globally as lethal forces by utilising the lacunae in the global financial system networked through electronic and communication technology. In fact, the new economy of terror has made these terrorist groups and their operations more lethal and deadly comparing to the state sponsorship phase. Due to this growing lethality and global threat to peace and security posing by the terrorist groups based in Pakistan, several scholars have labelled the ungoverned tribal areas of Pakistan as the "global epicentre of terrorism." Therefore, choking the funding sources would incapacitate the terrorist groups in carrying out their organisations and meeting their organisational and functional requirements to a great extent.

Situation of Terrorism in Pakistan and Funding Sources

During and after the Afghan Jihad, many structured and organised terrorist or insurgent groups were formed in Pakistan. Lashkar-e-Taiba (LeT) was one of these organisations that were involved in the anti-Soviet jihad in Afghanistan in the 1980s and early 90s. After the withdrawal of the Soviet forces from Afghanistan, the LeT was actively promoted by Pakistan's intelligence body i.e. the Inter-Services Intelligence (ISI) in carrying out proxy wars in Indian administered Kashmir as well as other parts of India (Swami 2005: 62). However, Pakistan was forced to stop supporting these organisations with the coming of it in the grip of United States led "War on Terror" (WoT) as a "frontline state" to root out the Al-Qaeda militants and its facilitator Taliban regime from Afghanistan following the 9/11 terrorist attacks in the United States. Eventually, the National Assembly of Pakistan, under pressure, proscribed many of these groups since

2002 after the launch of the WoT including the Lashkar-e-Jhangvi (LeJ), Sipah-e-Muhammad Pakistan (SMP), Jaish-e-Muhammad (JeM), LeT, Sipah-e-Sahaba Pakistan (SSP), Al-Qaeda (AQ), Tehrik-e-Taliban Pakistan (TTP) and Tehreek-e-Nifaz-e-Shariat-e-Mohammad (TNSM) (*The Express Tribune* 24 October 2012).

Although the state proscription have not turned to be very stringent as there are incidences of continued support of Pakistani state to many non-state actors, a declining trend of state sponsorship to these groups can be seen with the increasing international pressure to counter the problem of terrorism. In such a situation of drying up of state funding, the terrorist organisations have learnt to make use of new ways to survive and keep their funding means undamaged and intact. Many of them have established their front organisations to perform as public welfare bodies or charity organisations in order to foster their public image and evade government regulation in fundraising as banned organisations. This strategic move of the terrorist organisations has facilitated them in gaining public acceptance in the society as well as in the expansion of their support base and means of raising funds (Rana 2014: 150). In order to diversify their financial strength, many militant organisations have set up private commercial institutions like hospitals, schools, colleges, transportation companies and media groups. The LeT manages about 200 mainstream "Dawa" schools, mobile clinics, blood banks and ambulance service 11 madrassas, 2 science colleges and their services have penetrated to far-flung rural areas in Pakistan, where the state-run public welfare services have not penetrated properly. In fact, the social welfare services mainly through educational institutions helps them in strengthening their organisation as it brings them closer to the potential recruits (Shelly: 2015: 43).

TTP is one of the major terrorist organisations waging a war against the Pakistani state and Military. It is a well organised and well-financed terrorist group generating revenues from varied sources like ransom from abductions, bank robberies, volunteer donations, forced taxes and funding from anti-Pakistan forces (Gunaratna and Iqbal 2011: 51). The major portion of its organisational funding is generated through organised criminal activities. It has nexus with the well-established transnational criminal groups in various parts of Pakistan. Moreover, it has also recruited a large number of criminals into their organisation to make their organisational operations and attacks more perfect and mistake-free as the organised criminals have expertise in such crimes and it keeps them away from the reach of the security and police agencies. It is imperative to mention that like many other Islamic terrorist organisations that generates a major portion of their profits through criminal activities, the TTP justifies its involvement in criminal activities by giving the rationale to their cadre members that involvement in acts like bank robbery, extortion from rich and wealthy people are not crimes since the banks, and such wealthy people have accrued all these assets through un-Islamic ways, including charging interest.[1] It also rationalises their involvement in criminal activities as they are waging a "holy war" against the Pakistani state forces and the combined forces of US, NATO and ISAF (Pakistan Institute of Peace Studies 2009: 16). In fact, it was estimated that annual expenses of Baitullah Mehsud, the founder of TTP, at about USD 4 Million (Gunaratna and Iqbal 2011: 51-52).

Thenceforth, the terrorist and militant organisations are running a parallel administration in Pakistan with regular attacks and killings of both the security personnel and civilians and continuously deteriorating the law and order and security situation of the state. As a result of this, many parts of the state especially the tribal areas of FATA and Khyber Pakhtunkhwa Province (KPP) are considered as the "epicentre of global terrorism" (Gunaratna and Iqbal 2011: 17). However, the threats emanating from these terrorist organisations and their operations are not completely confined to Pakistan and Afghanistan but have cross-border implications especially in Europe and North America. A number of external forces like the Al-Qaeda and its affiliates are utilising the 'safe havens' in these lawless areas of Pakistan as base for their both operational and logistical requirements, while the local Taliban i.e. TTP and its affiliates raises funds mostly within the state (Acharya, Bukhari and Sulaiman 2009: 95). Though it is believed that the TTP is mainly operating against the Pakistani state, it would be a big misunderstanding to consider it as a terrorist organisation having local operations. In fact, the TTP has become one of the major global terrorist organisations by launching many deadly global ghastly attacks and threatened the global peace and security to a large extent. It has developed a deep nexus with the Al-Qaeda militants to wage "international jihad" (Iqbal 2010: 135). This is evident from the deadly gun attacks in the Peshawar based Army Public School (APS) on 16 December 2014 in which killed at least 144 persons- most of them were innocent children- the attack was carried out in retaliation to the military operation in North Waziristan and the killing of militants in government custody (Khan 2014). This gun running on the innocent children have raised the eyebrows of all the people and governments across the world along with the government of Pakistan in countering the problem of insurgency in Pakistan (Briggs, 16 December 2015, *Al Jazeera*). This massacre had such a global impact in the security and terrorism studies that Pakistan was ranked as one of the most vulnerable countries in the world. The Global Terrorism Index Report 2015, has categorised the Peshawar based Army School attack as one of the most fatal attacks out of total 20 that took place all the over the world in 2014 (Global Terrorism Index Report 2015: 13).

In the following section a detailed analysis has been given on the funding sources of the terrorist groups operating and based in Pakistan having their global reach in terms of funding and their operations.

Narco-money

The profit generated from the narcotics trafficking is one of the prime sources for financing the terrorist groups. The sharing of an open porous border with Afghanistan, the world's largest illicit opium producer, Pakistan is geographically vulnerable to drug trafficking (UNODC-a). Afghanistan is at the centre of illicit drug trade globally, with more than 90 percent of the world supply originating there and Pakistan serves as the main conduit for narcotics, heroin and opium as approximately 43 percent of the Afghan drugs are trafficked through Pakistan (*Daily Times* 2016). As large amount of Afghan origin drugs is traded through Pakistan, the mafias and terrorist groups have diverted a significant portion of it for their own funding. Tehrik-e-Taliban Pakistan is the major terrorist group operating in Pakistan and it earns huge revenues from the illicit drugs moving through their controlled areas. Even the United States' Officials believe that the Pakistani Taliban is using drug money as a major source to finance their organisation and activities (Iqbal 9 December 2014). An investigation conducted by the Ministry of Counter Narcotics of Afghanistan showed that out of the USD 70 billion received by the Afghan drug mafias and terrorist groups, nearly USD 2 billion of this amount is going to Pakistani Taliban which is one of the causes behind the rising incidences of insurgency both in Afghanistan and Pakistan (Moosakhail 3 June 2015).

Although the volume of narcotics-trade has not reached the level of Afghanistan, Pakistan seems to be edging towards becoming another "narco-state" due to the continuous deterioration of the law and order situation in the border areas with the involvement of TTP and Baluchistan-based insurgents in narcotics smuggling. The profits earned from narcotics smuggling have been empowering the terrorists that may destabilise the Pakistani state or government (Arhari 2009: 47). Recognising the crucial link between drugs and terrorism, the Interior Minister of Pakistan Chaudhry Nisar Khan has stressed the need to eliminate drug-funded terrorism from the country (*Dawn* 9 April 2015). Despite this, the personnel of the Anti-Narcotics Front (ANF), Pakistan's anti-drugs agency, have been denying the role of drugs in funding the terrorist groups in Pakistan (Gishkori 2015).

Kidnapping for Ransom

Kidnapping is a preferred terrorist tactic. Kidnapping influential and wealthy people can force the government in acceding to terrorist demands in order to safeguard prisoner release. Kidnapping for ransom also helps the organisations to finance their activities.

Through this criminal act, the terrorists extort money from states, rich individuals and corporations, who seek to have family members and employees returned. The Financial Action Task Force (FATF) suggests that kidnapping by terrorist differs from that undertaken by criminals. Terrorists often espouse a political position before focusing on the financial benefits. On the basis of financial success, terrorist groups may choose to target particular nations (Shelly, Loiuse 2014: 184).

In many urban centres of Pakistan like Karachi, Peshawar and even the more secure cities of Lahore and Islamabad, the kidnapping for ransom incidences have been rising at an alarming rate over the last few years. The Pakistani Taliban militants have a major role in this rising trend of kidnappings in the major urban centres as well as in other parts of Pakistan like KPP and Balochistan, though some other militant groups and criminal organisations are also found to be involved in this quick method of raising money. According to the police, though about 10 percent of kidnappings have the connection with the Pakistani Taliban, they generate USD 60,000 to USD 2,50,000 for releasing the each abducted (*New York Times* 28 August 2009). On 5 December 2011, three TTP militants were killed by the police in an encounter when the police raided a house targeted to rescue Riaz Chinoy, an industrialist who was kidnapped by the militants. The militants had initially demanded a ransom amount of Rs. 70 million for his release, but were brought down to Rs 20 million after negotiations (*The Express Tribune* 6 December 2011).

The situation is even scarier in the lawless and poorly governed Federally Administered Tribal Areas (FATA) bordering Afghanistan where the several proscribed militant groups have the safe hideout. In November 2016, six Pakistani citizens working for a Polish oil and gas surveying company were kidnapped by the militants from the Dera Ismail Khan area of FATA. In 2008, a Polish engineer working for the same firm was kidnapped by the Pakistani Taliban near the northwestern city of Attock and beheaded several months later (Mehsud 27 November 2016).

Apart from being a highly lucrative activity in financing their organisational and operational requirements, the militants are also involved in high profile kidnappings to bargain for the release of the prisoners. In a very high profile kidnapping, a former officer of Inter-Services Intelligence (ISI) Khalid Khwaja, Retired Colonel Sultan Ameer Tarar and Asad Qureshi, a journalist were abducted by the Asian Tigers[2] terrorist group demanding the release of three core leaders of Afghan Taliban from the Pakistani government's captivity namely Mullah Abdul Ghani Baradar, Maulawi Kabir and Mansoor Dadullah. When the government had not met its demand to release these top Afghan Taliban leaders, Khwaja was executed by the Asian Tigers (*Dawn* 1 May 2010). However, the demand for releasing their leaders continued but also ordered the freeing of 120 more militants held by Pakistan. The group also insisted on USD 10 million ransom for the release of Qureshi (*The News* 15 May 2010).

Hence, the increasing incidences of kidnappings by the militants have severely threatened the safety of the people and security of the state. The global risk and crisis management agency NYA International in its report of 2016 ranked Pakistan among the top 5 global kidnapping hotspots and the majority of the abductions were primarily made by the terrorist organisations rather than criminal groups (NYA International 2016: 10).

Bank Robbery

When the Pakistani Taliban found them cut off from the traditional sources of money, they turned back to bank robbery to supplement their meagre and sporadic income flows. The TTP-affiliated terrorists rob banks to increase their terrorist activities. As per data given by Police, from 2009 to May 2012, the TTP militants robbed several Karachi based banks and generated a sum of USD 18 million (Mahmood 2012). The Afghan Taliban is also involved in bank robberies in Pakistani cities as Pakistan has more wealth than Afghanistan. Although some of the robberies are conducted to cause social disruptions and weaken the capabilities of the police forces, their primary motive is to steal money and finance their organisation (Silinsky 2014: 129-130).

Extortion

Extortion is one of the major financial crimes having a national concern as no major urban centres in Pakistan seems to be free from this menace. Extortion provides financial strength to militant organisations. The terrorists turn to extortion as a source of making money whenever other funding sources dry up. Many militant organisations in Pakistan have established their research wings to execute the extortion business without any flaws. It is because the extortion activities require a wide variety of information about the person to be extorted in order to put them in real threat or pressure. In one such incident, a Karachi based doctor received an extortion phone call where the caller reeled off a list of personal details of the doctor (the hospital where he works, the registration number of his car etc.) and demanded 5,00,000 Pakistani rupees (*Dawn* 2 July 2013).

Initially, Karachi has been a centre of extortion activities being the country's financial hub. Its financial significance attracts many terrorist/ militants groups and transnational criminal organisations to have their bases in the city. The terrorist groups like TTP, Lashkar-e-Jhangvi (Le-J), Harkat-ul-Jihad-al-Islami (HuJI) Arakan, Harkat-ul-Mujahideen al-Alami (HuMA), Tehrik-e-Islami Lashkar-e-Muhammadi (TILM), Sipah-e-Sahiba Pakistan (SSP), Sipah-e-Muhammad (SM), Sunni Tehrik (ST) and many others (Pakistan Institute of Peace Studies 2009: 10-17). However, the TTP has been the major group active in the city and involved in many criminal activities like collecting money from Karachi business persons. In fact, TTP has ramped up the extortion operations in Karachi in the past few years and has been blamed for attacking and killing of police personnel. It has converted the financial city to a centre of extortion racketing (*The Express Tribune* 2 July 2013).

But in the recent past, extortion cases have significantly increased in Pakistan and incidences have also been reported from other cities like Peshawar, Islamabad and Rawalpindi. The wealthy shop owners and traders are the prime victims of extortion demands. Most of the time, the terrorists employ the unique style for extorting money by rolling a bullet in a piece of paper with a number mentioned (the amount of money demanded) on it. If the person refuses to pay the money, the bullet is meant for him. Due to the lack of confidence of people on Police and fear to an extent, the complainants initially do not report the matters to the law enforcing personnel. Many businessmen and traders quietly oblige the extortion rackets instead of suffering the "dire consequences" (Shah 10 February 2015).

Stolen Vehicles

Stolen vehicles provide terrorists with a means of delivering explosives that will be traced back to the original car owner and not to the terrorist organisation. Transportation is a critical need of a terrorist group, offering speed to get the target, insertion and extraction, or a firing platform. Terrorists, like criminals, prefer to use untraceable vehicles for their missions. Some may opt to rent vehicles. Vehicles are not limited to cars or trucks (Nance 2014: 105).

An estimate says that in Pakistan, around 41 percent of suicide bombings are carried out using Suicide Vehicle Improvised Explosive Devices (SVBIEDS)- a delivery method for suicide bombings that include cars and trucks as well as other motorized vehicles like ambulance (Marcovic 2013: 34).

Car bombings have been used by the terrorists and militants as the most preferred means as vehicles packed with explosive can do considerable damage and kill and wound many people. Car bombs have one advantage for terrorists in that one vehicle can easily blend in with a large number of similar vehicles on a street, in a parking facility or in a parking area. It will be difficult for the local authorities to continuously check all such vehicles (Lutz, James M. and Brenda J. Lutz 2008: 29).

Small bombs designed to injure bystanders or cause disruption in a transportation system might be carried by hand. But large bombs require some other form of transportation, usually a vehicle. However, transporting a bomb of larger size also presents security problems for the terrorists to move it on the public roads without detection. To escape the detection, the terrorists mostly use stolen vehicles with false registration plates.

In January 2010, the Islamabad Law Enforcement Agencies has detained Israr Amin alias Imran, a top gun of the banned Tehrik-e-Taliban Pakistan (TTP) who used to steal military vehicles for his outfit to launch suicide bombings. During interrogation, the investigating officials came to know about snatching of a number of military vehicles by him which were used to launch suicide attacks on the law enforcement agencies officials and Pakistan Army (Abbasi, Kasif Ali, *The Nation* 2010).

In February 2015, the TTP launched a deadly terrorist attack in the Peshawar based Imamia Mosque that killed 23 persons. The investigating officials found that the vehicle used to transport the terrorists (perpetrators) was stolen from the Wah Cantonment of Punjab (*The Express Tribune,* 22 February 2015). In another incident, a suicide bomber of TTP struck near a police team in Lahore killing more than 26 people and wounding more than 50 who are mainly policemen. The suicide bomber had used a motorcycle bomb to target the on-duty police officials.

In a failed attempt to detonate a car bomb targeted to implode the Times Square, a US-born citizen (originally from Pakistan) Faisal Shahzad was arrested in May 2010. It was found that he was an affiliate of the TTP and spent more than a month during which he was trained for launching suicide attacks. In fact, Shahzad was given USD 5,000 by TTP to execute the attack (*CNN* 2010).

As per the estimate released by Overseas Advisory Security Council (OASC) on 'Pakistan 2017 Crime and Safety Report', the crime statistics of the Lahore City only portrays a very unstable situation. The total cases of stolen vehicles have been registered at 6881 in 2016-an increase of approximately 9 percent than 2015 (OASC, 30 January 2017).

Money Laundering

The speedy developments in the financial information, technology and communication facilitate money to move anywhere in the world with great ease. The deeper "dirty money" gets into the international banking system, the more difficult it is to trace or identify its origin. Globally the total estimated amount of laundered money is 2-5 percent of global GDP (Gross Domestic Product) or USD 800 billion-USD 2 trillion. The major developments in the international financial system during recent decades have made three F's- finding, freezing and forfeiting of criminally derived incomes and assets, all the more difficult. These are mainly the "dollarization" or the use of US dollar in transactions in black marketing; the general trend towards financial deregulation; the forward-motion of the European financial market; and the expansion and proliferation of the financial secrecy tax havens (UNODC-b).

Money laundering is the changeover of incomes generated by criminal activities into assets that cannot be traced back to the underlying crime (Reuter, P., 1: 2004). The terrorist organisations also heavily rely on money laundering techniques like the criminal organisations to hide their money. Although the terrorists use the money derived from laundering for numerous purposes, they primarily use this technique to get cash to buy arms that help them in perpetrating their violent activities and operations they are intended to do (UNODC-c). Money laundering not only finances crime, it also pollutes the international banking and financial system, occludes the international fight against corruption, distorts economies, undermines honest government and threatens international peace and security by being associates with international terrorism (Aydin 2007: 242).

Money Laundering has been one of the crucial funding sources of many terrorist organisations based and operating in Pakistan. It is evident from the recently released Basel Anti-Money Laundering Index (2017) commissioned by the Based Institute on Governance that ranked Pakistan among the top 50 countries with high terrorist financing and money laundering risks (Basel Institute of Governance 2017: 3).[3]

Money laundering in Pakistan hampers both the formal and informal financial systems of the country. The absence of strict control over its international borders, mainly along the Afghan border, has served as a facilitator in the easy flow of illicit goods and monies into and out of Pakistan. As per an estimate of the United States Department of State Report, 2017, Pakistan has received total USD 19.7 billion in the year 2016 from its expatriates as Diaspora remittances via the formal banking sector, an increase of 2.3 percent from 2015 (USD 16 billion) (US Dept of State 2017: 181). Moreover, unlicensed hawala/hundi operators are widely prevalent in Pakistan besides the existence of formal financial transactions systems. In fact, the region is prominent for using the illegal unlicensed hawala operations which are used to transfer and launder illicit money. Some of the operators are found to be involved in financing several terrorist groups in meeting their organisational and logistical needs. The Altaf Khanani Money Laundering Organisation (MLO), a transnational criminal organisation, based in Pakistan is known for its illicit money transfer and movement between, among others, Pakistan, the United Arab Emirates (UAE), the United States, the United Kingdom, Canada and Australia. It is also held responsible for laundering billions of dollars annually via proceeds of organised criminal activities. The Khanani MLO provides money laundering services to the notorious organised criminals of Columbia and Mexico and individuals associated with the terrorist organisations like Hizballah and other UN-designated terrorist organisations. It has also been involved in the movement of funds for the Taliban. Interestingly, it is to be noted that Altaf Khanani, the leader of the organisation, has nexus with the Pakistan based terrorist organisations like Lashkar-e-Taiba (LeT), Dawood Ibrahim, Al-Qaeda and Jaish-e-Mohammad (ibid.).

Apart from this, the trade sector also serves as a crucial lucrative medium for the terrorist and militant organisations to transfer money and goods by showing as a legitimate activity. On10 March 2006, the Special Investigation Group (SIG) of Pakistan's Federal Investigation Agency (FIA) revealed the nexus of a sugar trading company with the Taliban organisation. The owner of the Afghan-based sugar trading company namely, Fazal Karim Maidanwal Limited, imported sugar to be sold in Pakistan, but eventually diverted and delivered to the local markets in Afghanistan with the help of the custom clearing agents to make huge profits as it resulted in rise of sugar price in the markets of Pakistan. The SIG had also discovered that Abdul Bari, the founder of the Company, had transferred approximately USD 6,00,000 to the Taliban leaders. During the course of investigation, the investigating agency also found that the founder had close association and business partnership with Mullah Omar, the founder of the Afghan Taliban. In fact, Abdul Bari and his brother Abdul Taqi were in the most wanted list of the INTERPOL[4] on charges of moving money to the Afghan Taliban (*Dawn,* 11 March 2006).

Funding Through Donations

Private donations have always been one of the major sources for the terrorist organisations to fund their organisational activities and operations. There is a trend prevalent among the Pakistani, and more particularly among the people in Punjab, Khyber Pakhtunkhwa Province (KPK) and the FATA, to donate money in the name of religion. The terrorist organisations having their bases in Pakistan like TTP that raise a major share of their total funds from the local donors or sponsors. As per a rough estimate, the TTP raise between 55 percent and 65 percent of its funding through the local donors (Rana 2014: 151). Moreover, there are several organisations existing in Pakistan in the form of charities or religious seminaries (madrassas) those are involved in collecting donations from urban business centres and door to door campaigns for charity. However, many times, they are found to be involved in raising funds for different militant organisations. Jammat-ud-dawa (JuD), the public wing of the Lashkar-e-Taiba (L-e-T), raises funds in Pakistan and the Middle East, more particularly Saudi Arabia, in the name of Islamic charity. The JuD collected a huge amount of money for relief work in the wake of the 2005 Muzaffarabad earthquake and diverted a major portion of it to the affiliated terrorist organisation (Greig 2016: 33).

Responses of the Pakistani State in Countering Terrorists Financing

In order to comply with these mechanisms developed by the international community, the Pakistani state has engaged in diverse efforts to check money laundering and counter the financing of terrorist activities. In this section a brief analysis has been made to the measures initiated by the Government of Pakistan.

Pakistani Government has enacted the first instrument of countering terrorism in the form of the Anti-Terrorism Act, 1997. However, it lacked the provisions for freezing the financial sources or aspect of the terrorists that have been a crucial element of all international and national instruments in countering terrorism (Anti Terrorism Act 1997). In fact, in Section 6 of the Act that defined the acts of terrorism, no reference was made to include the financial aspects of the terrorists groups.[5] However, Section 11-O of the Act has provided for freezing and seizing money or other property owned, directly or indirectly, by a proscribed person.

The 11 September 2001 incident became a turning point for the Pakistani Government in its journey of CFT missions. Following the 9/11 incident, the Pakistani Government was pressurised by the United States and the world community to cut the monetary aspect of the terrorist groups operating from and within Pakistan as money has been a crucial element in financing the terrorist groups that executed this tragic incident.[6]

The State Bank of Pakistan (SBP) supports global efforts to check money laundering. The State Bank of Pakistan (SBP) has been playing a significant role in countering the financial sources of the terrorists in Pakistan.[7] In 2004, the SBP initiated a provision under which all the hawaladars are required to register themselves as authorised foreign exchange dealers and meet the minimum standards and capital criteria set by the SBP. Not all the hawaladars, however, have registered even now, they operate illegally in different parts of the country without being offered any challenge by the law enforcement apparatus. By exploiting the lapse in this law, the tax evaders, corrupt figures and sponsors of terrorism used to transfer black money or illegal funds in and out of the country (Taj, 2 June 2012). Recently, in a major move to squeeze the financial sources of terrorist groups, the SBP has directed all the banks based in Pakistan to freeze accounts worth of millions of rupees linked to 2021 individuals listed on the Fourth Schedule of the ATA, 1997 (Syed, 25 September 2016).

Pakistan is one of the key members of the Asia Pacific Group (APG) on Money Laundering established in 1997. Pakistan joined the Group in May 2000 (APG official Website). It may be stated here that the APG aims to effectively implement and enforce the internationally accepted standards against money laundering and the financing of terrorism, in particular, the FATF recommendations. On 7 July 2007, the APG issued a warning to dismember Pakistan from the group as it was not up to the mark in the implementation of the global standards of anti-terrorism and anti-money laundering (Taj, 2 June 2 2012).

Following this warning, the Pakistani Government enacted its first act to check money laundering known as the "Anti-Money Laundering Ordinance, 2007" which is shortly abbreviated as AMLO, 2007.[8] Under Section 6 of the Ordinance, a separate Financial Monitoring Unit (FMU) was established in October 20007. It was mainly established to ensure compliance with the Financial Action Task Force's (FATF) recommendations on AML, safeguard the interests of the depositors from risks arising out of money laundering and terrorist financing and to reinforce the measures being taken by the banks and DFIs to strengthen their KYC/AML procedures (State Bank of Pakistan, 2007: Website).

However, the AMLO 2007 suffered from many major discrepancies. Some of the features of the ordinance stood in sharp contrast to the core FATF standards and the ordinance did not contain any provisions to report terrorist financing and therefore had to be amended.[9] Due to these defects of the AMLO, it was replaced by the Anti-Money Laundering Act, 2010 popularly known as the AMLA 2010 and it amended many provisions of the 2007 Ordinance. The definitions and list of "predicate offences" were expanded and certain provisions of the Act were later on modified to bring into conformity with the core recommendations of the FATF and the APG (AMLA 2010). Under this new act on money laundering, various offences of 15 major legislation (as against 11 in the 2007 ordinance) including all offences of the ATA, 1997 were listed as predicate offence (Taj, 2 June 2012). The AMLA 2010 in section 3 has defined the offence of money laundering in a detailed way that makes it more significant than to the AMLO 2007.[10] But it also lacks the countering of terrorist financing provisions as it is mainly concerned with anti-money laundering in Pakistan.

Thus, Pakistan's anti-terrorism mission did not contain the provisions relating to counter terrorist financing. Pakistan has partially implemented the United Nations Security Council (UNSC) UNSC Resolution 1373 and has taken some action against domestic entities in the banking sector. The freezing of assets in pursuant to the 1373 Resolution was done mainly by using powers under the Anti-Terrorism Act 1997 to proscribe entities considered to be "concerned in terrorism". However, the imposition was limited to organisations and freezing action was limited to the sealing of the offices of the entity, the freezing of the bank accounts and the detention of any cash found in its possession. But this was not a comprehensive freeze within the framework of the 1373 resolution (APG on Money Laundering 2009: 3)

On 16 February 2012, the FATF added Pakistan to its Public statement reflecting its lack of progress in implementing the terrorist financing laws and blacklisted for its poor performance in checking terror funds (US Dept. of State 2014: 326). Acting on fears of the imposition of sanctions by the United Nations in 2013 for failing to comply with the standards of the FATF and UNSCR 1373 on curbing money laundering and terrorist financing, the Government of Pakistan was to make necessary amendments to the Anti-Terrorism Act 1997.[1]

However, the major development in the course of counter-terrorism policy formulation took place in the aftermath of the ghastly terror attack in the Peshawar based Army Public School in December 2014. It is the first comprehensive policy framework of the country initiated to counter-terrorism and counter-terror financing namely, the National Action Plan 2015 popularly known as the NAP. The NAP comprises a "20-Point Programme" covering the issues like:

1. The UN slapped sanctions on Iran and North Korea due to its failure to comply with the global standards initiated by FATF and UNSCR 1373.

i) Implementation of death sentences of those convicted of terrorism;

ii) special trial courts under the supervision of Army whose duration would be 2 years;

iii) Militant outfits and armed gangs will not be allowed to operate in the country;

iv) NACTA, the anti-terrorism institution, will be strengthened;

v) Strict action against the literature, newspapers, and magazines promoting hatred, extremism, sectarianism and intolerance;

vi) Choking financing for terrorist and terrorist organisations;

vii) Ensuring against the re-emergence of proscribed organisations;

viii) Establishment and deploying a dedicated counter-terrorism force;

ix) taking effective action against rebellious persecution;

x) registration and regulation of religious seminaries;

xi) Ban on glorification of terrorist and terrorist organisations through print and electronic media;

xii) Administrative and development reforms in FATA with immediate focus on repatriation of IDPs;

xiii) Communication network of terrorists will be dismantled completely;

xiv) Measures against abuse of social media for terrorism;

xv) Zero-tolerance for militancy in Punjab;

xvi) Ongoing operation in Karachi will be taken to its logistical end;

xvii) Balochistan government to be fully empowered to be fully empowered for political reconciliation with complete ownership by all stakeholders.

(South Asia Terrorism Portal, satp.org)

The Pakistan People's Party-led government's post-2008 moratorium on the death penalty for terrorism cases was lifted after the APS attack and included it a crucial mandate in the 20 Point Programme. A number of bodies have been formed to look into the implementation of NAP.

In February 2015, the FATF has removed Pakistan from its grey list owing to its improvement in developing policy frameworks in combating the twin menaces of money laundering and terrorist financing. The adoption has been a major factor in getting this recognition. In a recent move, the State Bank of

Pakistan inaugurated a high-technology equipped data centre to assist the Financial Monitoring Unit (FMU)[11] in tracing the trail of money laundering and terrorism financing. It is established with the financial assistance of the UK Department for International Development (Alam, 11 February 2017).

Conclusion

It is seen that following the Peshawar APS attack, the Pakistani government has shown an imperative attitude to eliminate the problem of terrorism, its financing and other related issues primarily by formulating the comprehensive NAP which was absent earlier. But political will and intent of the government is somewhere lacking in implementing that comprehensive policy. There are huge gaps in the implementation of the NAP because of which the incidences of terrorist attacks and violence have not come down at all. Pakistan is still facing the risk of terrorism financing as around 223- national and international- terrorist organisations have been generating continuously billions of rupees in terms of their annual operating budgets in the country. As per a recently released confidential report of the Pakistan's Financial Monitoring Unit titled "National Risk Assessment on Money Laundering and Terrorism Financing, 2017" discovered by a newspaper agency, it is estimated that an annual operational budget of these terrorist groups is between Rs.5million to Rs.6 million and average cost of operation per incident or attack varies from Rs. 0.5 million to Rs. 2.5 million depending on the magnitude of the incident (Gishkori, 23 March 2017). The report also says that the major sources of terrorist funding in Pakistan includes foreign funding, drug trafficking, kidnapping for ransom, extortion from business, vehicle snatching, hawala/ hundi, cash couriers, dealings in foreign exchange, contraband items in FATA and sale of items looted from NATO and ISAF containers (ibid.). Moreover, the lack of political will on the part of the government is evident from its manner of handling the National Counter-Terrorism Authority (NACTA). Strengthening of NACTA is one of the major agendas of the NAP formulated in 2015, whereas the budgetary allocation for the authority is very small. Thus, expecting much from a less-funded agency to counter terrorism will be a distant dream as countering terrorism involves heavy expenses that rely on high technology management, personnel management and so on.

Besides these, dismantling communication networks of terrorist organisations through print media and electronic media is a key agenda of the NAP. It puts ban on the glorification of the terrorist organisations through these media. As per an online investigation carried out by the *Dawn* has revealed that 41 of Pakistan's 64 banned outfits are using their social networking pages and some of the major outfits are namely Ahle Sunnat Wal Jammat (ASWJ) with 200 pages and groups, Jeay Sindh Muttahida Mahaz (JSMM) with 160 pages, Sipah-e-Sahaba (SSP) with 148 pages, Baloch Student Organsiations etc. The major banned outfits still using the facebook, though at a smaller scale, comprise Lashkar-e-Jhangvi (LeJ), TTP, Tehrik-e-Taliban Swat, TNSM, Jamat-ul-Arhar, 313 Brigade etc (Haque and Bashir, 14 September 2017).

Muhammad Amir Rana, an expert on security issues and director of the Islamabad based Pakistan Institute for Peace Studies (PIPS) notes that the order to freeze terrorist financial sources primarily focuses on the leadership of the sectarian groups, while several hardcore terrorists are absent from the list. Moreover, accounts of individuals have been frozen, whereas no action has been taken against accounts of banned groups (Syed, Baqir Sajjad 2016). Hence, there is a need to adopt a comprehensive action covering both traditional and non-traditional source is required instead of just targeting the normal banking. Along with this, the government and other actors indulged in the administrative machinery should develop a mature political culture having a strong political will and commitment to eliminate the problem of terrorism, and then only the mechanisms developed to trace the money trail of the terrorist organisations can be implemented in the true sense.

Endnotes

1. Charging interest is considered as an un-Islamic act as viewed from the perspective of the Qu'ran.
2. Asian Tigers was an offshoot of the banned Lashkar-i-Jhangvi (LeJ comprising mostly Punjabi Taliban.
3. The Basel Anti-Money Laundering (AML) Index is an annual ranking that assesses the countries having risks regarding money laundering and terrorist financing. It emphasises on anti-money laundering and counter-terrorist financing (AML/CTF) regimes and frameworks and other related factors. In the 2017 Report, Pakistan has been placed on the 46th position in the list of 146 countries with a score of 6.64 (though the risks of Pakistan is lower than the other South Asian countries namely Afghanistan (2nd Position); Nepal (14th Rank) and Sri Lanka (25th Rank).

4. Interpol is the world's largest international police organisation with 192 member countries. It mandated to enable the police forces around the world to work mutually to ensure a safer world.
5. The Section 6 (a) of the Anti-Terrorism Act, 1997 defined : "A person is said to commit a terrorist act if he, in order to, or if the effect of his actions will be to, strike terror or create a sense of fear and insecurity in the people, or any section of the people, does any act or thing by using bombs, dynamite or other explosive or inflammable substances, or such fire-arms or other lethal weapons as may be notified, or poisons or noxious gases or chemicals, in such a manner as to cause, or be likely to cause, the death of, or injury to, any person or persons, or damage to, or destruction of, property on a large scale, or a widespread disruption of supplies of services essential to the life of the community, or threatens, with the use of force public servants in order to prevent them from discharging their lawful duties" (Anti- Terrorism Act, 1997, p. 3)
6. The total financial cost for the Al-Qaeda led 9/11 attack was estimated around US USD 4,00,000 - 5,00,000 (9/11 Commission Report Monograph, p.3).
7. State Bank of Pakistan is the Central Bank of Pakistan that issues currencies and regulates the financial institutions in Pakistan.
8. AMLO was promulgated in September, 2007 by the then President of Pakistan General Pervez Musharraf.
9. The AMLO, 2007 did not designated all the form of crimes or offences as predicate offences as designated by the FATF. The Ordinance only designated the offences like arms smuggling and trafficking, sexual exploitation and trafficking in persons as predicate offences.
10. Section 3 of the AMLA, 2010: A person shall be guilty of offence of Money Laundering, if the person:

    a. acquires, converts, possessed, uses or transfers property, knowing or having reason to believe that such property is proceeds of crime;

    b. conceals or disguises the true nature, origin, location, disposition, movements, or ownership of property, knowing or having reason to believe that such property is proceeds of crime;

c. holds or possesses on behalf of any other person any property knowing or having reason to believe that such property is proceeds of crime; or

d. participate in, associates, conspires to commit, attempts to commit, aids, abets, facilitates, or counsels the commission of the acts specified in Clause 3a, 3b and 3c.

11. The FMU is the financial intelligence unit of the Finance Ministry responsible for countering money laundering and terrorist financing.

References

Abbasi, Kasif Ali (2010), "Top TTP Man Caught", *The Nation,* 10 January, 2010, available at: http://nation.com.pk/politics/08-Jan-2010/top-ttp-man-caught .

Acharya, Arabinda, Syed Adnan Ali Shah Bukahri and Sadia Sulaiman (2009), "Making Money in the Mayhem: Funding Taliban Insurrection in the Tribal Areas of Pakistan", *Studies in Conflict & Terrorism,* 32(95), 95-108.

Adams, James (1986), "*The Financing of Terror: Behind the PLO, IRA, Red Brigades, and M-Stand the Paymasters: How the Groups that are Terrorizing the World Get the Money to Do It",* New York: Simon and Schuster.

Alam, Kazim (2017), "Data Centre to Tackle Money Laundering, Terror Financing", *Dawn, 11* February 2017, available at: https://www.dawn.com/news/1314123 .

APG on Money Laundering (2009), "Anti-Money Laundering and Combating the Financing of Terrorism", Pakistan Mutual Evaluation 2, *Mutual Evaluation Report.*

APG on Money Laundering, available at: http://www.apgml.org/members-and-observers/members/details.aspx?m=8fc0275d-5715-4c56-b06a-db4af266c11a .

Arhari, Ehasan (2009), "The Dynamics of Narco-Jihad in the Afghanistan-Pakistan Region", in National Bureau of Asian Research, *NBR Special Report 20.*

Aubrey, Stefan M. (2004)," *The New Dimension of International Terrorism*", Schriftenreihe: Strategie und Konfliktforschung.

Aydin, Suleyman (2007), "Money Laundering and Financing of Terrorism", in H. Durmaz et al. (Eds.) *Understanding and Responding to Terrorism,* Amsterdam: IOS Press, 242-251.

Basel Institute of Governance (2017), "Basel AML Index 2017 Report", *Basel Institute of Governance,* Basel, available at: https://index.baselgovernance.org/sites/index/documents/Basel_AML_Index_Report_2017.pdf .

Biersteker, Thomas J. (2002), "Targeting Terrorist Financing", in Ken Booth and Tim Dunne (eds.) *Worlds in Collision: Terror and the Future of Global Order,* New York: Palgrave Macmillan.

Briggs, Billy (2015), "Remembering the Peshawar School Massacre", *AlJajeera, 16* December 2015, Peshawar, http://www.aljazeera.com/indepth/features/2015/12/remembering-peshawar-school-massacre-151215071631624.html .

Dawn (2006), "Taliban-Linked Traders Found Involved in Illegal Sugar Sale", *Dawn, 11* March 2006, Karachi, available at: https://www.dawn.com/news/182554 .

Dawn (2009), "Nisar Calls for Choking Drug Trade to Cut Terrorists Funding," (9 April 2015) available at: https://www.dawn.com/news/1174802 .

Dawn (2010), "Militans Kill Khalid Khwaja dead in FATA", *Dawn,* 01 May 2010, available at: https://www.dawn.com/news/851939.

Dawn (2013), "Growing extortion menace haunts Karachi", *Dawn,* 2 July, 2013, available at: https://www.dawn.com/news/1022242.

Daily Times (2016), "Drug Trafficking from Afghanistan," *Daily Times,* 24 August 2016, available at: http://dailytimes.com.pk/editorial/24-Aug-16/drug-trafficking-from-afghanistan.

Financial Action Task Force (2008), "*Terrorist Financing*", available at: http://www. fatf-gafi.org/media/fatf/documents/reports/FATF%20Terrorist%20Financing%20 Typologies%20Report.pdf.

Feyerick, Deborah (2010), "Times Square Bomb Plotter Sentenced to Death", *CNN,* 5 October, 2010, available at: http://edition.cnn.com/2010/CRIME/10/05/new. york. terror.plot/index.html.

Gishkori, Zahid (2015), "Pakistan Spends Rs.4 a Year on Each Addict, says ANF," *The Express Tribune,* 6 July, 2015, online available at: https://tribune.com.pk/story/915729/8-9-million-get-addicted-to-drugs-every-year-in-pakistan-senate-body-told/.

Gishkori, Zahid (2017), "Terror Outfits Continue to Generate Billions", *The News,* March 23, 2017, available at: https://www.thenews.com.pk/print/194044-Terror-outfits-continue-to-generate-billions.

"*Global Terrorism Index-2015: Measuring and Understanding the Impacts of Terrorism*", Institute for Economics and Peace.

Govt. of Islamic Republic of Pakistan, Anti Terrorism Act, 1997.

Government of Islamic Republic of Pakistan, "Anti-Money Laundering Act, 2010".

Greig, J. Andrew (2016), "Riding the Tiger: The Threat to Pakistan from Terrorism", in Ravi Kalia (eds.) *Pakistan's Political Labyrinths: Military, Society and Terror,* New York: Routledge.

Gunaratna, Rohan and Khurram Iqbal (2011), "*Pakistan: Terrorism Ground Zero*", London: Reaktion Books.

Haque and Bashir (2017), "Banned outfits in Pakistan Operated Openly on Facebook", *Dawn* , 14 September 2017,available at: https://www.dawn.com/news/1335561 .

Horgan, John, 2005: 114) (Horgan, John (2005), "*The Psychology of Terrorism,* London: Routledge.

Iqbal, Anwar (2014), "TTP Using Drug Money to Fund Activities", *Dawn,* 9 December, 2014, available at: https://www.dawn.com/news/1149674.

Iqbal, Khurram (2010), "Tehrik-e-Taliban Pakistan: A Global Threat", *Conflict and Peace Studies,* 3(4), 127-140.

Jenks, David A. and John Randolph Fuller (2004), "*Global Crime and Justice*", New York: Routledge.

Khan, Ismail (2014), "Taliban massacre 131 schoolchildren: Principal among 141 dead in attack on Army Public School, Peshawar", *Dawn, 17* December 2014, Peshawar, available at: https://www.dawn.com/news/1151361.

Lutz, James M. and Brenda J. Lutz (2008), "*Global Terrorism*", London: Routledge.

Mahmood, Javed (2012), "Taliban Bank Robberies Total USD 18m in Karachi Since 2009", *Central Asia Online, 21* May 2012, available at: http://archive. is/20140301023815/centralasiaonline.com/en_GB/articles/caii/features/pakistan/main/2012/05/23/feature-01.

Marcovic, Vesna. (2013), "Suicide Terrorism: The Special Case of the Suicide Bomber" in *Future Trends and New Approaches in Defeating the Terrorism Threat* (eds.) Ugur Gurbuz, Amsterdam: IOS Press.

Mehsud, Saud (2016), "Militants Kidnap Six Pakistanis Working for Polish Oil Firm," *Reuters,* 27 November 2016, available at: http://www.reuters.com/article/us-pakistan-kidnapping-poland/militants-kidnap-six-pakistanis-working-for-polish-oil-firm-idUSKBN13M077?il=0.

Moosakhail, Zabihullah (2015), "Mafia, terrorists annually receive USD 70 billion from narcotics in Afghanistan," *Khamma Press,* 3 June, 2015, available at: http:// www.khaama.com/mafia-terrorists-annually-receive-70-billion-from-narcotics-in-afghanistan-3426.

Nance, Malcom W. (2014), "*Terrorist Recognition Handbook: A Practitioner's Manual for Predicting and Identifying Terrorist Activities*", Boca Raton: CRC Press.

NYA International (2016), "*The Global Kidnapping Review 2016*", available at: http://presswire.com/pr/nya/160203-NYA-January-Kidnap-Review.pdf .

OASC (2017), "Pakistan 2017 Crime and Safety Report: Lahore", *OASC,* 30 January 2017, available at: https://www.osac.gov/pages/ContentReportDetails.aspx?cid=21143 .

Pakistan Institute of Peace Studies (2009), "Profiling the Violence in Karachi", *Conflict and Peace Studies,* 2(3), 16).

Rana, Muhammad Amir (2014), "Choking Financing for Militants in Pakistan", in Moeed Yusuf (eds.) *Pakistan's Counter-Terrorism Challenge,* Washington D.C.: Georgetown University Press.

Reuter, P. (2004), "*Chasing Dirty Money: The Fight against Money Laundering*", Washington D.C.: Institute for International Economics.

Shah, Sabir (2015), "Pakistan is not Lone Target of Extortion, Gangster Crimes", *The News,* 10 February, 2015, available at: https://www.thenews.com.pk/print/23313-pakistan-is-not-lone-target-of-extortion-gangster-crimes .

Shelly, Louise (2014), "*Dirty Entanglements: Corruption, Crime and Terrorism*", Cambridge: Cambridge University Press.

Shelly, Louise I. (2015), "Corruption and Youth's Recruitment into Violent Extremism", in M. Lombardi et al. (eds.) *Countering Radicalisation and Violent Extremism Among Youth to Prevent Terrorism,* Amsterdam: IOS Press.

Silinsky, Mark (2014), "*The Taliban: Afghanistan's Most Lethal Insurgents*", California: Praeger.

Swami, Praveen (2005) "Lashkar-e-Taiba", in Wilson John and Swati Parashar (eds.) *Terrorism in Southeast Asia: Implications for South Asia,* New Delhi: Pearson.

Syed, Baqir Sajjad (2016), "SBP Tells Banks to Freeze Terror Financing Accounts", *Dawn,* 25 September, 2016, available at: https://www.dawn.com/news/1285955 .

Taj, Affran (2012), "Financial Crime and Our Laws", *Dawn,* 2 June, 2012, available at: http://www.dawn.com/news/723431/financial-crime-and-our-laws .

Tavernise, Sabrina (2009), "Organized Crime in Pakistan Feeds Taliban", *New York Times,* 28 August, 2009, available at: http://www.nytimes.com/2009/08/29/world/asia/29karachi.html .

The Express Tribune (2011), "Kidnapped: Industrialist Riaz Chinoy Found", *The Express Tribune,* 6 December, 2011, available at: https://tribune.com.pk/ story/302772/kidnapped-industrialist-riaz-chinoy-found/.

The Express Tribune (2012), "List of Banned Organisations in Pakistan", *The Express Tribune, 24* October 2012, Islamabad, available at: https://tribune.com.pk/ story/456294/list-of-banned-organisations-in-pakistan/ .

The Express Tribune (2013), "For Karachi, 2013 Will be A Record Year of Extortion Demands: Police", *Dawn, 2* July 2013, Karachi, available at: https://tribune.com.pk/story/571302/for-karachi-2013-will-be-a-record-year-of-extortion-demands-police/.

The Express Tribune (2015), "Investigation Under Way: Terrorist Used Stolen Vehicle in Imamia Mosque Attack", *The Express Tribune,* 22 February, 2015, available at: https://tribune.com.pk/story/842611/investigation-under-way-terrorists-used-stolen-vehicle-in-imamia-mosque-attack/.

The News (2010), "No Real Effort by Govt, Tribal Leaders to Secure Release of Col Imam, Qureshi", *The News,* 15 May, 2010, available at: https://www.thenews. com.pk/archive/print/237092-no-real-effort-by-govt-tribal-elders-to-secure-release-of-col-imam-qureshi.

State Bank of Pakistan (2007), "Establishment of Financial Monitoring Unit", *State Bank of Pakistan, 09* July , 2007, available at: www.sbp.org.pk/bprd/2007/c7.htm.

South Asia Terrorism Portal (n.d.), "National Action Plan 20 Points", available at: http://www.satp.org/satporgtp/countries/pakistan/document/papers/National_ Action_Plan_20_Points.htm .

Syed, Baqir Sajjad (2016), "SBP Tells Banks to Freeze Terror Financing Accounts", *Dawn, 25* September 2016, Islamabad, available at: https://www.dawn.com/news/1285955

UNODC-a, "Country Profile", *UNODC,* available at: https://www.unodc.org/pakistan/en/country-profile.html.

UNODC-b, "Money Laundering and Globalisation", available at: https://www.unodc. org/unodc/en/money-laundering/globalization.html .

UNODC-c, "*Introduction to Money Laundering*", United Nations Office on Drugs and Crime, available at: https://www.unodc.org/unodc/en/money-laundering/introduction.html .

US Deptt of State, "International Narcotics Control Strategy Report: Money Laundering and Financial Crimes, 2017: 181.

CHAPTER 12

Origin and Growth of Madhesi Movement in Nepal

Subodh Chandra Bharti

Abstract

In Nepal, recently after promulgation of the New Constitution (20 September 2015), people of Terai-Madhes region started a movement based on their ethnic identity. This movement called a complete blockade at the border from Indian side and stopped the transportation of the essential goods which Nepal imports from India. Hundreds of lives have gone in several clashes between the protesters and the state military/ police. Though the blockade have been lifted up the movement has not stopped yet and still moving gradually. People are raising slogan like; "Not Our Constitution" and demanding a huge amendment to the constitution before the local elections which have scheduled to be held in May. The Madhesi movement has both the violent and nonviolent organisations active since the interim Constitution of Nepal (2007) was promulgated. A secessionist movement is also going on parallel to the peaceful democratic movement.

Here the study tries to explain Madhes as a region, ethnic Identity of Madhesis, socio-political conditions of Madhesis and perceptions about the Madhesis among the hill people. The paper also discusses the factors responsible for the origin of the Madhesi movement like; language issue, citizenship issue, socio-political and economic unfairness, state-centric nationalism, etc. The study discusses four phases of Madhesi movement and its growth and finally analyses of all the facts, events and the current political situation in Nepal.

Introduction

In the 21st century post-globalization, there are several issues emerges in the world politics challenging the state autonomy and state nationalism. In the phase of globalization, identity has become a very crucial element within a state. The question of identity politics can be seen both in the old and new democracies as well in non-democratic countries. In South Asia, ethnic identity-based conflicts begin with the end of the British colonialism. Kashmir and northeast issues in India, Tamil issue in Sri Lanka, Baloch and Bengali issues in Pakistan where the Bengali ethnic movement (1952-1971) led to a succession of East Pakistan and formation of Bangladesh as a separate nation-state. Very small countries like Nepal and Bhutan are also experiencing ethnic movements within their territories.

Very recently the people of Terai-Madhes region of Nepal started a movement after the promulgation of a new 'Federal Democratic Republic' Constitution on 20 September 2015. The movement called a complete blockade on the border from Indian side and stopped the transportation of the essential goods in Nepal. Hundreds of lives have gone in several clashes between the protesters and the state military/ police. Though the blockade have ended but still the demand of constitution amendement is going on. People are raising slogans like; "Not Our Constitution" and demanding a huge amendment to the Constitution. This movement has violent and nonviolent organizations active since the interim Constitution of Nepal (2007) has promulgated. A secessionist movement is also going on parallel to the peaceful democratic movement.

The Madhesi movement has its roots in socioeconomic and political discrimination which Madhesis have been facing since the integration of Nepal. This study tries to explain Madhes as a region, ethnic Identity of Madhesis and the sociopolitical conditions of Madhesis. It also highlights perceptions about the Madhesis among the hill people. The language issue, citizenship issue, socio-political and economic unfairness, state-centric nationalism all factors responsible for the movement have discussed. The study discusses the four phases of Madhesi movement and concludes after analyzing all the facts and events.

Tarai/Madhes Region

The southern plain of Nepal is known as *Madhes* (the middle state), and people who live in this region are known as 'Madhesis.' The word 'Madhesi' originates from the word *'Madhya-deshi'* (people from the middle state), in other words, those people who live in the middle state (Jha 1993). "The ethnonym Madhesi refers to residents of the *Terai/Madhes* who share common languages and cultures with various communities across the border in north India."[1] This *Terai* Region is very fertile land in between the Himalayan Hills and the *Indo-Gangetic* plains and "it forms about a quarter of the country's total area, in an 885km strip stretching from the Mahakali River in the west to the Mechi River in the east, with a width varying from four to 52km. The Terai also includes some low hills (the Siwalik range) and valleys to their north (the inner Terai)"[2] which is near about 23,068 Km².

Madhes region is dominated by the high Hindu castes and follows the caste-based hierarchy. In this region, people speak the languages such as Maithili, Bhojpuri, Bajjika, Awadhi, and Hindi which also spoken in Indian border districts of the states Bihar and UP. Their way of celebrating festivals, cuisines, style of clothing, arts, customs, etc. all are same like border Indians have. Even their social caste structures are same as border side Indians. They also have a kinship with people from Bihar, UP and other border states of India.

All Hindu caste groups, Muslims and Hindu Dalits of the Tarai considered as Madhesis. Some time 'Tharus,' 'Dhimals' and 'Rajbanshis' (other indigenous tribal groups from the Tarai), also considered in this group, but many Tharu peoples and some writers do not consider them as Madhesis. Madhesis have a problem with the term Terai, and the Tharus don't want to consider this region as Madhes so "to manage this contention, the decision-makers came to a negotiated settlement by naming the region as 'Terai-Madhes.'[3] Out of 75 districts of Nepal, 20 districts come under this region. Here "Madhesi form 16.59 percent of the population but when Dalits and indigenous nationalities from the Tarai region added, this rise to 32.29 percent."[4]

Map of Nepal and Madhes region

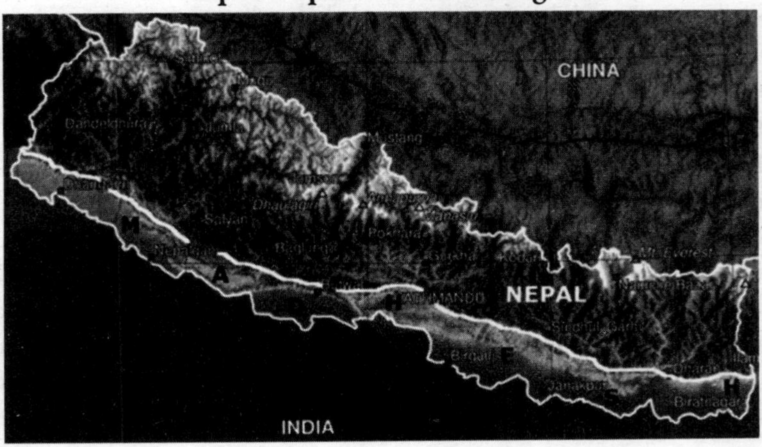

Source: madhes.com

Constituents of Ethnic Identity and Madhesis

The identity of an Individual and a group as a whole can be defined in terms of being alike (from within a group) as well as being different from others (from other individuals or groups). Ethnic identity is a social identity of a group or an individual. According to Charles Taylor (1994), "our identity is partly shaped by recognition or its absence, often by the misrecognition of others, and so a person or group of people can suffer real damage, real distortion, if the people or society around them mirror back to them a confining or demeaning or contemptible picture of themselves."

According to Paul Brass (1985) an ethnic identity formation is based on 'three sets of struggles': (1) 'control over its material and symbolic resources' among themselves; (2) 'Competition for rights, privileges, and available resources' between different ethnic groups; and (3) 'Control over local territories and population' and administrative control, between the State and the dominating groups, 'on the one hand, and the populations that inhabit its territory.' Primordialists believes that an ethnic identity is a natural biological phenomenon and according to them, culture plays a most important role in the formation of an ethnic group. Anthony Smith gives six 'bases' or foundations of ethnic identity: (1) A distinct group name; (2) A shared belief by group members; (3) The presence of historical memories among group members; (4) A shared culture; (5) An attachment to a specific territory or homeland (6) A sense of common solidarity. Other hand constructivists who say ethnic identity is socially constructed, human actions and choices led to the construction of ethnic identity. Max Weber held that ethnic identity is more based 'on a set of beliefs about common ancestry' rather than 'shared language, religion, and especially biological traits' (Phadnis 1989).

In Nepal by race or descent there may be three types of ethnic categorization: 'Mongoloid' or Tibeto-Burman,' 'Indo-Aryan' and Austro-Asiatic' can be seen. Similarly from the religious point of view: 'Hindu, Buddhist, and non-Hindu religious beliefs, customs, and practices among several ethnic groups' can be seen. According to language basis, there are two distinct groups one is Hill areas' people who speak Nepali (*Khas-Kura*) and the other side Tarai people, mostly bilingual Hindi (Maithili, Bhojpuri, Awadhi, and Vajjika) and Nepali speaking (Phadnis 1989).

Madhesi ethnic identity has constituted by the Tarai 'caste-based groups' 'who are of non-*Pahadi* origin'; The Tarai Hindus (upper castes and Dalits), Tarai Muslims and Tarai Janjatis (indigenous people from Tarai, Tharus, Rajbanshis, Dhimals, etc.). Madhesis are basically 'Indo-Aryan' race-based people and their culture, customs, language, and beliefs are different from *Pahadis*. The Madhesi movement has an important role in the emergence of its ethnic identity at the international level, "it is a manifestation of historical marginalization and alienation experienced by Madhesis at the hands of a succession of ruling elites of Nepal."[5]

It appears very clear that Madhesis are an ethnic group in Nepal. Their identity is based on their race, language, culture, and also on the historical-cultural commonalities and common solidarity among themselves, control over a certain territory, recognition by other distinct identity groups and conflict on the control of the resources with other ethnic groups.

Chart No. 1. Ethnic Diversity in Nepal

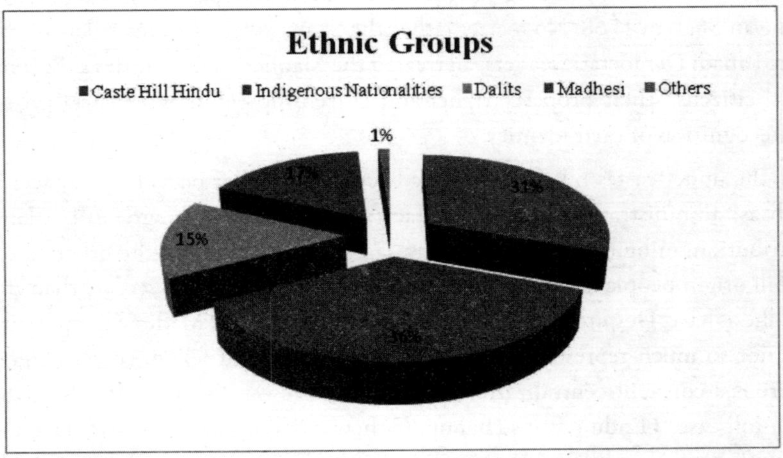

Source: 2011 Census of Nepal

Perception About Madhesis

The *Pahadis* do not recognize the Madhesis as full citizens of Nepal. They consider them as 'less Nepali' than them (Hangan and Lawoti 2013). They believe that Madhesis are not indigenous people of Nepal as they have a different and distinct culture and have different physical appearances ('dark-brown complexion' and they wear Dhoti'). Madhesis use to speak mostly Indian origin languages and have their kinship with the Indians, so they aren't considered as equal citizens as *Pahadis*, even the Pahadis consider Madhesis 'to be people who have few manners and culture.' They are called '*Dhotis*,' '*Black-folks*' and '*Madhesiya*.' Pahadis question the loyalty of Madhesis towards Nepal.

Some historical facts and evidence are there which also promote the perception of *Pahadis* regarding Madhesis. Such as Madhesis are those who came from India (the businessmen and labors from Bihar and UP) during the Rana regime for cleaning forest land and developing markets that would further increase the revenue of Nepal's ruler (Regmi 1961).

Factors Responsible for Madhesi Movement

Socioeconomic Conditions and Political Representation of Madhesis

There is a large history of sociopolitical and economic discrimination, what the Madhesi community is facing since the annexation of Terai by the King Prithvi Narayan Shah in 1768. No matter either the Shaha rulers or Rana rulers or the 'elite Pahadi Democratic leaders', all treated the Madhesi communities as 'second class' citizens. Their property rights and citizenship rights were curtailed by misrecognition of their identity.

The upper castes hill Hindus have been given higher posts in every sector such as; administration and bureaucracy, education sectors, agricultural land distribution, military and police forces, Jagirs and Birtas. And the other castes of hill origin people also have greater representation in all the sectors than the Madhesis have. Despite being significant in the number, the Madhesi community has not so much representation as some of the selected fellow citizens enjoy. There is a constant centralization of power and resources in the hands of the high hill caste Hindu groups (Bahun, Chhetri, Thakuri and Sanyasi) since the formation of Nepal. The *Birta* and *Jagir* lands which were non-tax payable lands given to the military officials and the Administrative officials of high hill castes. The condition of land labours and the peasants were not good. The Rana family, Newars, Thapas, Pandeys, Thakuris and other upper castes have had the ownership of the land and resources (Regmi 1961).

The conditions of Dalits– Mushar, Dom/Halkhor, Paswans, Chamars, etc. are bad. They have deprived of all the facilities, resources, positions which are enjoyed by other Tarai people. Even many of them are landless in Siraha, Mahottari and Dhanusha districts. "The Tarai leaders, particularly the leaders of the Nepal Sadbhavana Party, claim that about Four million people in the Tarai have not obtained the Nepali citizenship even today."6 Most of them are Dalits who are uneducated and landless, and there is no awareness of their rights and toward these official papers of citizenship or any other cards or papers. In the Tarai region the proportion of educated is also very low, and mostly the people from Tarai worked in Indian Cloths mills, Factories, in the fields of Punjab, in the coastal areas of India, also they migrate to Malaysia, Saudi Arabia and in the South East Asian regions. They don't have much government jobs.

The condition of Muslim Madhesis is not equal to the Brahmans, Kshatriya, Kayasths, and Yadavs. They are again economically and educationally backward than the upper caste Hindus of Madhes. The condition of Madhesi women is also bad in a sense that most of the Madhesi people excluding upper caste Hindus they do not send their daughters to schools or they just provide them a primary education. Especially the Muslim and Dalit Hindu women are more deprived and subordinated by the male-dominant society.

The Political Representation of Madhesis is low compared to Hill people; the political parties have 'used Tarai as entry points to launch various political struggles as well as to maintain a presence in Nepal while in exile in India.' Their representation in the military has been 'almost non-existent' compare to other 'excluded groups' such as hill *Janjatis*, because the elite class perceives the Madhesis as they are 'not loyal to the Nepali state' and they would act according to Indian interests (Sijapati 2013). In the Madhesi society, women's representation in politics and social decision making is almost zero; hardly any female Madhesi leader can be seen in the elections or giving speeches. "Although Madhes contributes 70 percent of the agricultural production of Nepal, 65 percent of the GDP, and 76 percent of the country's total revenue, the infrastructure in this region is considered to be poorer than in the hill areas."7 The table No. 1, 2 and 3 shows the statistical data of discrimination against Madhesis.

All the above factors: marginalization, misrecognition, homogenisation and underdevelopment lead the people to mobilise and to demand the equal rights, equal status, proper representation, the control over the resources and provincial autonomy to self-rule. The Madhesi, Dalits and the indigenous nationalities started identity-based movements.

Table No.1: Percent distribution of the jure population by wealth quintiles, according to caste/ethnicity and regional identity, Nepal 2006

Caste/ ethnicity and regional identity	Electri-city	Private latrine	Improved drinking water	Radio	Television	Any means of transportation	Number of Households
Brahaman/ Chhetri	60.7	52.0	76.7	75.3	33.4	30.3	2,659
Hill Brahman	75.8	66.3	81.1	83.7	45.8	41.3	991
Hill Chhetri	50.4	42.5	72.9	70.9	25.0	21.7	1,600
Tarai/ Madhes Brahaman/ Chhetri	82.9	65.7	98.8	57.7	49.7	71.5	68
Tarai Madhesi/ Other castes	43.4	81.1	97.3	38.8	24.5	71.4	806
Dalits	33.0	16.4	80.2	45.0	15.5	32.0	940
Hill Dalit	32.7	23.2	70.3	53.3	13.3	13.6	600
Tarai/ Madhes Dalit	33.7	4.6	97.5	30.2	19.4	64.4	340
Newar	72.6	71.6	90.5	82.8	61.4	46.4	348
Janjati	46.3	35.5	80.9	61.8	25.6	34.2	2,539
Hill/ Mountain Janjati	49.6	42.4	76.7	64.8	26.5	17.6	1,795
Tarai Janjati	38.3	18.6	91.0	54.6	23.4	74.1	744
Muslim	63.2	26.6	92.3	47.6	28.8	53.6	250
Other	76.4	46.6	93.3	69.8	65.3	23.7	139
All Hill/ Mountain Groups	54.3	46.6	76.5	70.0	30.4	24.7	5,334
All Tarai/ Madhes Groups	43.6	18.7	94.7	44.4	24.6	69.2	2,208
All Nepal	51.6	38.6	82.1	62.7	29.4	37.5	7,681

Source: Bennett et al. (2008).

Table No.2: Representation of Various caste/ethnic groups in national legislature (prior to the Constituent Assembly)

Caste/Ethnic Groups	National Legislature (a)					Total Population (b)	Proportional Share Index (Ratio of a and b)	
	1959	1981	1991	1999	2007	2001	1999	2007
Bahuns	27.5	13.3	38.1	39.6	32.8	12.7	3.12	2.58
Chhetri/ Thakuri	31.2	36.3	18.2	17.3	17.9	17.3	1.0	1.04
Newar	3.7	8.1	8.3	8.3	7.3	5.5	1.51	1.33
Sub Total	62.4	57.7	64.6	65.2	58.0	35.5	1.84	1.64
Tarai	22	18.5	19.6	19.6	21.9	33	0.53	0.66
Hill Social Groups	15.6	23	14.7	14.7	20.1	29	0.51	0.69
Others	-	0.7	1.2	1.5	-	2.5	0.6	-
Sub Total	37.6	42.2	35.5	33.6	42.0	64.5	0.52	0.65
Total	100	99.9	100.1	98.8	100.0	100		

Source: Bandita Sijapti (2013).

Table No.3: Representation of various caste/ethnic groups in different sectors 2005

Sector	Upper-caste hill[1]	Janjati	Madhesi	Dalit	Newar	Others	Total
Public	82	7	9	2	14	0	114
Political	93	20	11	1	14	0	139
Private	21	3	30	0	42	0	96
Civil Society	94	9	18	1	19	0	141
Total	290	39	68	4	89	0	490
Percent (a)	59.2	7.9	13.9	0.8	18.2	0.0	100.0
Percent of Total Population (b)	30.9	23.1	31.5	7.9	5.5	1.2	100.0
Proportional Share Index (Ratio of a and b)	1.9	0.3	0.4	0.1	3.3	0.0	6.0

Source: Bandita Sijapti 2005.

The Language Issue

In the Terai-Madhes region there are some languages spoken by Madhesis namely; Maithili, Bhojpuri, Awadhi, Bajjika, Tharu, Rajbansi, Urdu, and Hindi. Some of these languages were used as 'the language of court' during the 17th and 18th centuries. The language was not a problem there in Nepal. Even Maithili was used in Kathmandu Valley as the language of the court during the reign of Malla Kings. Even during the reign of King Prithvi Narayan Shah, local languages used for the administrative purpose. In 1951 when the NEPC9 formed, it recommended that only Nepali would be the sole medium of instruction in schools and no other languages would be taught even at primary level. Therein census report, it was shown that Nepali speaking people are large in number and the non-Nepali speaking population is very less. The Census (1952-54) report, which published in 1958, shows that only 3 percent people have Hindi as their mother tongue. Again in the 1962 census report further reduced the number of Hindi speaking from 80,181 (1952-54)) to 2,867 and in 1971 and 1981 census report there nowhere Hindi was mentioned. The Terai Congress (TC) which established in 1951 demanded that Hindi should be the second national language of Nepal. Several committees formed; many people meetings demonstrations happened, and several political parties like NC, CPN, and UDP supported the "Save Hindi" campaigns, movement and protests led by TC. The denial of the recognition of Hindi perceived by the Madhesi leaders as 'disrespect to the Terai people' (Jha 1993).

Chart No. 2. Linguistic Diversity in Nepal

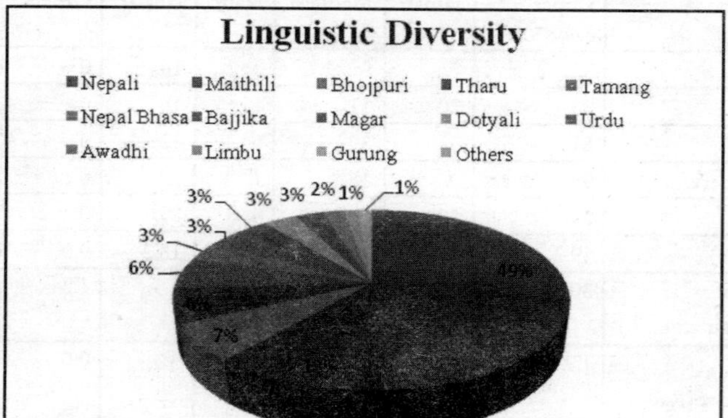

Source: 2011 Census of Nepal

Issue of Hill Migration to Terai

Jha (1993) mentions that "Madhesi people had their own identity... they sometimes resisted against the British East indie Company and sometimes against the Gorkha rulers" because "during the war between British East India Company and Nepal in 1815, they resisted in favor of British Government." Then After the defeat of Gurkha in Anglo-Nepalese War (1814-16), by the Treaty of Sugauli (1816) Nepal loses the Kumayun, Garhwal, and Sikkim as well as some part of Tarai. Some Part of Tarai was returned to Nepal by British India for helping the British East India Army to suppress the rebellion of 1857 (Gupta 1964; Shrestha and Singh 1972; Dahal 2001)

Migration from Hills to Terai started since the 1950s as a consequence of growth in population, redundancy, underemployment, scarcity of resources, etc. Other factors are also involved in the migration of the Hill people in Terai. These are 'malaria eradication program, job opportunities, some institutional level efforts by Rapti Valley Development Plan (RVDP 1954), Nepal Resettlement Company (1964) and the Department of Resettlement of His Majesty's Government of Nepal (HMG/N). Several resettlement projects ran; Jhapa, Sarlahi, Nawalparasi, Taratal, Kailali, Kanchanpur settlement projects (Jha 1993). Since 1952-54 when the population of hill origin people (Pahadis) was only near about 6 percent of the total population of Madhes increased to about 43 percent in the year 1981 and remain significant in numbers in the year 1991 and 2011. But the Madhesi population increased merely two-fold over the last five decades while the Pahadi population increased many folds (Shah 2006 Table No.4).

There was a huge migration from Hill to Terai which ultimately led to the migration of native Terai people to Indian states Bengal, Bihar, Uttar Pradesh and Punjab, Haryana and different other parts of India. In search of jobs during certain seasons, and because of the 'Kamaiya System'10 several Tharus and other people forced to migrate permanently and settled to Indian states Bihar and UP. The migration from hill to Terai resulted in deforestation, unemployment, cultural assimilation and migration of Terai people to Indian states (Jha 1993).

Table No.4: Terai Population: Increasing percent of Hill People Population in Terai

Year	Pahadis	Madhesis	Total	Percent of Pahadis	Percent of Madhesis
1952/54	142,000	2,246,000	2,388,000	5.9	94.1
1981	2,795,000	3,762,000	6,557,000	42.6	57.4
1991	3,444,000	5,262,000	8,706,000	39.6	60.4
2001	4,120,000	7,092,000	11,212,000	36.7	63.3

Source: Shah (2006)

Citizenship Issue

Jha (1993) maintains that discriminatory policy of King Prithvi Narayan Shah while assigning important positions, the Terai-Madhes people left behind, and from here the seeds of citizenship issue can be traced. He further says that until 1958 the Madhesi people used to carry a passport with them while entering to the Kathmandu Valley. After 1950s very complex citizenship laws were made to control the "influx of population from India" and many genuine Nepali Madhesi people were denied to acquire citizenship.

A very large section of the Madhesi population is without citizenship certificate an issue causing great anxiety for Madhesis.[11] "The Citizenship Act of 1964 and the constitution of 1990 decided that citizenship would be given by 'descent' and ability to speak and write Nepali. In the absence of valid documents (birth certificates and land ownership documents), Hindi speaking people were denied citizenship certificates. Without a citizenship certificate, they could not get land titles and were deprived of government benefits."[12]

State-Centric Nationalism

The formation of Nepal through the integration of small principalities of the Himalayan region by Gorkha conquered became successful because of the one most important factor, and that was the concept of Hindu Monarchy. Hindu kings or Rajas ruled all the smallest kingdoms, so the people did not question the integration of Nepal. The core idea of the Nepali nation-state was "the king is the incarnation of God on the earth" as the traditional Hindu religious scriptures prescribe, and no one can question the king. The State used Hindu symbols in Nepali flag (the sun and the moon) and the size of the Nepalese flag which unique in the world. Nepalese *Rajkiy Mohar* and later on coins and in currencies have the Hindu symbols like *Sankha, Chakra, Gada, and Padma*. The Hindu festivals are the national festivals; the Cow announced as *Rashtriya Pashu* (national animal) and the state declaration of Hindu state in 1962 by King Mahendra. All shows that a complete Hinduisation of the State of Nepal.

The second thing what the Nepalese Kings and Ranas did, that they started the homogenization of the culture of the hill high caste Hindu and an idea of 'homogeneous Nepali Nation' was constructed. Promotion of the *Pahadi* Hindu culture, language (*Khas-Kura*-Nepali*)* and the partial high-caste Hindu oriented history-based education. During the period of Panchayat with Monarchy (1962-1990), there was a slogan raised by the politicians –*"Ek Bhasha, ek dharma, ek bhes, ek desh"* – 'one language, one religion, one form of dress, one country' to create a kind of cultural uniformity. In 1962 Nepal became the Hindu Kingdom, all the national symbols like red color, the cow, and the signs of Lord Vishnu on the coins all referred to Hindu Monarchy. Nepali (*Khas-Kura)* was the language to give education in the schools, and the state published books they excluded the cultures, histories, and languages of Madhesis and other indigenous nationalities. Because of the main aim of the state, was the assimilation of diversity in a unified nation based on one religion, one language and one culture (Hangan and Lawoti 2013).

All lead towards the construction of a 'Nepali-Hindu Nationalism. This nationalism was exclusive, and the 'Notion of the Nation' was '*Uniformity among Diversity*.' And the cultural assimilation was promoted by the rulers of Nepal. This was a top-down model of constructing a nation-state which comes from the authority: the monarch, the Ranas, and the high-caste hill Hindu elites.

Movement and its Growth

Since Madhesis have been ill recognised by the political elites of the hill they face discrimination. Madhesis are now asking for a 'people-centric nationalism.' Not defined by the political elites of the hill but a bottom-up approach. They reject the state-centric nationalism and hill centric developmental approach. They are asking for recognition of their identity, their nationalism and their role in the economic development of Nepal. They are asking for a redistribution of resources according to their contribution and need.

First Phase of the Movement (1950s-1960s)

Movement in Terai-Madhes has seeds during the early 50s and 60s though the nature of the movement was not as violent as can be seen today. The first phase of the Madhesi movement (linguistic identity based) mainly starts in 1951, with the formation of the Nepal Terai Congress (TC) in the leadership of Vedanada Jha (founder of TC) demanding state autonomy, Recognition of Hindi and adequate representation of Terai people in the civil services. Bishnu Pathak and Devendra Uprety (2009) see the Madhesi movement as a result of discriminatory and exploitative nature of the state machinery, political parties and elites with the core issues of linguistic, cultural, citizenship and recruitment in the military. The movement further strengthened by 'Madheshi Mukti Andolan' (1956) lead by Raghunath Thakur, against the discriminatory and exploitative nature of the state. Raghunath Thakur visited India in 1971, looking for support to the movement and met the then head of the state President Sarvapalli Radhakrishnan and the then head of the government Prime Minister Smt. Indira Gandhi but the Indian leaders showed their concern over the injustice to Madhesis only. Despite the anti-India riots in South Nepal which also discussed in the Indian Parliament, the Indian government refused to interfere in this saying that it is the internal matter of Nepal (Nayak 2011).

Second Phase of the Movement (1970s-1980s)

As with most other the groups, Madhesis also remained largely politically inactive during the 1960s and 1970s due to the restrictions imposed by the autocratic Panchayat regime.13 The second phase of the Madhesi movement started in the late 80s and continued till the early 90s when the multiparty system restored in Nepal. Nihar Nayak (2011) maintains that Sadbhavana Council (1985) later became Nepal Sadbhavana Party (1990) founded by Gajendra Narayan Singh (a prominent Madhesi leader), started a movement raising voice for the citizenship rights, language issue, Madhesi culture, "representation in state agencies and a federal system." But post-1990 when the multiparty democracy restored they made "alliances with Hill-based political groups," and party lost its credibility, and Madhesi movement vanished.

Third Phase of the Movement (1990s-2000s)

After the end of the civil war (started in 1996) in 2006 with the signing of Comprehensive Peace Accord between the Unified Communist Party of

Nepal and the His Majesty Government of Nepal (HMG/N), the Madhesi leaders started a movement. They called for a bandh, Chakkajam and other demonstration saying that Maoists has betrayed. Madhesi organizations started agitations and demonstration by using both violent and nonviolent means. Several Bandhs, Chakkajaams, demonstrations called in different towns of Dhanusha (Janakpur), Saptari (Rajbiraj), Rautahat (Gaur), Parsa (Birgunj), Bara (Kalaiya) districts of the Terai-Madhes region. They started protesting against the interim Constitution of Nepal which promulgated in 2007. The Madhesi Janadhikar Forum (MJF), one of the main protesting groups, presented a list of their demands some of the major demands were: federal structure; proportionate electorate system; autonomous Madhes region and self-determination; abolition of internal colonization; citizenship to all Madhesis without discrimination.

Earlier the CPN (Maoist) ethnicized the Maoist movement with the ethnic upsurge of different groups during *Jan Andolan* of the 1990s; *Madhesi, Dalits* and *Janjati* movements. The CPN (Maoist) inculcated the ethnic concerns in their demands carefully. They asked for "Declaration of Nepal as a secular state, Equal treatment to all languages of Nepal, Ethnic and regional based autonomy and the right to self-determination, End of caste, ethnic, regional and gender-based discrimination and Special policy for the promotion of the interest of Dalit and women" (Basnet 2009). CPN (M) lobbied for federal ethnic structure during war-time with a targeted strategy of winning heart and mind of ethnic groups. And a sudden change in the political aspiration of the Maoist brings them in a condition of distrust among Madhesis (Upreti et. al. 2012).

Deepak Thapa (2011) argues that there are about 109 subversive groups active in Nepal and most of them are working from the Terai-Madhes and fighting for the rights and the grievance of Madhesis. He also explains that how the Maoists used the Young Madhesis and pulled them into militancy through spreading the situation as "internal colonialism," and Pahadis have control over the state and they are exploiting the Terai-Madhes region and not providing any political rights.

Nihar Nayak (2011) says that "During the People's War period, the CPN-Maoist established a Madhesi Rashtriya Mukti Morcha (MRMM) in 2000 under the leadership of Jai Krishna Goit to expand the Maoist presence in the Terai." The demand of "single autonomous province under the new constitution" by Madhesi political parties which was partly supported by the Maoists to some extent (favoring to the creation of two Madhes provinces) threatened other political parties. That if this demand gets fulfill it might give rise to the "demand for separate states in future."

A study by Conflict Study Centre Nepal (2007) explains that the Madhesi movement after 2006 has several conspiracies by different organizations against each other. "In the early February 2007, the arson to NC office in Sunsari was disclaimed by MJF, as it was campaigning then. Similarly, in Gaur incident, 30 Maoist cadres were killed in clashes between MJF and Maoists. Prabhu Sah, General Secretary of the Madhesi Rashtriya Mukti Morcha (sister organization of Maoists) in a press release regarding the incident stated that Indian criminals were hired by MJF." The study further claims that all the armed or unarmed groups of Madhesi movements assembled in Patna (Bihar) and prepared a set of agenda:

- To protect Tarai, the motherland of Madhesis, identify throughout the globe as a separate country with facts and figures;
- Advancement to liberate Tarai by preparing a 10-year plan uniting all the Madhesi forces;
- Acquire foreign support from UN, China, Pakistan, US and especially India is pertinent for liberation of Madhes and build cordial relationship with them;
- To build cordial relation with Indian Embassy at Kathmandu for advancing the war in Tarai;
- Understanding of aims and objectives of the different Madhesi groups fighting in Tarai;
- Develop strategy on common problem identification, common concept, common demand, common consensus and common tactics;
- Establish Common National Madhesi Morcha or Sajha Tarai Mukti Morcha offices in each district to carry out political and administrative functions;
- To make the media – press, and radio – realize their rights and duties to succeed Madhes Movement; and;
- Change the strategy from Tarai Bandh (strike) to Kathmandu Bandh;

Ram Raja Prasad Singh who was chairing the meeting refused the demand of separate Madhes state from Nepal and said it is impossible and even India will not support for this. This study further maintains that most of the Madhesi movement groups neither have any sound ideology nor political means and visions to reach any destination. Different Madhesi groups do not accept the existence of each other and always fight with each other.

Bishnu Raj Upreti et al. (2012) maintain that there a kind of mutual mistrust developed between the two communities (Pahadi and Madhesi) during the violent Madhesi uprising started in early 2007. The anger they showed that the hill-people are responsible for the long discrimination against them. There were some cases where Madhesi protesters vandalized the properties of the hill originated people, any Madhesi leaders did not show their responsibility nor did the state machinery take it seriously. The Madhesi leaders also threaten to call for secessionist movement in Terai-Madhes. They also denied the ethnic and linguistic Identity of Tharu people of this region by saying that there is no any separate language of Tharus exists and they speaks what the dialect of the other Madhesi languages is; Bajjika, Maithili, and Bhojpuri. The Seven Party Alliance (SPA) was in power, and they were defusing the demand of a single autonomous Madhes, and this demand was perceived as a threat to the national integration and backed by several other opposition parties also.

Bandita Sijapti (Lawoti and Hangen eds. 2013) maintains that very surprisingly the movement which was limited earlier started from Sirha and Dhanusha districts got spread to central and eastern Terai. After two weeks disturbance then Nepali PM Girija Prasad Koirala called a meeting with the protestors, but they rejected. Again PM Koirala made a second attempt to talk with the Madhesi protesters and on 8 February 2007 there some concessions made by him; "federal system of governance by amending the constitution, increase in electoral districts in Terai, a system of proportional representation and MJF suspended the movement. But the govt. Failed to fulfill the promises and a fresh protest started from 19 February 2007. The MJF led by Upendra Yadav and the Interim Government of Nepal leader Ramchandra Paudel reached a '22 point Agreement' on 30 August 2007 which provided some political space to the MJF, and the agitation stopped.

The three major Madhesi political parties MJF, Sadbhavna Party (SP-Mahto) and Terai-Madhes Democratic Party (TMDP) made a coalition UDMF

(United Democratic Madhesi Front) and put the demand of "single autonomous Madhes with the right to self-determination," and called several strikes. Finally, the Government came to talk with them and an Eight-point Agreement signed. UDMF decided to go for the CA elections with the slogan "Ek Madhes Ek Pradesh" (one Madhes, one province) (Upreti et al. 2012).

The CA elections took place on 10 April 2008, and CPN (Maoist) appeared as a big party with 229 seats out of 601. This CA elections' result took the Maoists in the mainstream politics and with the help of smaller political parties the Maoist leader Prachanda became the PM of Nepal. UDMF got 81 seats in the CA and became the coalition partner of the government. However, the political instability uncertainty to take decisions lead to the resignation of Prachanda and Madhav Kumar Nepal became the PM. But the political and governmental instability remain same, and the CA failed to give a new Constitution (Upreti & Pyakurel 2012).

Table No. 5: Madhesi Parties' Position in CA Elections 2008

SL No	Madhesi Political Parties	Seats
1	MJF-Nepal (Upendra Yadav)	12
2	MJF-Gantantrik	13
3	MJF-Loktantrik (Gachhadar)	28
4	Terai Madhes Democratic Party (Thakur)	11
5	Terai Madhes Democratic Party-Nepal (Raya Yadav)	09
6	MJF-Madhesh (Bhagyanath)	00
7	Nepal Sadbhawana Party (Mahato)	09
8	Nepal Sadbhawana Party-A (Sarita Giri)	02
Total		84

Source: Nihar Nayak (2011)

Fourth Phase of the Movement (Post second CA elections)

The fourth phase of the Madhesi movement starts with the announcement of the promulgation of the New Constitution of Nepal by Constituent Assembly in September 2015.

The new Constitution came on 20 September 2015 and adopted by a majority of 507 out of 598 CA members. This Constitution has republican, federal, secular and inclusive characters. The preamble holds the principle of "socialism based on democratic values." "It incorporates proportional representation to ensure that women, untouchables (Dalits), and marginalized groups like the Janjatis and the Madhes find representation in the national legislature and the other institutions of the state. In spite of having these prominent characters, this Constitution has been "disapproved by the large constituencies of the marginalized groups—the Madhes, Janjatis, and women." "The Madhes parties, the Janjati groups, women, monarchists, Hindu fundamentalists and splintered extremist Maoists" all are agitating and saying that their aspirations have not been considered. Most of the MPs voted this Constitution were the representatives of these groups, but they voted because of the fear of their political career, under the pressure of their respective political bosses of different political parties. In these five areas having the difference between the agitators and the political parties: "(i) the carving of federal provinces, (ii) proportional representation, (iii) citizenship rights, (iv) the identity of the Nepali State, and (v) its ideological parameters." The Madhes parties have rejected the federal structure of Nepal which has divided seven provinces. "The Tharu leader Gachchdar of the Madhes Forum, who had joined hands with the dominant parties, also withdrew from the process when six provinces were changed to seven provinces, but without the accommodation of Tharu majority districts (Kanchanpur and Kailali) in the western Terai province." The Janjati groups have been denied their identities and the Hill caste dominating boundary structure. Their proportionate representation in parliament has been reduced to earlier 58 percent to now 45 percent. On the question of citizenship, the provisions that the children of those who get married to other nationals would not be appointed to the higher post in Nepal and the citizenship will not be given on maternal basis; have created fear among the Madhesis who have marital relations with India. On the other side, the "monarchists and Hindu fundamentalists are working together to ask for making Nepal a Hindu state and reinstating the monarchy." They have "extensive moral and material support from India, particularly from the Hindutva sections of the ruling Bharatiya Janata Party (BJP)." This agitation has led "violence and disruption of normal life in the Terai region." "The agitating parties are blocking the supply of essential goods from India to Kathmandu, resulting in scarcity of petrol and other commodities" (Muni 2015).

Nirabh Koirala and Geoffrey Macdonald (2015) maintain that the new constitution has a discriminatory provision regarding the children of a Nepali citizen and a foreign National and the Madhesi community is going to be badly affected since they have marital relations with Indians. Very few seats are under the "proportional representation rules" which would affect "their power in national politics," even they have not been provided a majority in any provinces. They further say that the supply of oil and petroleum has been completely stopped at the border and Nepal's government claims it is "retaliation for the new constitution, which India has strongly criticized, while India is saying Nepal's internal conflict is disrupting the border transport. Again they maintain that the denial of Madhesis in the process of constitution-writing has "cross-border implication" and "the discrimination against Madhesis is an affront to India's ethnic identity and democratic ideals, and the resulting protests have created instability on its border. However, India risks overplaying its hand." There is anti-India sentiment on the rise because of the very "critical public comments of the Indian officialdom on the new constitution" and the "unofficial economic blockade."

Human Rights Watch Nepal (October 2015) report says there were several incidents happened in these districts and many lives gone. Here bellows are some incidents:

Kailali Incidences: Between 24 August to 11 September 2015, 25 people lost their lives including 9 police officials and 16 public. In the Tikapur incident which took place on 24 August 2015, 8 people including 7 policemen and a 18-month old baby were killed by the armed protesters who identified themselves to be associated with the Tharu Struggle Committee. Whereas on other different occassions, 16 people were killed by the police where two were already injured and laying on the ground, and they intentionally killed, and six of them were bystanders not even protestors, according to eyewitnesses.

The report further maintains that most of the incidents happened in this region were not reported in the rest of the country and media described the protesters as violent. But no any police atrocities and violence despite some illegal killings (by the police having been witnessed and even filmed by numerous journalists was reported. This is described by the editors of the Newspapers "protecting social harmony."

Parsa Incidents: Birgunj, the headquarter of the Pars district is the main transit point of the goods from India to Nepal and not only the supply of fuel, petroleum, and LPG but also several essential goods transported to Kathmandu, blocked by the protesters. Till the early 16 days when the protest was non-violent the entry of loaded trucks done at night. Bijaya Gachhadar-led Madhesi

People's Rights Forum – Nepal (MPRF-N) party's leader Upendra Yadav wanted to continue the protest until 5 p.m., while the Sharad Singh Bhandari-led Rashtriya Madhesh Samajwadi party's leader Rajesh Man Singh wanted to stop the transportation of goods completely. The rising public opinion was the same as Rajesh Man Sing was asking for because there "was having no political impact due to the free passage of goods by night to Kathmandu."

The local administration of Birgunj declared a "prohibited zone" from 8 p.m. to 6 a.m. from 26th of August. People started violent agitation in these places; Naguwa, Ghanta Ghar, Murli Chowk, and Radhemai after a police attack on Upendra Yadav on 31st August. "Dilip Chaurasiya, a student at the Birgunj Institute of Technology" involved in the protest, was killed by the police. "No goods were able to leave Birgunj for Kathmandu on the night of August 31. That day the local administration received reinforcements of about 200 extra Nepal Police and APF members from nearby Pathlaiya, Hetauda, and Chitwan."

Curfew was imposed at Birgunj; some of the people who were not throwing stones were killed by the police. "On 1 September various protests took place against the curfew in areas outside the curfew area such as Maniyari and Jaganathpur. Protesters vandalized government buildings." According to a member (Sudip Lama) from the Narayani Hospital Birgunj on 2 September "a group of protesters was on the street about 200 meters away. The police arrived and charged at the protesters" and "a police officer set his shotgun on the top of the hospital wall and deliberately fired one shot into the compound. Buckshot hit Lama, who was standing six to seven meters away, and three other people."

Bara Incidents: Hifajat Miya (19) was killed in Kalaiya (Headquarter of Bara district) on 1 September when there was a protest by about 150 members was going on. "According to numerous witnesses, 60 to 70 members of the Nepal Police arrived at about 2 p.m. and attempted to disperse the gathering with tear gas" and then bullets.

Mahottari Incident: On 9 September four people were shot dead by the police in Mahottari district near Mahendra Chowk while involved in the protest.

Dhanusha Incidents: In Janakpur, a large protest on 11 September 2015 by local people was planned by the UDMF under the slogan, "Let's go to Janakpur. Let's fill Janakpur." "to thwart the protest the administration issued a curfew order in the city for the first time. That day live ammunition was used at Kadam Chowk on the eastern side of the city." First 20-25 both police and APF confronted with the thousands of protesters with tear gas and crowd was dispersed but again gathered soon then the police started "fire with live ammunition without any verbal warning" and two peoples hit by bullets. In a similar at Pirari Chowk, (on the western side of Janakpur) a 13-year-old Dilip Yadav was killed while going toward his home.

All these events show that the police atrocities took so many lives during mass movements that lasted for months, in these Terai-Madhes districts.

A secessionist movement to create a sovereign Madhes as a nation state is also going parallel to the Madhesi movement. C K Raut is the leader of this movement 'Independent Madhes Movement' and the alliance called 'Alliance for Independent Madhes' (AIM)[14]. They call Nepali rule as a colonial rule over Madhes motherland. He has been arrested several times.

Political instability in Nepal has become a big challenge and affected and still affecting the state-building as well the nation building process in Nepal. It is affecting the peace and stability in the country and the development and economic growth as well.

Conclusion

After analysing all the above literature, it can be concluded that Madhesi movement is an identity-based movement against the misrecognition of their identity and maldistribution of resources. So they are asking for self-determination, recognition, and redistribution. If the government fails to satisfy the aspirations of the Madhesi community and constantly remain to do with partisan politics, it will lead to greater secessionist movements. This would challenge the national integration and sovereignty of Nepal.

The people of Madhes are demanding amendment in Constitution and protesting against the announced local elections. This is further escalating the political instability. Now there is time for taking some strong and sound policy steps to satisfy the aspirations of the identity groups, promotion of mutual trust and cooperation of all the stakeholders in the decision making, and only that would help Nepal to overcome this issue.

Endnotes

1. Mahendra Lawoti and Susan Hangen eds. (2013); Nationalism and Ethnic Conflict in Nepal: Identities and Mobilization after 1990; Routledge, Abingdon, p.11

2. Nepal's Troubled Tarai Region Crisis Group Asia Report N°136, 9 July 2007; p.2
3. Upreti, Bishnu Raj (2012) eds., Ignored or ill-represented? : The Griviance of Terai-Madhes Conflict in Nepal, New Delhi, Adorit Publishers, p. 3.
4. Mahendra Lawoti and Susan Hangen (2013); Nationalism and Ethnic Conflict in Nepal: Identities and Mobilization after 1990; Routledge, Abingdon; p.9
5. Mahendra Lawoti and Susan Hangen (2013 – Bandita Sijapati); Nationalism and Ethnic Conflict in Nepal: Identities and Mobilization after 1990; Routledge, Abingdon p.149
6. Gellner David and Krishna Hachhethu (2008); Local Democracy in South Asia; Sage Publication, New Delhi; p. 142
7. Nayak Nihar R (2010), *Madhesi Movement in Nepal: Implications for India*; Online Web Accessed URL: http://www.idsa.in/event/ Madhesi Problem and Implications for India
8. Bahun/Chettri
9. National Education Planning Commission
10. The Tharu community usually lives in the forests and is mostly illiterate and very submissive and the elite Hill migrants used the Tharu community to work as slaves or Kamaiyas on their own land. This system was very oppressive and still prevalent in the far western Terai districts namely; Banke, Bardia, Kailali and Kanchanpur.
11. Yadav, Ram Prakash (2010), *Madhesi: A Disadvantaged Social Group*, [Online: Web] Accessed 12 April 2016, URL: http://www.socialinclusion.org.np/userfiles/ file/Madhesi_by_Ram_Prakash_Yadav.pdf
12. Nayak Nihar (2011), The Madhesi Movement in Nepal: Implications for India, *Strategic Analysis,* Vol. 35, No. 4, July 2011, 640–660
13. Lawoti, Mahendra and Susan Hangen (edt.2013), Nationalism and Ethnic Conflict in Nepal: Identities and Mobilization after 1990, Abingdon: Routledge, p. 21.
14. AIM is an alliance of Madheshi people, activists, parties and various organisations working for establishing an independent and sovereign Madhesh.

References

Basnet, Yurendra (2009), "From Politicization of Grievances to Political Violence: An Analysis of the Maoist Movement in Nepal" [Online: Web] Accessed 23 Nov. 2016, URL: http://www.lse.ac.uk/internationalDevelopment/pdf/WP/ WP78.pdf

Bennett et al. (2008), *Caste, Ethnic and Regional Identity in Nepal: Further Analysis of the 2006 Nepal Demographic and Health Survey*, Calverton, Maryland, USA: Macro International Inc.

Brass, Paul R. (Edt.1985), *"Ethnic Groups and State"*, Beckenham: Croom Helm Ltd.

Conflict Study Centre (2007), *Nepal's Madhesi Movement: Against Khas Chauvinism?* August 2007, Kathmandu: Nepal. [Online: web] Accessed 12 March 2017, URL: http://www.cscenter.org.np/uploads/doc/110627200853_Situation%20 Update%2045- Madhesi%20movement.pdf

Crisis Group Asia (2007), *Nepal's Troubled Tarai Region*, Report N°136, 9 July 2007, [Online: web] Accessed 12 April 2016, URL: http://www.refworld.org/ pdfid/4693304c2.pdf

Dahal, Ram Kumar (2001), *Constitutional and Political Development in Nepal*, Kathmandu: Ratana Pustak Bhandar.

Gaige, Frederick (1975), *Regionalism and National Unity in Nepal*, Berkeley: University of California Press.

Gupta, Anirudh (1964), *Politics in Nepal: A Study of Post-Rana Political Developments and Party Politics*, New Delhi: Allied Publishers.

Hangen, Susan (2010), *The Rise of Ethnic Politics in Nepal: Democracy in the margins*, Abingdon: Routledge.

Human Rights Watch (2015), *"Like We Are Not Nepali": Protest and Police Crackdown in the Terai Region of Nepal*, Printed in the U S A.

Jha, Hari Bansh (1993), *The Terai Community and National Integration in Nepal*, Kathmandu: Modern Printing Press.

Koirala, Nirabh and Geoffrey Macdonald (2015), "India in the Madhesi Movement", *Economic and Political Weekly*, 50 (45): 9.

Lawoti, Mahendra and Susan Hangen (edt.2013), *Nationalism and Ethnic Conflict in Nepal: Identities and Mobilization after 1990*, Abingdon: Routledge.

Madhes Tarai Profile, [Online: web] Accessed 12 April 2016, URL: http://madhesh. com/ files/2013/02/madhesh_tarai_profile.pdf

Muni, S. D. (2015), "Nepal's New Constitution", *Economic and Political Weekly*, 50 (40): 15-19.

Nayak, Nihar (2011), "The Madhesi Movement in Nepal: Implications for India", *Strategic Analysis*, 35 (4): 640–660.

Pathak Bishnu and Devendra Uprety (2009), "Tarai-Madhes Searching for Identity Based Security", *Conflict Study Centre*, Kathmandu: Nepal, [Online: Web] Accessed 16 March 2017, URL: http://www.cscenter.org.np/uploads/ doc/100524052535_ SituationUpdate88Tarai-Madhes-SearchingforIdentitybased Security.pdf

Phadnis, Urmila and Rajat Ganguli (1989), *Ethnicity and Nation-building in South Asia*, New Delhi: Sage.

Regmi, D. R. (1961), *Modern Nepal: Rise and Growth in the Eighteenth Century*, Calcutta: Firma K. L. Mukhopadhyay.

Shah, Govind (2006), *Social Inclusion of Madheshi Community in Nation Building*, Kathmandu, [Online: web] Accessed 12 March 2017, URL: https://madhesi.files.wordpress.com/2006/07/social-inclusion-of-madheshi-community-in-nation-building.pdf

Shrestha, D. B. and C.B. Singh (1972), *History of Ancient and Medieval Nepal: In Nutshell with Some Comparative Traces of Foreign History*, Kathmandu: HMG Press.

Upreti, B. C. and Uddhab Pd. Pyakurel (eds.2012), *Contemporary Nepal*, Delhi: Kalinga Publication.

Upreti, Bishnu Raj et al. (2012), Ignored or Ill-Represented? The Grievance of Terai-Madhes Conflict in Nepal, New Delhi: Adroit Publishers.

World Bank (2011), *Nepal*, World Development Report, by Deepak Thapa, [Online: web] Accessed 11 March 2017, URL: http://web.worldbank.org/archive/website01306/web/pdf/wdr_2011_case_study_nepal_04dbd.pdf?keepThis=true&TB_iframe=true&height=600&width=800

Yadav, Ram Prakash (2006); "Madhesi a Disadvantaged Social Group", [Online: web] Accessed 12 April 2016, URL: http://www.socialinclusion.org.np/userfiles/file/Madhesi_by_Ram_Prakash_Yadav.pdf